Better Homes and Gardens®

501 QUILT BLOCKS

A Treasury of Patterns for Patchwork & Appliqué

BETTER HOMES AND GARDENS® BOOKS
Des Moines, Iowa

501 QUILT BLOCKS

Authors and Designers: Joan Lewis and Lynette Chiles, Flower Mound, Texas
Editor: Sylvia Miller
Art Director: Jerry J. Rank
Pattern and Illustration Graphics: Chris Neubauer
Graphic Production Coordinator: Paula Forest
Photo Styling: Jill Mead
Photography: Perry Struse

BETTER HOMES AND GARDENS® BOOKS

An Imprint of Meredith® Books
President, Book Group: Joseph J. Ward
Vice President and Editorial Director: Elizabeth P. Rice
Executive Editor: Nancy N. Green
Art Director: Ernest Shelton

MEREDITH CORPORATION CORPORATE OFFICERS:

Chairman of the Executive Committee: E. T. Meredith III
Chairman of the Board, President and Chief Executive Officer: Jack D. Rehm
Group Presidents: Joseph J. Ward, Books; William T. Kerr, Magazines; Philip A. Jones, Broadcasting;
Allen L. Sabbag, Real Estate
Vice Presidents: Leo R. Armatis, Corporate Relations; Thomas G. Fisher, General Counsel and Secretary;
Larry D. Hartsook, Finance; Michael A. Sell, Treasurer; Kathleen J. Zehr, Controller and Assistant Secretary

WE CARE!

All of us at Better Homes and Gardens® Books are dedicated to providing you with the information you need to use the patterns in this book. We are particularly concerned that all of our instructions for making the projects are clear and accurate. We welcome your comments and suggestions. Please address your correspondence to Better Homes and Gardens Books, Craft Editorial Department, 1716 Locust Street, Des Moines, IA 50309-3023.

If you would like to order additional copies of any of our books, call 1-800-678-2803 or check with your local bookstore.

Library of Congress Catalog Card Number: 94-75959
ISBN: 0-696-01997-3

QUILT TALK

PREFACE

We came to write this book because we have three things in common.

First, we both collect things. (Lynette is by far the more dedicated collector.) We have developed our own rules about collections: One of anything is, well, just one. Two is a set. And three of anything is a collection, therefore requiring additions as often as possible. (One exception: We both decided that a collection of three children is to be regarded as complete!) As we became friends, and later business partners, we noticed that many of our designs were samplers. But they were samplers of a different sort: they had themes. Themes are a lot like collections, so it is not surprising that the samplers we designed were collections—of trees, or houses, or baskets, for example.

Second, we are fascinated with sewing small things. Little quilts are intriguing—so fast to make, so challenging to do. Finding a way to reduce the size of a quilt often requires more than just making smaller templates. In the beginning we learned like most other new quilters: we made samplers with large blocks, set together rather unimaginatively. But we both knew there was more to it than that: we began to make smaller blocks.

Finally, we have very limited patience with making the same thing over and over again—we find making the same quilt block sixty times mind-numbing.

So here we are, weaving together the three things we love most as a quilting duo: themed collections, small things, and the pleasing assurance of variety.

The blocks in this book are four-inch squares. While we didn't invent the four-inch block, we did discover its wonders. In 501 patterns, we have explored the variations and mapped a road for you. The patterns are grouped by theme (collections!), and we offer forty ideas for setting them together in small or full-size quilts and other projects: clothing, home decorations, seasonal decorations, and personal accessories.

Some of the blocks are more challenging than others. If you haven't worked with small pieces before, start out making blocks with fewer and larger pieces. Later, at your own pace, you can graduate to more and more ambitious blocks.

Most important, don't be intimidated or discouraged by small pieces. Remember that with ¼-inch seam allowances on all sides, the pieces you are working with will be a little bigger than they appear in the patterns.

As you travel through these pages, please be sure to stop and try a block now and then. We want you to have as much fun as we did when we made each one. And we dedicate this book to those of you who really don't want to make the same quilt block over and over and over again!

A GUIDE TO THE BOOK

This book begins with *why*. Before we show you how, we want to make sure you understand why it is worthwhile to make four-inch quilt blocks, and why you should make each one different.

The first section (pages 6–51) shows the projects we created from the block patterns in this book. You'll see many options: projects using one block, two blocks, or two hundred blocks. There's only one project where we repeated a block pattern. (See if you can find it!) Of course, you may know exactly what you want to do with your quilt blocks. But if you need inspiration, we know you'll find it among these projects, together with all the instructions you need on putting them together.

Beginning on page 52 you'll find the patterns for the blocks—501 of them. These are actual size: Just lay your template plastic over them and trace.

We've included the *how* right along with the block patterns. While our directions may not be the only way to make each block, we've shared the method we found easiest as we made each one.

The Tips and Techniques (beginning on page 305) will refresh your memory if you haven't used a specific technique for a while, or never learned it. Again, we simply want you to have the advantage of our experiences and share in our discoveries as we made each block.

Our objective is to show you why and how to make these quilt blocks so you'll be inspired to do it. We hope you will have years of fun as a result.

Lynette Chiles and Joan Lewis

BALTIMORE ALBUM

A showpiece of appliqué skills, this little wall quilt is ideal for using some of those precious pieces of hand-dyed or marbleized fabrics you have collected.

Finished Size

20" x 25"

Block Patterns

12 Baltimore Album appliquéd blocks (B57–B68, pages 124–29)

Fabric Requirements

1 yd. for background and sashing

⅛ yd. for swag border

Small pieces of hand-dyed, marbleized, or solid colors for appliqué

Construction

Note: Add ¼-inch seam allowances to all measurements and templates.

Cut the following sashing and border pieces:

Cut 8 pieces 4" x 1"

Cut 2 pieces 21" x 1"

Cut 2 pieces 20" x 2"

Cut 5 pieces 14" x 1"

Cut 2 pieces 21" x 2"

Join 3 blocks with 4" x 1" strips into a row (4 times). Join rows with 14" x 1" strips (adding strips to top and bottom as well). Add 21" x 1" strips to sides. Finally, add 21" x 2" strips to each side and 20" x 2" strips to top and bottom.

Use the full-size pattern provided to appliqué swags and flowers onto border.

Back, quilt, and bind as directed on page 312.

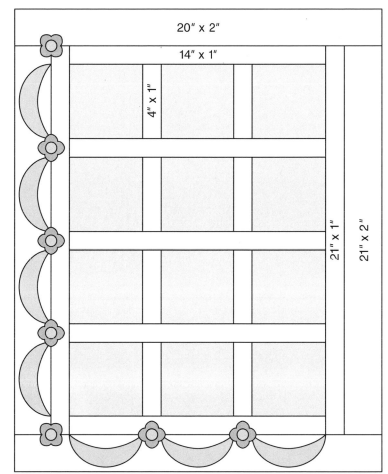

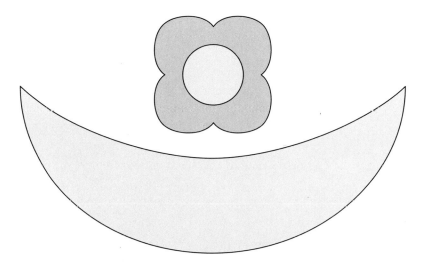

CATS IN THE ATTIC

Quilters and felines seem to have an affinity.
Twelve kitty blocks make a wonderful wall hanging.
Four make a pillow.

Finished Size

24" x 30"

Block Patterns

12 cat blocks (G13–G24, pages 281–6)

Fabric Requirements

¼ yd. each of 2 colors for sashings

¼ yd. each of 2 colors for borders

⅓ yd. for binding

1 yd. for backing

Construction

Note: Add ¼-inch seam allowances to all measurements and templates.

Cut 12 of the window sashing piece (Pattern A piece) in one color and 12r (template reversed) in a second color.

Join the sashings to each block as shown in the diagram. Do not stitch into the seam allowance at the point where the 2 sashing pieces meet; miter the 2 sashing pieces, starting from the outside point. (For help with mitering, see page 309.)

Join the sashed blocks into rows, then join the rows. Add the outer borders. Note that they, too, are mitered.

Back, quilt, and bind as directed on page 312.

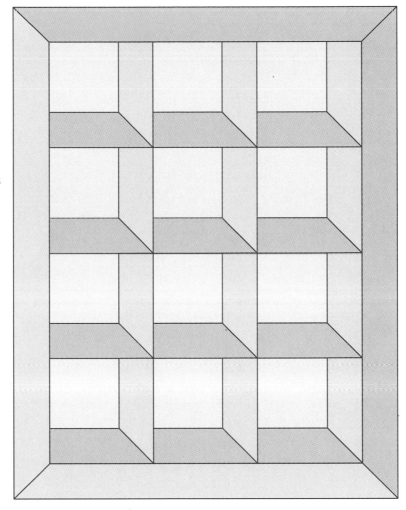

We used 2 Attic Window blocks (A56, page 81), Barn Cat and Mouse block (F42, page 273) and our Dog and Bone block (F45, page 274) for a fun pillow. We added ceramic kitty buttons to the Attic Windows (button source on page 320). Use sashing strips to make pillow top desired size.

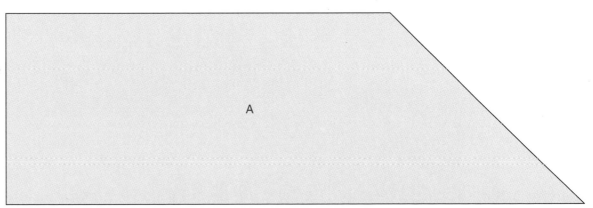

A

TIMELESS TREASURES

This quilt is a collection!
224 four-inch blocks speak of your skills and
look beautiful on a king-size bed. However,
this simple setting makes it easy to showcase
a collection of any size.

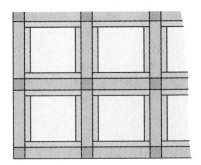

Finished Size

85" x 97" without outer borders

Block Patterns

224 blocks of your choice

Note: This quilt was made with
14 blocks across and 16 down.
You can make your quilt as large
or as small as you wish using this
setting.

Fabric Requirements

3¼ yds. for ½-inch borders for
every block

½ yd. for 1-inch squares

2¾ yds. for 1" x 5" strips

Additional fabric for outside border, binding, and backing, as
desired

Construction

Note: Add ¼-inch seam
allowances to all measurements
and templates.

For the king-size quilt cut:

224 strips ½" x 4"

224 strips ½" x 5"

255 squares 1" x 1"

478 strips 1" x 5"

Frame each block with ½-inch
strips.

Make horizontal rows of
framed blocks joined with 1" x 5"
strips (begin and end each row
with a 1-inch strip).

Make horizontal rows of 1" x
5" strips joined by 1-inch squares
(begin and end each row with a
1-inch square).

Join the rows, beginning and
ending with strip/square rows.

Add border strips on all sides,
as desired.

Back, quilt, and bind as directed on page 312.

11

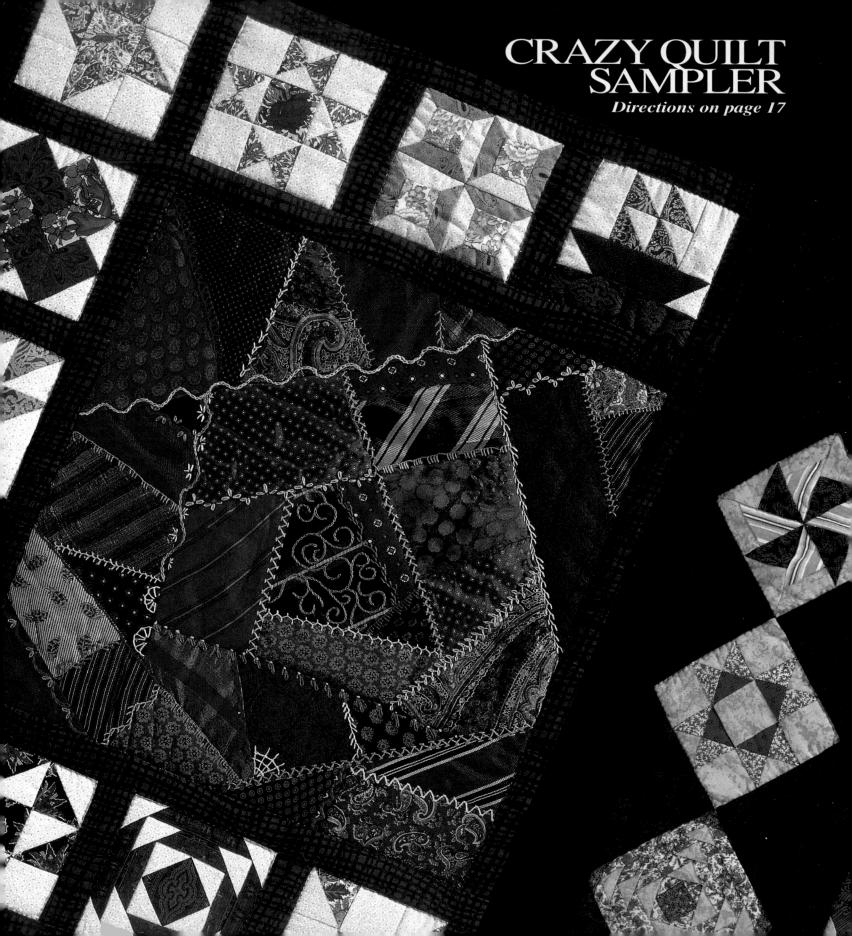

CRAZY QUILT
SAMPLER
Directions on page 17

MAGIC CARPET
Directions on page 14

MAGIC CARPET

A dark print background for 144 four-inch blocks creates a magical effect. The mosaic-style setting, with some blocks straight and others on point, highlights every block.

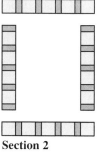

Section 1

Section 2

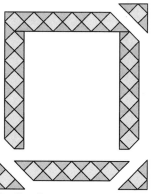

Section 3

Finished Size

73" x 93¾"

Block Patterns

144 blocks of your choice

Note: This quilt was made in sections, beginning in the center. You can make the quilt as shown, or add or delete sections to achieve a different size.

Fabric Requirements

4 yds. for sashings and borders

6 yds. for backing

1 yd. for binding

Note: Add ¼-inch seam allowances to all measurements and templates.

Construction: Section 1

This section uses 12 four-inch blocks of your choosing.

Background fabric required:

Cut 6 four-inch squares

Cut 10 Pattern A

Cut 4 Pattern B

Note: Be sure to cut Pattern A pieces with the long edge of the triangle (the hypotenuse) straight with the fabric grain (shown by arrows).

Piece the rows together diagonally, then add a 1" x 22½" border to each side and 1" x 19" borders to top and bottom edges.

Construction: Section 2

This section uses 18 four-inch blocks of your selection.

Background fabric required:

Cut 18 sashing pieces 1¾" x 4"

Cut 2 border pieces ½" x 32¾"

14

Cut 2 border pieces ½" x 28"

Sew 4 blocks together with sashing between each and on each end. Make 2 of these units; join to sides of center section.

Sew 5 blocks together with sashings between each; make this unit 2 times and attach to top and bottom of center section.

Sew ½" x 32¾" borders to sides and ½" x 28" borders to top and bottom.

Construction: Section 3

This section uses 26 four-inch blocks of your choice.

Background fabric required:

Cut 48 pieces of Pattern A

Cut 8 pieces of Pattern B

Cut 124 pieces of Pattern C in various fabrics.

Cut 2 border strips 1" x 45"

Cut 2 border strips 1½" x 41⅜"

Cut 2 border strips 1½" x 45"

Follow diagrams to assemble and attach Section 3.

Then attach a 1" x 45" border to each side, and a 1½" x 41⅜" bor-

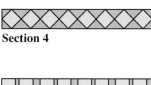
Section 4

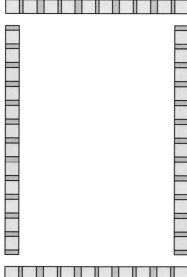
Section 5

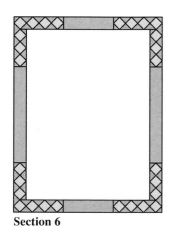
Section 6

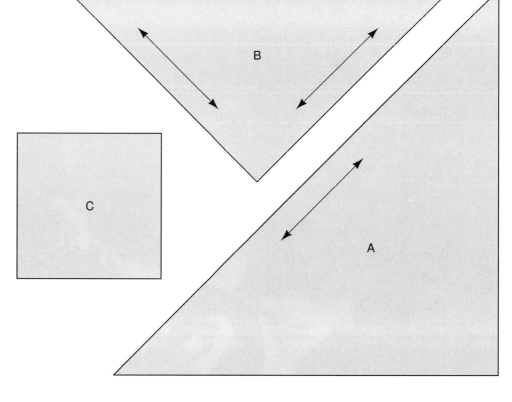

der to top and bottom.

Sew a strip of 32 pieces of Pattern C, alternating selected fabrics. Make this unit 2 times and attach to each side of the center section. Make 2 units of 30 pieces of Pattern C and sew to top and bottom. Add 1½" x 45" borders to top and bottom only.

Construction: Section 4

This section uses 16 four-inch blocks of your choice. Background fabric required:
Cut 28 pieces of Pattern A
Cut 8 pieces of Pattern B
Cut 2 strips ⅞" x 65¼"
Cut 2 strips 1⅛" x 46¾"

Make 2 units as shown in the diagram for Section 4. Attach these units to top and bottom.

Add ⅞" x 65¼" sashings to sides and 1⅛" x 46¾" sashings to top and bottom.

Construction: Section 5

This section uses 44 four-inch blocks of your choosing.
Background fabric required:
Cut 36 pieces 1¼" x 4"
Cut 8 pieces 2" x 4"
Cut 2 border strips 1½" x 75½"
Cut 2 border strips 1½" x 57⅝"

See the Section 5 diagram. Sew 1¼-inch sashing pieces between each block and on each end of the side units; add to center section. Sew sashings between each block for the top and bottom units, alternating the narrow and wider sashings as shown in the diagram. Add to top and bottom of

main section.

Add 1½" x 75½" borders to the sides, and 1½" x 57⅝" to top and bottom.

Construction: Section 6

This section uses 28 four-inch blocks of your choice.
Background fabric requirements:
Cut 44 pieces of Pattern A
Cut 24 pieces of Pattern B
Cut 2 strips 5⅝" x 44¾"
Cut 2 strips 5⅝" x 23⅞"
Cut 2 strips 2" x 89¾"
Cut 2 strips 2" x 73"

See the Section 6 illustration to assemble and attach pieces. Then finish with the 2-inch borders on sides and top and bottom.

Back, quilt, and bind as directed on page 312.

15

SAMPLER STYLE

Think of the medallion center, framed by forty little sampler blocks, as your canvas, waiting for creative ideas to show off your collectibles. Using the same setting, we made a nostalgic crazy quilt from a collection of men's ties; then we went contemporary with our op art showcase of buttons.

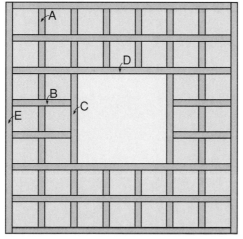

CRAZY QUILT SAMPLER

Shown left and on page 12

Finished Size

36" x 36"

Block Patterns

40 blocks of your choice

Fabric Requirements

1¼ yds. for border and sashing

1⅛ yds. for backing

½ yd. for binding

14" square for center

Construction

Note: Add ¼-inch seam allowances to all measurements and templates.

Using the 14-inch square, we fashioned the crazy-quilt block from silk ties and embellished it with crazy-quilt stitches. Add extra seam allowances to this center block. This is especially necessary when using crazy-quilt technique (it's called *crazy* for good reason!).

Referring to diagram, cut the following 1-inch strips:

  30 A pieces: 1" x 4"

   4 B pieces: 1" x 9"

   2 C pieces: 1" x 14"

   6 D pieces: 1" x 34"

   2 E pieces: 1" x 36"

Assemble the sampler blocks with the A strips in horizontal rows, referring to the diagram. Piece the rows with B strips and D strips. Add C strips to sides of

center block. Join center block to short rows.

Sew all rows together as shown. Add E strips to sides.

Back, quilt, and bind as directed on page 312.

OP ART SAMPLER

The Sampler, shown opposite, was designed around a specific fabric with a button collection in mind. Its construction is the same as the Crazy Quilt Sampler, with an extra border.

Finished Size

45" x 45"

Fabric Requirements

1¼ yds. for sashing

1¼ yds. for inner border

1⅜ yds. for outer border

 ½ yd. for binding

2¾ yds. for backing

Construction

Follow directions for Crazy Quilt Sampler, adding a 1-inch border all around the assembled quilt and a 3½-inch border beyond that.

TEATIME ANYTIME QUILT

Directions on page 22

18

VERY VICTORIAN QUILT
Directions on page 20

VERY VICTORIAN

The too-much-is-almost-enough philosophy of Victorian decor
is what we had in mind as we designed this wall hanging.
Let's display everything! We used buttons, laces, tatting,
handkerchiefs, and buckles along with Liberty fabric pieces in
four-inch spool blocks.

Finished Size

52" x 35"

Block Patterns

6 Spool blocks (D29, page 192)
or 6 other blocks of your choice

Fabric Requirements

¾ yd. for bars

⅛ yd. for grape leaves

1¼ yds. for inner border and binding

1¾ yds. for outside border and sashings*

¼ yd. for appliquéd bow

1½ yds. for backing (used horizontally)

10 buttons for each grape cluster

* We used a striped fabric. If you
do the same, stripes should not
measure more than 2½ inches cut.

Construction

*Note: Add ¼-inch seam
allowances to all measurements
and templates.*

6 A pieces 4" x 24" black

6 B pieces 2" x 24"

8 grape leaves cut from pattern

Grape Clusters

Mark 2 black strips of fabric at
6-inch intervals. Then divide the
6-inch portions into 2 sections:
top 2 inches and bottom 4 inches.
Appliqué leaf, centered, in 2-inch
space; cluster buttons in 4-inch
space. (In this quilt, ½- to ⅝-inch
buttons were used in rows of 4, 3,
2, 1 to make the grape cluster.)

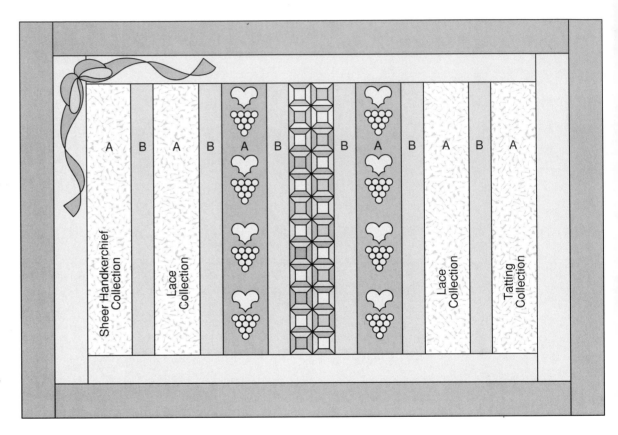

Construction

Sew strips together as shown in
the illustration above:
A/B/A/B/A/B/ Spool Blocks /
B/A/B/A/B/A.

Borders

Inner border: Cut 2 pieces 2½" x
40", add to top and bottom. Cut 2
pieces 3" x 29", add to sides.

Appliqué bow to top left corner. Bow could also be appliquéd
to opposite diagonal corner.

Add outer border. Cut 2 pieces
3" x 46", add to top and bottom.

Cut 2 pieces 3" x 35", add to
sides.

Back, quilt, and bind as directed on page 312.

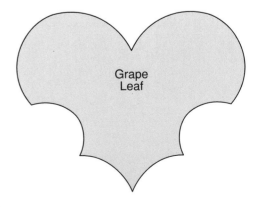

Grape
Leaf

20

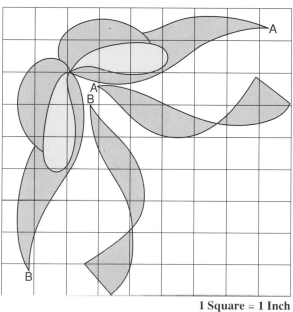

This appliquéd bow is a perfect finishing
touch to your Victorian collection.
Enlarge pattern pieces as indicated
(one square on grid equals one inch).
Bow streamers are completed by
matching the pieces at A and B.

We used a collection of ladies' belt buckles
to embellish our bow, sewing them to the
"twists" in the ribbon-like streamers.

1 Square = 1 Inch

TEATIME ANYTIME

We designed a small wall quilt and then thought about the white gloves! It was easy to add borders to accommodate our collection. (See photo on page 18.) Perhaps you have some linen napkins or other treasures that could be displayed this way.

Finished Size

20" x 26" without borders

34" x 47" with borders

Block Patterns

12 Teatime blocks (G1–G12, pages 275–80)

Fabric Requirements

¼ yd. dark for sashings

½ yd. light for sashings

1 yd. for background

For larger version with borders you will need 1⅜ yds. of background fabric plus the border pieces as specified.

Construction

Note: Add ¼-inch seam allowances to all measurements and templates.

From the dark fabric, cut 20 of Pattern A. (We used a teapot-printed fabric and centered a teapot in each square.) From the light fabric, cut 31 of Pattern C. From the light fabric, cut 80 of Pattern B.

For the sashing, sew B pieces to two oposite sides of A, then add B pieces to two remaining sides of A.

Join these AB units with the C pieces, referring to the diagram of the quilt to make the rows.

Join your 4-inch blocks with C pieces to form rows. Join the rows as shown in the diagram.

To make the larger wall quilt, add borders as follows:

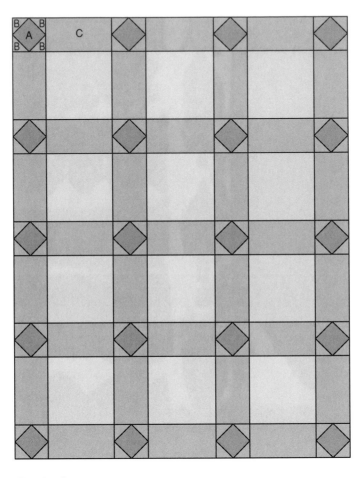

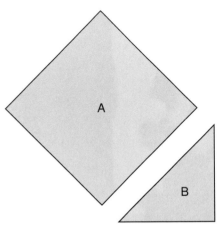

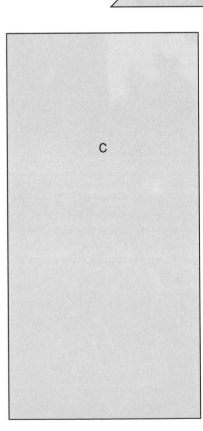

Border I

Add 5" x 26" borders to sides, and 5" x 30" borders to top and bottom.

Border II

Add 7" x 30" borders to bottom only.

Border III

Add 2" x 30" borders to top and bottom, and 2" x 47" borders to sides.

Back, quilt, and bind as directed on page 312.

WELCOME SPRINGTIME

*Just a few quilt blocks bring the freshness of a new season
to your home. To create the mantle/shelf quilt we enlarged our four-inch
basket quilt block to twelve inches and added appliquéd Easter eggs.
Apply some of your imagination to other seasonal projects!*

A single block framed by a grapevine wreath adds a picture of the season to your home. We added backing and binding to a delightful bunny block (C56, page 163) and tacked him inside a wreath decorated with a few flowers, buttons, and bows.

An Easter basket or an anytime basket is another great holiday project. See our notes on basket quilts on page 37.

MANTLE/SHELF QUILT

The mantle quilt shown here was made from one enlarged block pattern. We used D109 (page 232), but you could select another pattern instead.

Enlarge the block to 12 inches. Construct each block according to the directions for that block, but do not use background pieces around the bottom section of the basket.

Join the baskets at the sides, as shown in the diagram.

Measure the depth of the mantle or shelf you plan to use. Cut the mantle overlay that depth plus ½" x the length of the basket blocks measured from raw edge to raw edge. Add this overlay piece to the top of the constructed piece. Press seam toward the constructed piece.

Lay the quilt right sides togeth-er with the backing and very thin batting. Stitch around the whole piece, leaving an opening of about 6 inches for turning. Trim corners, clip notches at corners. Turn; close opening.

Machine- or hand-quilt in the ditch along the seam between the overlay and the hanging portion to help the quilt hang nicely.

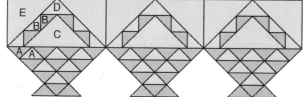

SWEET DREAMS

Block borders decorate linens. Here we used a band of nine appliquéd flower blocks on a sheet and embellished each pillowcase with a single block. These block patterns are all in the collection beginning on page 96.

SPOOLS FOR ALL SEASONS

We made our own block-of-the-month decisions for this calendar quilt. It demonstrates a way to establish a theme when combining block patterns. Here, we chose four blocks for each month, from sailboats and fans for July and August to hearts and pinwheels for February and March. The 48 blocks are joined in a spool setting.

COUNTRY CHARM

A simple chambray shirt is a
charm bracelet without the charms.
Four-inch blocks, yo-yos,
and ceramic buttons add that charm.
Button-on bibs provide even more
variety (find pattern and button
sources on page 320).
If you aren't wearing your quilting,
it's about time!

Sensational wearables are as simple as setting a sunflower on a knit top or as inspiring as constructing a fantastic Southwest shirt. For the colorful shirt we combined some great fabrics with twelve Southwest blocks (G37–G48 beginning on page 293). The blocks are joined with black sashing to form the back yoke and vertical strips on the pattern pieces of the shirt (see page 320 for pattern source).

WITH NO RESERVATIONS

RANCH DRESSING

Pour it on! Have fun with quilt-block apparel. We went crazy with barnyard blocks combined with a shirt sewn from farmland fabric. Then we used bright geometrics on a blue jacket. (You'll find sewing pattern sources on page 320.) You don't have to live in Texas to wear Western.

SIGNATURES

*Celebrate a special occasion with a signature quilt.
Blocks especially designed to include the autographs of friends,
relatives, coworkers, or family members begin on page 178.
These twelve album-block patterns can be showcased in any setting
to make a wall hanging of memories.*

STAR-SPANGLED BANNER

The wings of an eagle, spread protectively over flags and a shield of stars, make this a wall hanging for a hero. For a public office or the den in your home, this handsome wall quilt delivers a patriotic message.

Finished Size

50" x 50"

Block Patterns

12 Star blocks (D89–100, pages 222–7)

Fabric Requirements

2 yds. for background

1 yd. first navy for flags, shield, binding, border stars, and sashing

½ yd. second navy for border stars

1½ yds. first red for flag, eagle and borders

⅛ yd. second red for shield sashing

¾ yd. dark brown for flagstaffs

¼ yd. light brown for eagle

¼ yd. medium light brown for eagle

¼ yd. medium dark brown for eagle

¼ yd. dark brown for eagle

⅛ yd. green for olive branches

¼ yd. red, white, and blue stripe for USA letters

3 yds. for backing

Construction

Note: Add ¼-inch seam allowances to all measurements and templates unless otherwise directed.

The quilt is constructed in four parts: the appliquéd eagle, the flags, the shield and the star blocks, and the stars-and-stripes

32

border.

Eagle and Flag Sections

Cut border strips of red, white, and the background fabric before cutting anything else. Diagram 1 shows large pieces that you will need to cut to make the sections.

For the two flag sections you will need to cut the following pieces (patterns on page 36):

A: 8 white and 12 red

Ar: 8 white and 12 red

B: 8 background fabric

Br: 8 background fabric

To construct, first piece the top

portion with the large blue triangles. Next, piece the flag sections, noting that you must flip the template over to cut the reverse pieces of A and B—Ar and Br. Piece the flag sections in horizontal rows, referring to the diagram.

Once the piecing is done, appliqué the flagstaffs. Cut 2 bias strips of dark brown, 34" x 1¼". (This provides extra length.) Fold each strip lengthwise, wrong sides together. Stitch, using ¼-inch seam. Press the strip flat,

with the seam centered underneath the strip. Appliqué the poles, crossing them in the center block. The lower ends of the poles will end 3 inches from the side seam of the center block. (See Diagram 1 for placement.)

Now you are ready to appliqué the eagle. The pattern is drawn in three parts (pages 34 and 35), and this is the easiest way to appliqué it. Once the three parts are prepared, appliqué them to the top section of the piece. Finally, appliqué the letters USA and the leaves in position around the flagpoles.

Shield Unit with Star Blocks

To make the shield unit (Diagram 2) use pattern pieces on page 36 (add seam allowances):

C: Cut 21 red

D: Cut 32 navy

Join Cs and Ds with the 12 star blocks as shown. Add the side units (background piece with red B triangle).

Appliqué the navy shield piece (pattern on page 35) to a 5" x 39" background piece and then attach it to the block unit.

Border instructions follow on page 36.

Diagram 1

Diagram 2

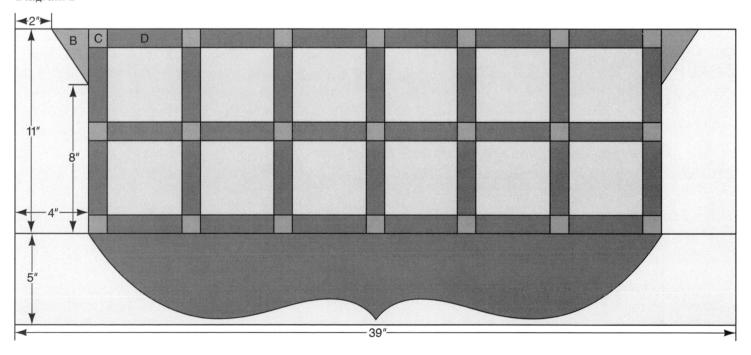

33

Fold

1 Square = 1 Inch

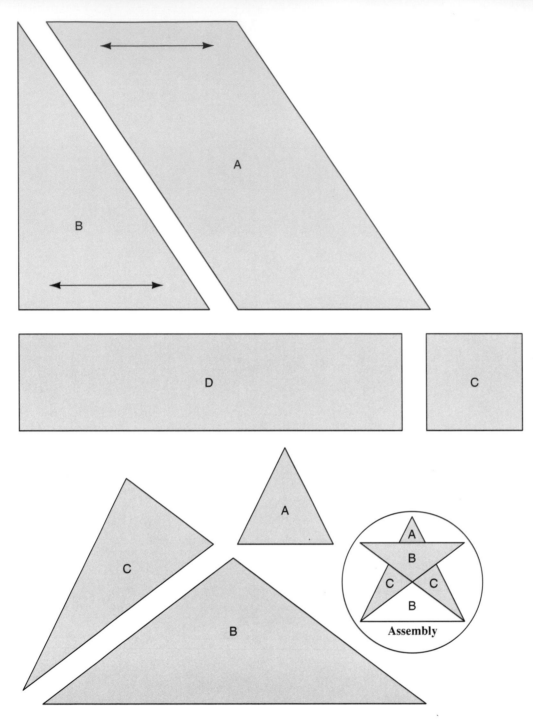

Assembly

Stars-and-Stripes Border

Cut the following strips for the border. *Note: The following measurements INCLUDE ¼-inch seam allowances and allow a little extra length.*

Red: 8 pieces 1½" x 52"

White: 4 pieces 1½" x 52"

Background: 4 pieces 3" x 52"

Sew pieces together in the following order:

1. Background
2. Red
3. White
4. Red

Fold a strip in half to determine center. Match center of border to center of quilt and pin, right sides together, sewing the background edge to the quilt. Leave ¼ inch free at each end of quilt. Stitch all four sides in this manner.

Now miter the corner (for help with mitering, see page 309). At each corner: Overlap one free end of the border over the other, working on the wrong side. When the strips lie at true right angles, make a mark where they cross.

Refold the top so that the borders match. Draw a line from the seam point on the quilt to the point you marked on the edge of the border. Check to be sure that the strips all match up. Now stitch along the line you drew. Open the quilt to be sure that strips match, then trim the seam and press.

Border Stars

Using the three-piece star pattern at left, make 16 stars. Cut pieces A and C from first navy; cut 1 C piece from second navy and the bottom C piece from background fabric.

Assemble stars with the pattern pieces, as shown in the diagram. Baste all raw edges except the background fabric edge.

Appliqué stars to quilt border. The stars on each end of the border are 6½ inches apart. We suggest you lay them out, then adjust if necessary.

Back, quilt, and bind quilt as directed on page 312. Quarter-inch binding will work best on this piece to prevent cutting the points off the stars.

KITCHEN WARE

The well-dressed kitchen wears four-inch quilt blocks in the colors of your choice. Select your favorite block patterns. We never use the same one twice! One for a hotpad, one for a towel, one for a tea cozy, plus enough to decorate a basket.

BASKET WRAPS

Baskets and quilts are natural partners. You'll find our Easter basket on page 23. Think about the other seasonal baskets you could create...especially Christmas!

The wrap just ties onto the basket, so you can use the same basket throughout the year with new clothes for the season.

Select a suitable basket. The sides must be perpendicular and flat for the wrap to fit properly.

Measure the depth of the basket and the circumference. Based on these figures, determine how many blocks you will need and the size of the borders.

Once you know how many 4-inch blocks you can use, select and make the blocks. Then add borders to the blocks to construct the size your basket needs.

Cut a backing piece for the wrap and back, quilt, and bind as directed on page 312.

Finally, add ribbons to each end of your basket wrap (we use three sets) and tie the wrap around the basket.

BLOCKS OF FUN

*Quilt blocks with spirit! Cheer the team, the sports' fans,
the school. Young-at-heart quilting is fun.
Select blocks to fit your family and make them bright!*

SPIRITED QUILTING

Top a family bulletin board with a strip of sports blocks.

Give your favorite golfer a special pillow.

Pad a notebook for school or personal use.

Design a quilt block sweatshirt with alphabet and activity blocks.

Put the alphabet in order for your favorite youngster.

ALPHABET SOUP

Finished Size

26" x 36"

Block Patterns

26 alphabet blocks (E1–E26, pages 234-46)

12 juvenile blocks (F10–F21, pages 257–62)

Additional Fabric

1¼ yds. for background and sashing

1⅛ yds. for backing

⅓ yd. for binding

Construction

Note: Add ¼-inch seam allowances to all measurements and templates .

Cut the following sashing pieces:

8 pieces 1" x 4"

2 pieces 4" x 4"

8 pieces 24" x 1"

2 pieces 36" x 1"

Join the blocks in rows as shown in the diagram. Join the rows with the 24" x 1" sashings,

then add the 36" x 1" pieces to the sides.

Back, quilt, and bind as directed on page 312.

Note: If you intend this quilt to be used by a child rather than displayed on a wall, omit the beads, snaps, buttons, or other embellishments that could scratch or be swallowed.

Kites	Top	Blocks	Bear	Wagon
A	B	C	D	E	F
G	H	I	J	K	L
M	N	O	P	Q	R
S	T	U	V	W	X
Doll		Y	Z		Soldier
Stick horse	Buggy	Ball	Drum	Cat

24"

36"

HOLIDAY HARVEST

October and November bring Halloween, Thanksgiving, family gatherings, rich, warm colors, and the spirit of harvest. Bring it all inside your home with an autumn quilt-block project.

HALLOWEEN MANTLE

Finished Size

42" x 9" plus shelf overlay

Block Patterns

6 blocks: Black Cat and Ghost (C83, page 177), Witch (C81, page 176), Bat (C77, page 174), Jack-o'-lantern (C74, page 172), Spider Web (C82, page 176), and Ghost (C76, page 173)

Additional Fabric

1½ yds. for background and backing

Scraps of various orange fabrics for 6 pumpkins

Scraps of green for pumpkin leaves

Note: Add ¼-inch seam allowances to all measurements and templates.

Block 1

Make 2 blocks (see diagram, page 43), using blocks C83 and C74. Construct each as follows:

Sew A piece to sides of block. Sew B piece to bottom of block; make CBC unit and attach to top of block. Make EDEr unit and sew to top. Sew 2" x 6" background piece to top edge.

Block 2

Make 2 blocks (see diagram, page 43), using Blocks C81 and C76, as follows:

Sew B pieces to sides of block; sew A piece to bottom of block. Make CAC unit and attach to top of block. Make DCE unit and add

to top of block.

Block 3

Make 2 blocks (see diagram, page 43), using Blocks C77 and C82, as follows:

Sew A and Ar pieces to all sides of block, mitering the A/Ar seams (for help with mitering, see page 309.) Add D pieces to top corners. Make BC unit and DEF unit, join and add to top of block. Sew 9" x ½" background piece to top of block.

Assembly

Join the blocks horizontally, as pictured on page 43.

Measure the depth of the mantle or shelf where the quilt will be displayed, add the width of the hanging portion plus ½ inch, and you have the width of the overlay from raw edge to raw edge.

Add the overlay piece to the top of the constructed piece. Press the seam toward the constructed piece.

Lay the quilt right sides together with a backing piece and a thin batting. Stitch around the whole piece, leaving an opening of about 6 inches for turning. Trim corners, clip notches at bottom of piece between pumpkins. Turn right side out; close opening.

Machine-quilt or hand-quilt in the ditch along the seam between the overlay and the hanging portion, to help the quilt hang nicely.

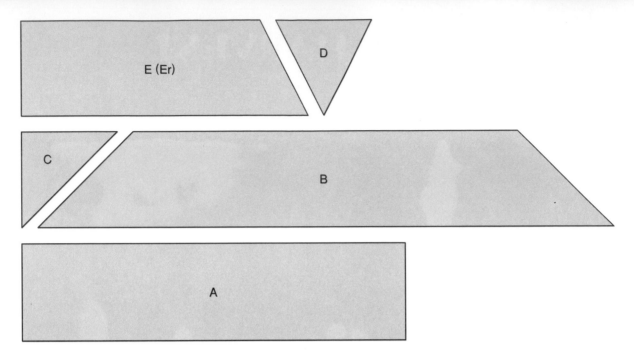

Block 1

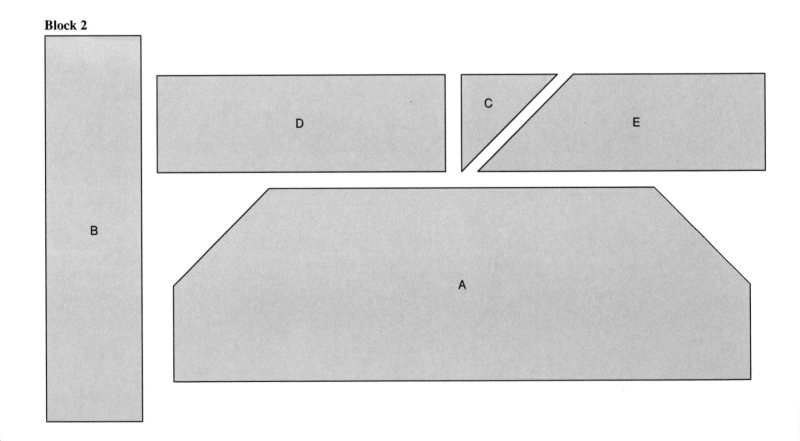

Block 2

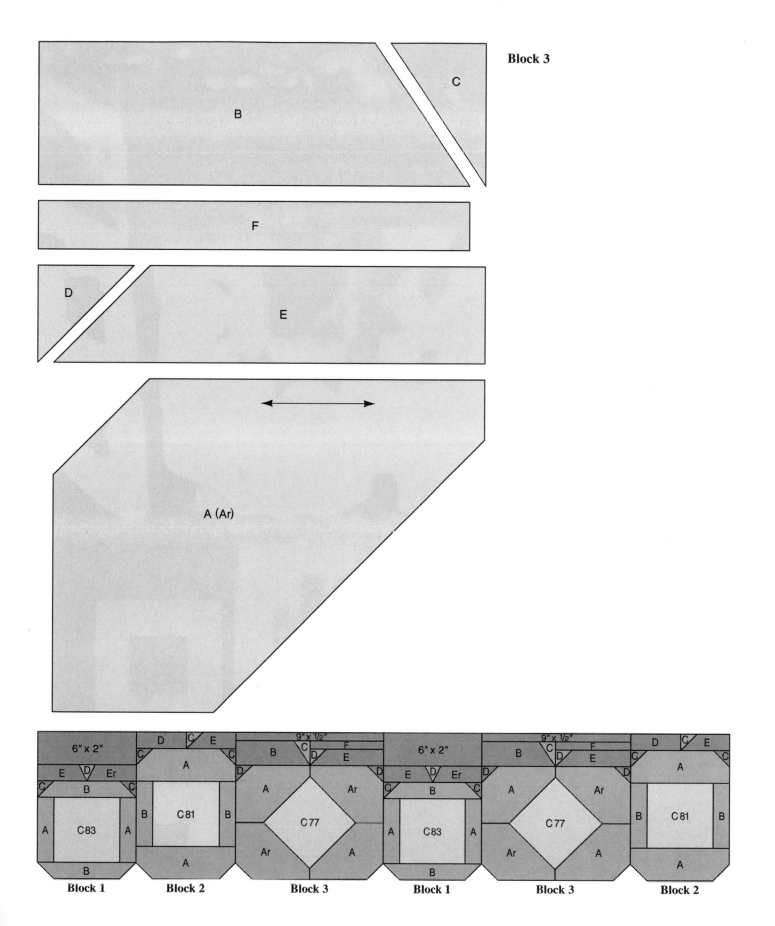

Block 3

B

C

F

D

E

A (Ar)

Block 1	Block 2	Block 3	Block 1	Block 3	Block 2

6" x 2"

E   D   Er

C   B   C

A   C83   A

B

D   C   E

C   C

A

B   C81   B

A

9" x 1/2"

B   C   F
D   E
D   D

A   Ar

Ar   A

C77

6" x 2"

E   D   Er

C   B   C

A   C83   A

B

9" x 1/2"

B   C   F
D   E
D   D

A   Ar

Ar   A

C77

D   C   E

C   C

A

B   C81   B

A

43

TABLE RUNNER

Finished Size

22½" x 74½"

Block Patterns

Six blocks: C73, C75, C78, C79, C80, and C84 (patterns begin on page 172)

Additional Fabric

1 yd. for background pieces

½ yd. background for leaf blocks

1⅛ yds. striped fabric for border

Scraps for leaf blocks

Buttons to embellish (optional)

Note: Remember to add ¼-inch seam allowances when cutting all background pieces.

Backing and binding

Note: This project includes an 8-inch square cross-stitched piece. See page 320 for pattern reference.

Block 1

Make 2, one with Block C79 and one with C80 in the center.

Make 3 ABB units, and 4 ACCD units. Join ABB to ACCD to ABB for the top row. Join ACCD to Block to ACCD for center row. Join ABB to ACCD to F for third row. Join rows.

Block 2

Make 2, one with Block C73 and one with C78 in the center.

Make 4 BCB units. Add BCB units to two opposite sides of block.

Join A pieces to each end of the other 2 BCB units, then add these strips to top and bottom of center block unit.

Block 3

Make 2, one with Block C75 and one with C84 in the center.

Make 4 BB units, join in pairs. Add 1 BB/BB unit to side of block. Attach A piece to second BB/BB unit and join to top.

Assembly

Assemble table runner as shown in diagram.

Embellish

Use buttons to embellish some of the leaf blocks, or try appliquéd and/or heat-transfer motifs of leaves and pumpkins.

Borders

Decide how wide you want your borders and then use the following formula to determine the

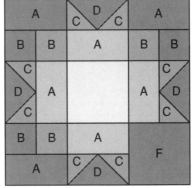

Leaf Block 1 (12″)

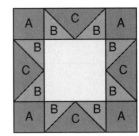

Leaf Block 2 (8″)

length of each border piece (W=width): Length of edge + 2W + seam allowance = total length of border. This formula works for all sides.

Back, quilt, and bind as directed on page 312.

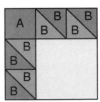

Leaf Block 3 (6″)

44

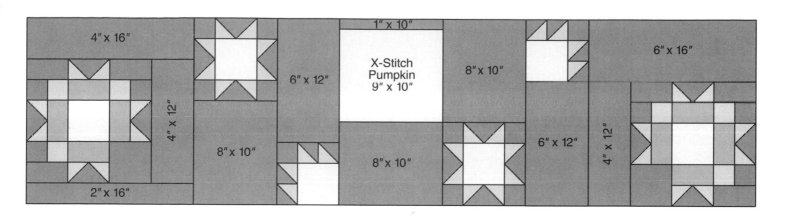

PIECEFUL CHRISTMAS

*Christmas quilt blocks are as much fun to make
as to receive. The projects we put together are designed to inspire your own
Christmas piecing. Try wall hangings and bell pulls
as well as the following special items.*

SANTA TREE SKIRT

A dozen Santas decorate this little tree skirt, designed for table-top display.

Finished Size

28" diameter

Block Patterns

12 Santa blocks (C61–C72, beginning on page 166)

Additional Fabric

½ yd. green

½ yd. red

⅞ yd. for backing

2½ yds. ribbon

Construction

Note: Add ¼-inch seam allowances to all measurements and templates.

Using the pattern pieces provided on page 48, cut the following:

A: 12 green and 20 red

B: 3 green

C: 4 green

D: 1 green

Dr: 1 green

Following the diagram, piece together in vertical rows. The numbers on the blocks in the diagram face the same direction as each Santa should face. Join the pieced rows, then add B, C, and D pieces.

Remove stitching in seam as shown by the double line in the diagram. Cut a 3-inch circle in the center. Cut 6 pieces of ribbon, 15 inches long. Baste in place at dots marked in diagram.

Sew tree skirt top and backing, right sides together, with batting. Leave opening to turn right side out, turn and close the opening.

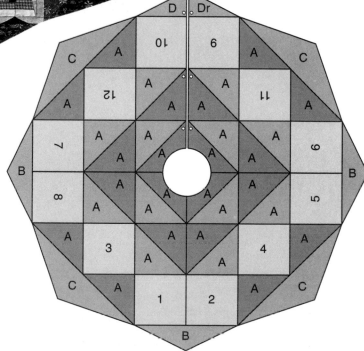

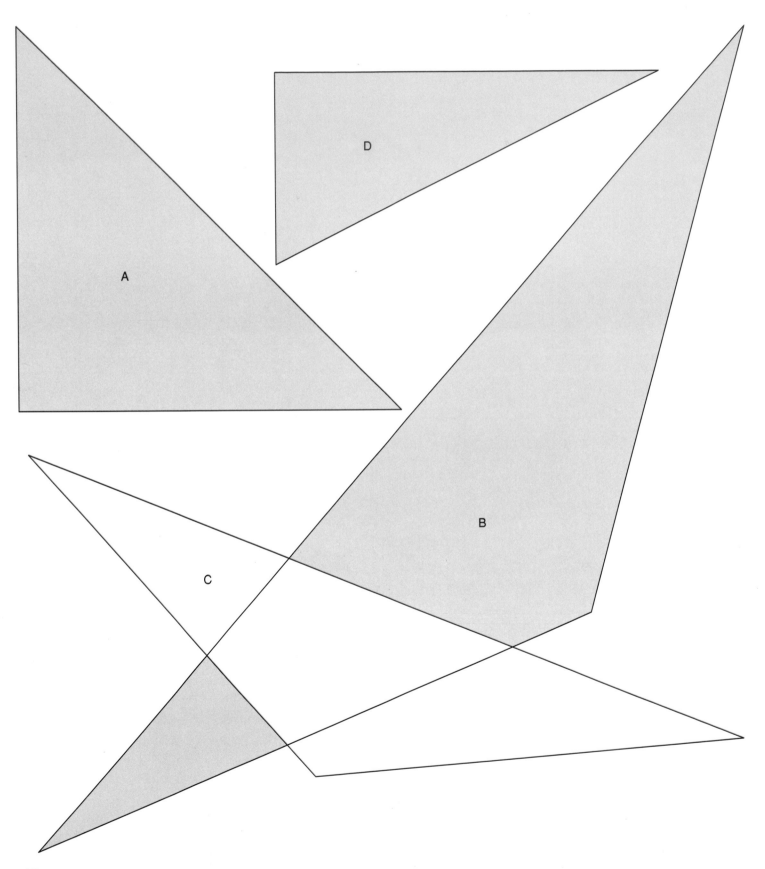

CHRISTMAS STOCKINGS

Use one, two, or three quilt blocks to make a Christmas stocking that just begs to be filled. *Note: Add ¼-inch seam allowances to all measurements.*

Stocking 1

One 4-inch block of your choice makes the smallest stocking. It requires ⅜ yd. of fabric, using the same fabric for stocking and lining.

Add ½" x 4" border to top of block, then add ½" x 4½" border to each side. Sew block with borders to edge of stocking (using Stocking 1 pattern provided on page 50). See Basic Stocking Directions to complete.

Stocking 2

This stocking uses 2 of the 4-inch blocks. You will need ½ yd. fabric for the stocking and lining.

The top of this stocking extends beyond the edge of the stocking bottom.

Join the 2 quilt blocks with a ½" x 4" strip to make a horizontal row. Add ½" x 8½" strip to top and bottom of block unit. Sew ½" x 5" border to sides.

Add stocking bottom, matching center of block section with center of stocking bottom section.

See Basic Stocking Directions to complete.

Stocking 3

Select 3 of the 4-inch blocks for this stocking. You will also need ½ yd. fabric for the stocking and lining.

Join the 3 blocks together in a vertical row with ½" x 4" sashing between blocks. Add 1" x 14" border to right side and 3" x 14" border to left side. Sew a 9" x 4" strip to bottom edge of block unit. Add 1" x 8" border to top of stocking.

Make a template of the bottom section of the stocking (Stocking 3 pattern) and trace around it to make stocking shape.

Basic Stocking Directions

The stocking templates provided are without seam allowances. The outline given is the sewing line.

Using the full stocking template, cut 1 back and 2 linings from your fabric. If your fabric is not reversible, remember to reverse the template to cut the back and one lining.

To make ribbon hanger for stocking, cut a piece of ¼-inch ribbon 6 inches long and fold in half. Position this loop about ½" from the side of the backing before stitching the lining to it. Catch ribbon in seam as you stitch backing and lining together, right sides facing.

Stitch lining and front together, right sides facing, as shown in the illustration on page 50. Lay lining/front unit on lining/back unit, right sides together, and stitch. Leave a 5-inch opening in the lining seam to turn. Trim seams, clip curves, and turn to right side. Close opening. Push lining into foot of stocking.

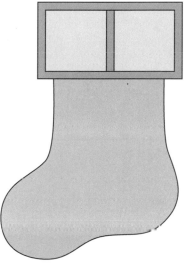

Stocking 1

Stocking 2

Stocking 3

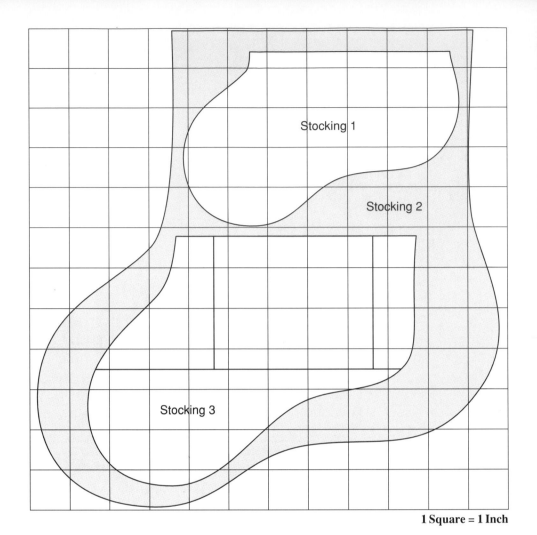

1 Square = 1 Inch

Stocking 1

Stocking 2

Stocking 3

Stocking Diagram

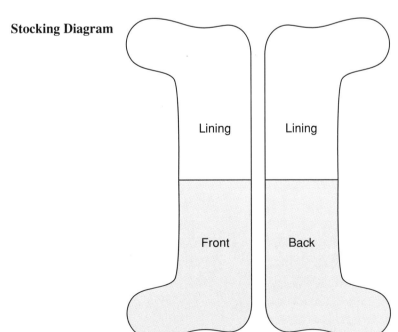

Lining

Lining

Front

Back

ORNAMENTS

A single 4-inch block can hang from your tree, a door knob, a wreath, or anywhere you want to add Christmas decoration.

Each ornament uses one 4-inch block plus backing and thin batting the same size as the block. Cut binding 20" x 2". Fold in half along the length and press. Layer block with batting and backing (right sides out, batting between).

Attach binding to edge of square, raw edges together. Fold over the end of binding before stitching. Stitch using ¼-inch seam. Bind as directed on page 312.

Use a 7-inch length of ribbon for each hanger.

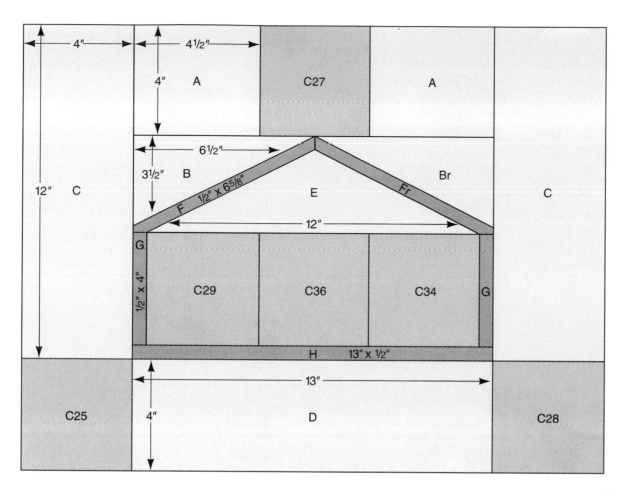

longer than the side seams, but will be trimmed later. Sew C25 and C28 to bottom edges of C pieces. Attach to right and left sides, stitch through all layers, matching raw edges at bottom.

Back, quilt, and bind as directed on page 312.

CARD HOLDER

The Nativity scene surrounds a pocket to display Christmas cards as they arrive.

Block Patterns

6 blocks: Angel on High (C27, page 149), Joseph (C29, page 150), Baby Jesus (C36, page 153), Mary (C34, page 152), Shepherd Tending Flock (C25, page 148), and We Three Kings (C28, page 149).

Additional Fabric

½ yd. for background
⅛ yd. brown for stable
⅛ yd. for binding

Construction

Sew blocks C29, C36, and C34 together in a horizontal row; add G piece to each side. Make

BFEFrBr unit; miter F/Fr seam (see page 309 for mitering directions); attach to top of first section. Join A pieces to sides of C27 block and sew to B/Br edge.

Sew 13" x ½" piece to bottom of Joseph/Baby Jesus/Mary blocks; attach a 13" x 4" piece (same fabric as stable) to bottom edge.

Cut two 13" x 4" pieces from background fabric and sew together along one 13-inch edge; turn and press with wrong sides together. Sew this piece to the lower edge of first section, matching raw edges at sides and bottom. (This will form pocket.)

Cut 2 C pieces 4" x 12½". These pieces will be slightly

51

BLOCK PATTERNS
Actual-size drawings for 501 four-inch quilt blocks are ready for your templates.

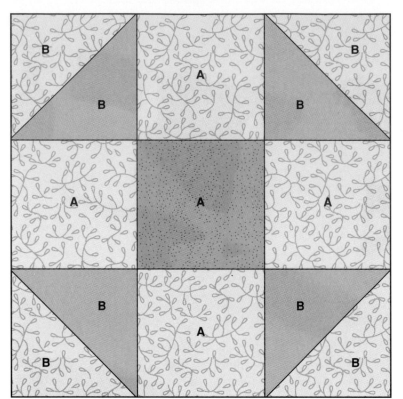

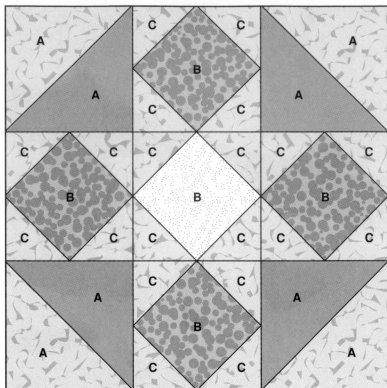

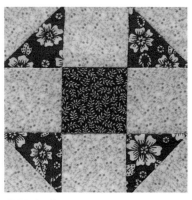

A1 Make BB unit (4 times). Join A pieces with BB units to form rows, referring to the diagram. Join rows to form the block.

SHOOFLY

A2 Attach C pieces to all 4 sides of B (5 times). Make AA units (4 times). Make rows A/BC/A, BC/BC/BC, A/BC/A. Join rows to make the block.

SAWTOOTH

PATCHWORK

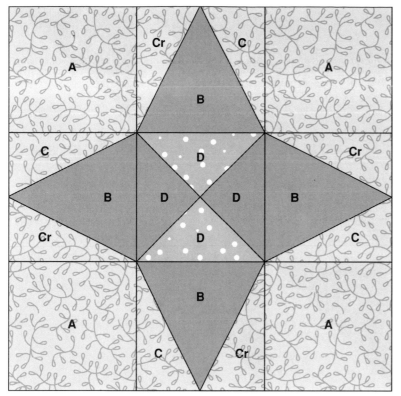

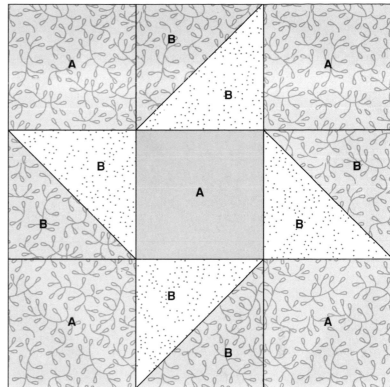

UNTITLED I

A3 Make center DDDD unit by joining 2 D pieces (2 times), then join 2 sets to form D unit. Add C and Cr to B (4 times). Make rows A/CBC/A, CBC/D/CBC, A/CBC/A. Join the rows to make the block.

FRIENDSHIP STAR

A4 Make BB unit (4 times). Join A pieces with BB units to form rows, referring to the diagram. Join rows to make the block.

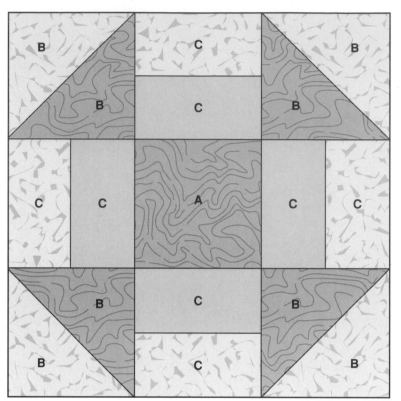

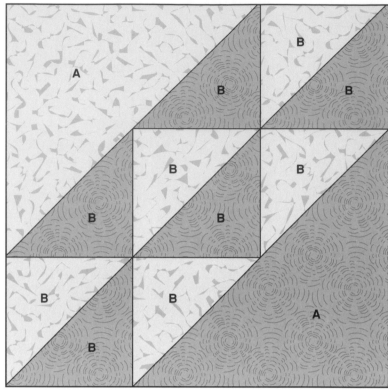

A5 Make BB units (4 times). Make CC units (4 times). Make rows BB/CC/BB, CC/A/CC, BB/CC/BB. Join rows to make the block.

CHURN DASH

A6 Form 2 diagonal rows of Bs. Add A to each B unit. Join AB sections to make the block.

NORTH WIND

PATCHWORK

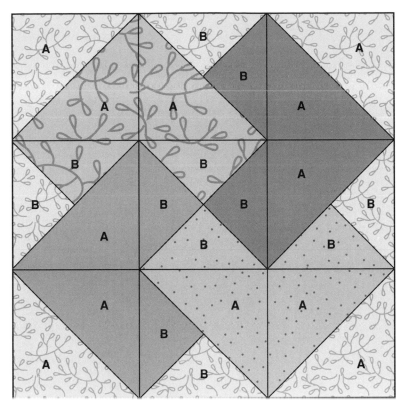

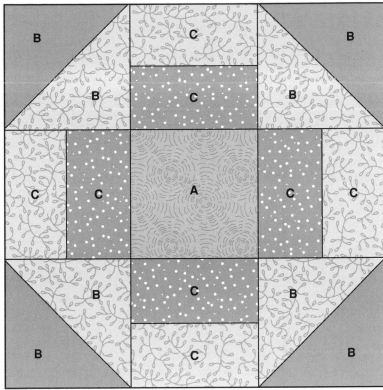

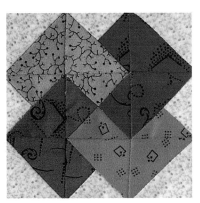

CARD TRICKS

A7 Make AA units (4 times). Make BBBB unit. Make ABB unit (4 times). Make rows AA/AB/AA, AB/B/AB, AA/AB/AA. Join rows to make the block.

GREEK CROSS

A8 Make BB units (4 times). Make CC units (4 times). Make rows BB/CC/BB, CC/A/CC, BB/CC/BB. Join rows to make the block. *Note: This is the same pattern as Churn Dash (A5), but it has a different look with this fabric/color sequence.*

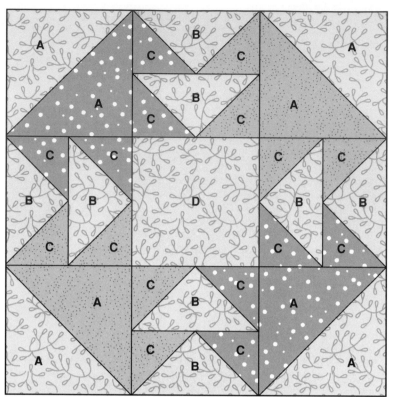

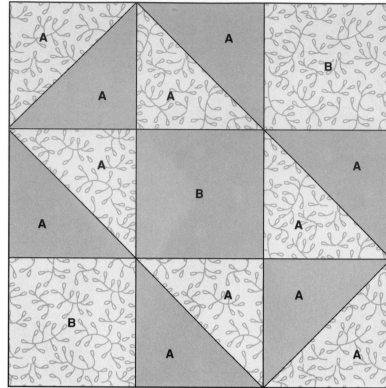

A9 Sew C pieces to B (8 times). Join 2 CBC units (4 times). Make AA unit (4 times). Make rows AA/BC/AA, BC/D/BC, AA/BC/AA. Join rows to make the block.

DOUBLE T

A10 Make AA unit (6 times). Make rows AA/AA/B, AA/B/AA, B/AA/AA. Join rows to make the block.

SPLIT NINE PATCH

PATCHWORK

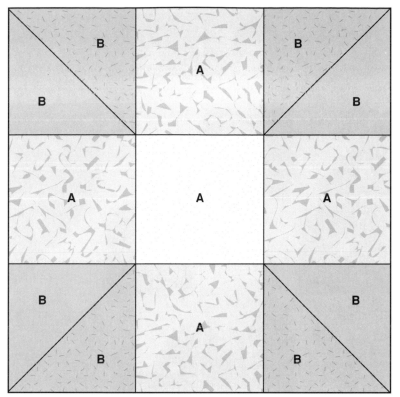

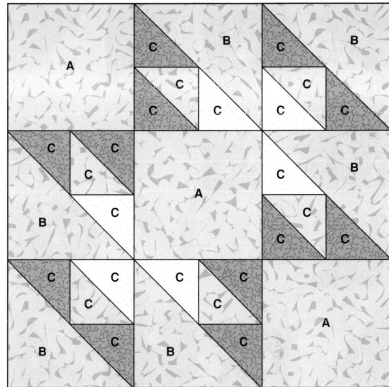

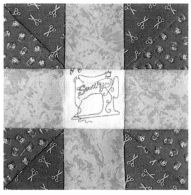

A11 Make BB unit (4 times). Make rows BB/A/BB, A/A/A, BB/A/BB. Join rows to make the block.

CALICO PUZZLE

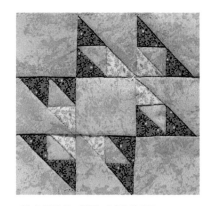

A12 Join 2 C pieces to make a square, add 2 C pieces to adjoining sides of CC square; add B piece to form square (6 times). Make rows A/BC/BC, BC/A/BC, BC/BC/A. Join rows to make the block.

CAT'S CRADLE

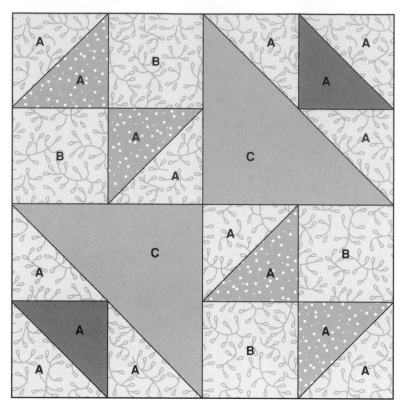

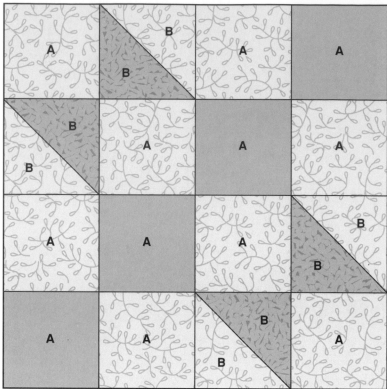

A13 Make AA unit (6 times). Add 2 A pieces to adjacent sides of AA unit, then add C piece to make a square (2 times). With 2 B pieces and 2 AA units make a square (for four-patch directions, see page 309). Make rows AB/AC, AC/AB. Join rows to make the block.

OLD MAID'S PUZZLE

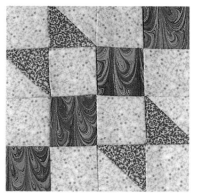

A14 Make BB unit (4 times). Make rows A/BB/A/A, BB/A/A/A/, A/A/A/BB, A/A/BB/A. Join rows to make the block.

ROAD TO CALIFORNIA

PATCHWORK

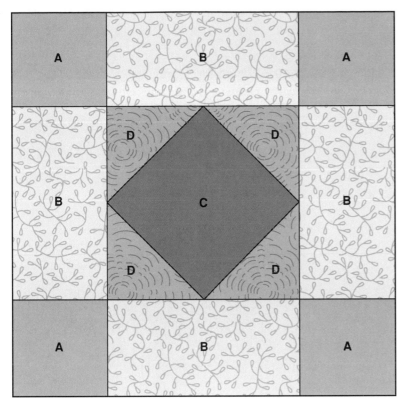

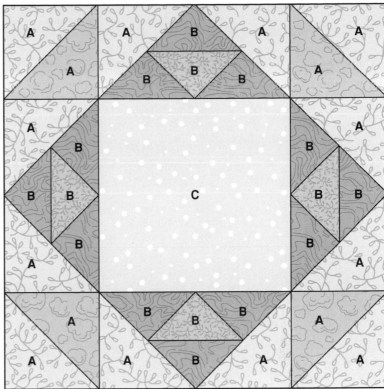

AMISH DIAMOND

A15 Add D pieces to 2 opposite sides of C, then to 2 remaining sides. Add B pieces to 2 sides of CD unit. Add A to each end of B (2 times); add AB units to each side of the first section to make the block.

GRANDMOTHER'S FAVORITE

A16 Make BB unit, then add B pieces to 2 sides (4 times). Add A pieces to B units. Attach 2 AB units to C. Make AA unit (4 times). Sew AA units to each end of 2 remaining AB units. Add AA/AB/AA sections to each side of center section to make the block.

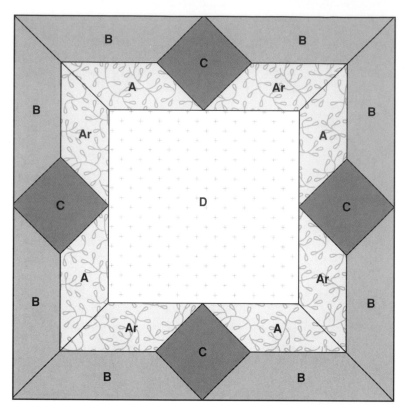

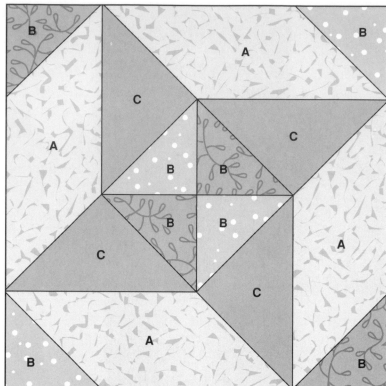

A17 Sew A and Ar, and 2 B pieces to C; miter AB edges (4 times). (See directions for mitering on page 309.) Add ABC units to D, then miter the corners.

UNTITLED II

A18 Make BBBB unit in center. Make ABC unit (4 times); add 1 unit to center unit using start-and-stop method. (For start-and-stop method, see page 309.) Add the next ABC units in counterclockwise order. Finish the first seam after the last unit has been added.

NEXT DOOR NEIGHBOR

PATCHWORK

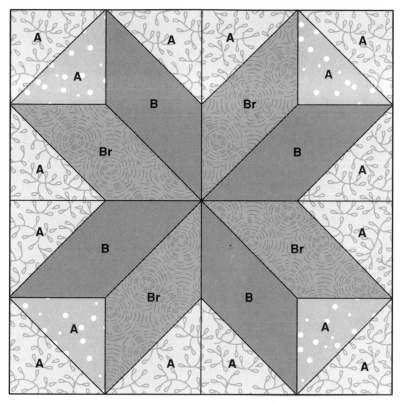

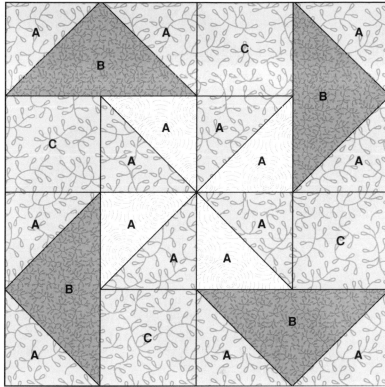

UNTITLED III

A19 Make AA unit (4 times). Sew A triangles to B and Br (4 times). Add AA unit to B and Br mitering edges. (See directions for mitering on page 309.) Join the 4 units into 2 rows, then join rows to make the block.

SEESAW

A20 Make AA unit (4 times), make ABA unit (4 times). Sew C to AA, add ABA (4 times). Join the 4 units into 2 rows, then join rows to make the block.

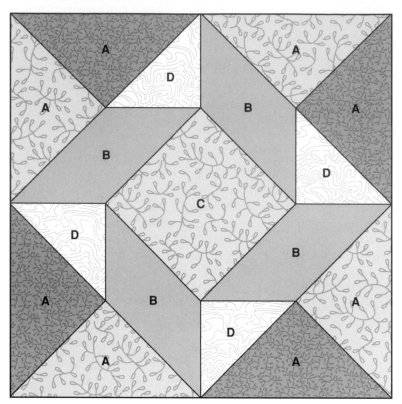

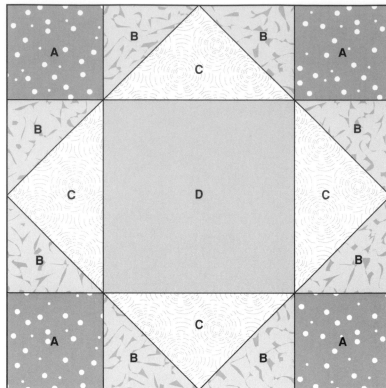

WINDBLOWN SQUARE

A21 Make BD unit (4 times), add to each side of C, then miter edges. (See directions for mitering on page 309.) Make AA unit (4 times); add to the BD edges to make the block.

KING'S CROWN

A22 Make BCB unit (4 times), attach 2 of these units to opposite sides of D piece. Add A pieces at each end of BCB unit (2 times). Sew ABCBA units to each side of center unit to make the block.

PATCHWORK

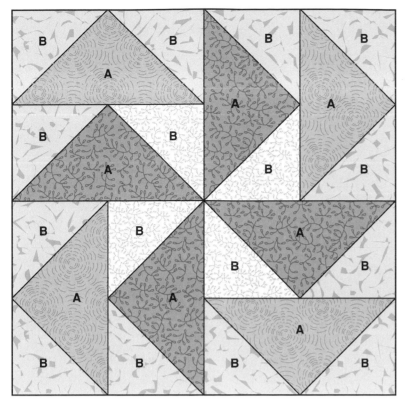

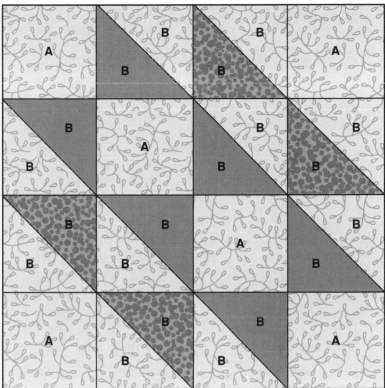

A23 Make BAB unit (8 times). Join units in pairs to make 4 sections. Join the 4 sections into 2 rows, then join rows to make the block.

DUTCHMAN'S PUZZLE

A24 Make BB unit (10 times). Join into rows A/BB/BB/A, BB/A/BB/BB, BB/BB/A/BB, A/BB/BB/A. Join rows to make the block.

HOVERING HAWKS

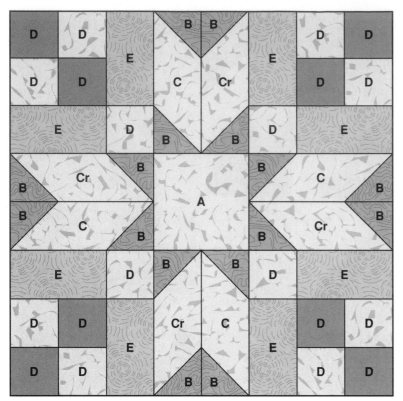

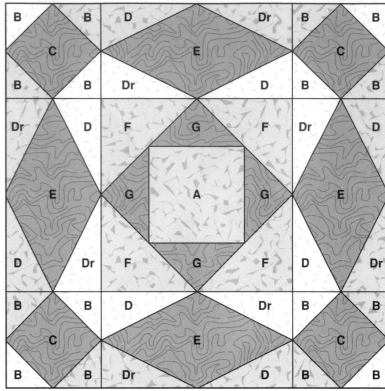

A25 Make DDDD unit (4 times); add E to each DDDD unit. Sew D to E (4 times); add to DE units. Make BCB and BCrB units (4 times each). Sew BCB to BCrB (4 times). Make 2 rows of DE/BCB/DE. Sew BCB to 2 opposite sides of A; add previous rows to each side to make the block.

BLACKFORD'S BEAUTY

A26 Sew G pieces to all 4 sides of A; sew F pieces to all 4 sides of AG unit. Sew B pieces to all 4 sides of C (4 times); sew D pieces to all 4 sides of E pieces (4 times). Make rows: BC/DE/BC, DE/AGF/DE, BC/DE/BC. Join rows to make the block.

STORM AT SEA

PATCHWORK

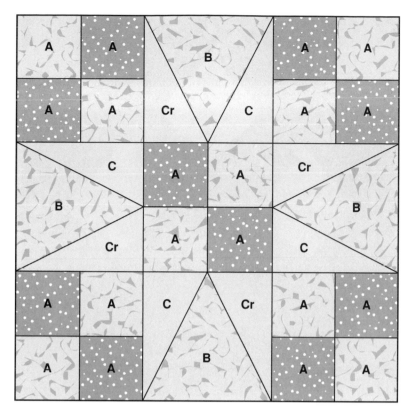

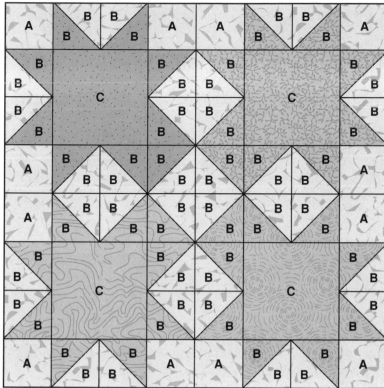

A27 Make AAAA unit (5 times). Make CBCr unit (4 times). Make rows A/CBCr/A, CBCr/A/CBCr, A/CBCr/A. Join rows to make the block.

54-40 OR FIGHT

A28 This block is made in 4 sections. For each section make BB unit (9 times), sew 2 BB units together (4 times). Make rows A/B/B/A, BB/C/BB, A/B/B/B. Join rows to form one section. Make 4 of these sections. Join rows to make the block.

DEVIL'S CLAW

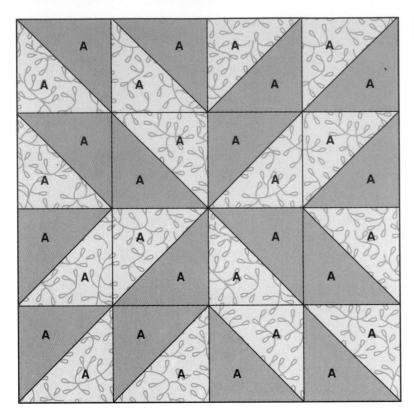

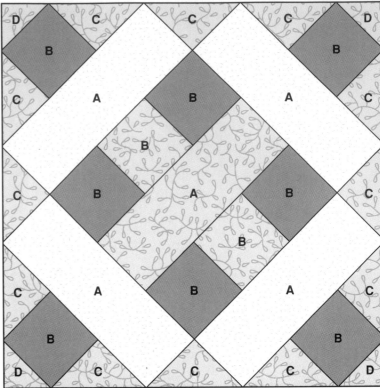

ANNIE'S CHOICE

A29 Make AA unit (16 times). Referring to diagram, join units into rows, then join rows to make the block.

ALBUM

A30 This block is pieced diagonally. Begin in center by making 2 BBB units. Sew B units to A; add A piece to each BBB side. Make BCDC unit (4 times); add one unit to each A edge. Make CAC unit (2 times); attach to ABABA edges. Attach BCDC units to make the block.

PATCHWORK

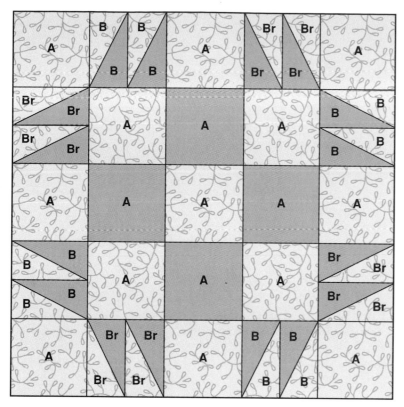

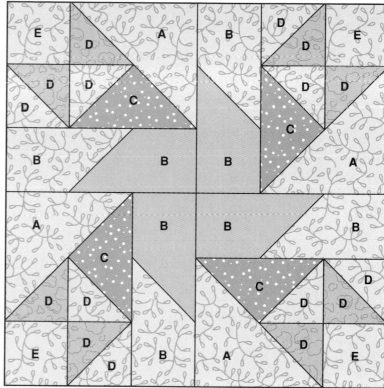

ROLLING PIN

A31 Make BB unit (8 times and 8 reverse). Join 2 BB units together (4 times). Join 2 BrBr units together (4 times). Join B units with A pieces to form rows. Join rows to make the block.

ROLLING PINWHEEL

A32 Make DDC unit; join to A. Make DD unit; join to E. Join DE unit to ACD unit. Make BB unit. Join to CD edge of first section to form unit. Repeat this unit (4 times). Join the 4 units to make the block.

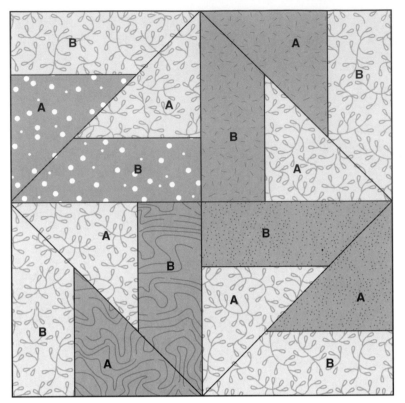

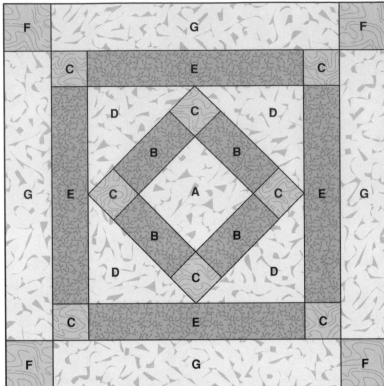

**TURN ABOUT
VARIATION**

A33 Make AB unit (8 times). Sew 2 AB units to form square unit (4 times). Sew the square units together to make the block.

AMISH DIAMOND

A34 Begin in center, sewing B to 2 opposite sides of A. Make 2 CBC sections and add to BAB. Sew D pieces to each side of center section. Sew E to 2 opposite sides of center section. Make 2 CEC units and add to opposite sides of center. Add G pieces to 2 opposite sides. Make 2 FGF units and add to 2 opposite sides to make the block.

PATCHWORK

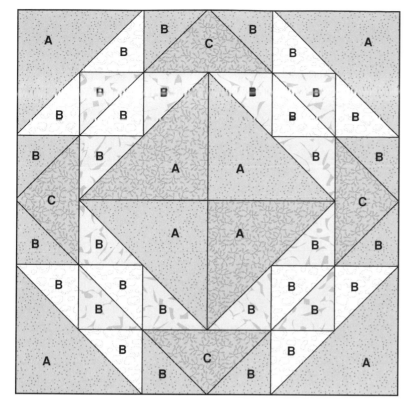

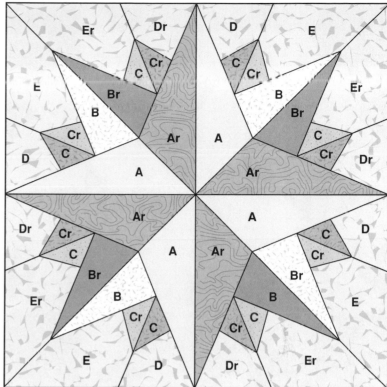

CORN AND BEANS

A35 Make AAAA section to form center. Make 4 BBB units; add to center on all 4 sides. Sew C pieces to all 4 sides of center as shown in diagram. Make BBBB-BA unit (4 times); sew to 4 sides of center section to complete the block.

MARINER'S COMPASS

A36 Join C to D, join Cr to E; sew CD to CrE; add B, then A. Make 4 units (called A units). Sew Cr to Dr, sew C to Er; join CrDr to CEr; add Br, then Ar. Make 4 units (called Ar units). Join A units to Ar units along the B edges (4 times). Sew resulting square units together in 2 rows, then join rows to make the block.

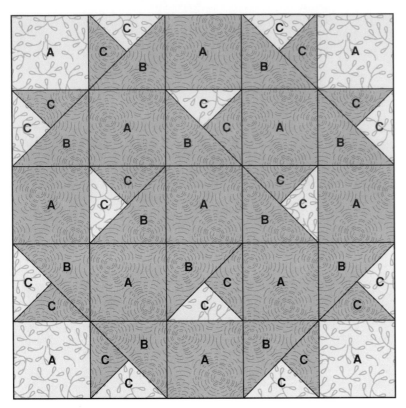

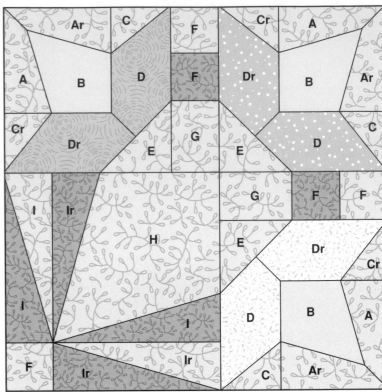

**CROSS UPON
CROSS**

A37   Make the CCB unit (12 times). Combine the CCB units with the A pieces to form rows. Join the rows to make the block.

STAR BOUQUET

A38   Miter A piece and Ar piece to B (3 times). (See page 309 for information on mitering.) Make CrDr (3 times) and CD (3 times); miter with AArB unit and then add E piece (3 times). Make FFG unit (2 times) Sew I and Ir pieces to 2 sides of H. Make II unit and add to HI unit. Make IrIr unit and add F piece; join to HI unit. Make top row by joining 2 ABCDE units with FFG unit. Make bottom row by sewing FFG unit to ABCDE unit; join with FHI unit and add to top section.

PATCHWORK

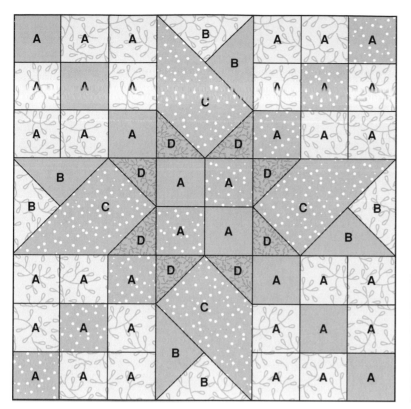

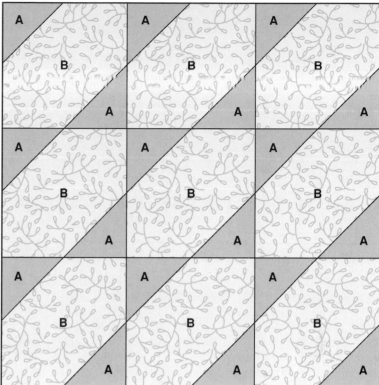

A39 Make nine-patch using A pieces (4 times). Make center four-patch using A pieces. (See page 309 for help in making nine-patches and four-patches.) Make BB unit (4 times), and DCD unit (4 times); join BB to DCD (4 times). Join together in rows, then join rows to make the block.

ARROWHEADS

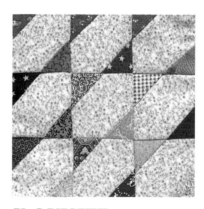

A40 Make ABA unit (9 times). Combine units to make nine-patch. (See page 309 for help in making nine-patches.)

X-QUISITE

73

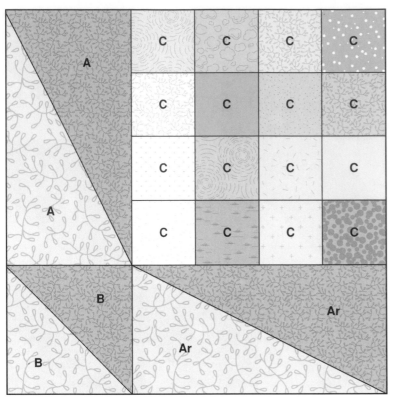

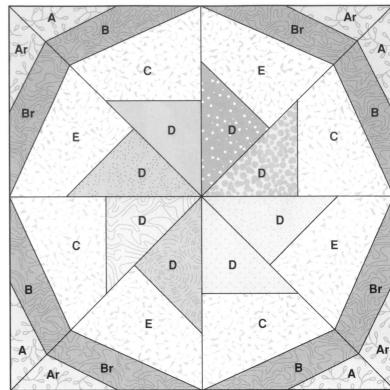

A41 Join C pieces into 4 rows, join the rows to make a square. Make AA unit, ArAr unit and BB unit. Add AA unit to C section. Sew BB unit to ArAr and add to main section.

NOSEGAY

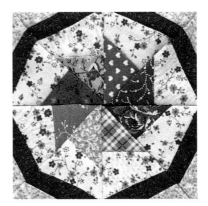

A42 Make ABCD unit (4 times), and ArBrED unit (4 times). Join into 4 pairs: ABCD to ArBrED. Join these squares into a four-patch to complete the block. (See page 309 for help in making four-patches.)

WHEEL OF FORTUNE

PATCHWORK

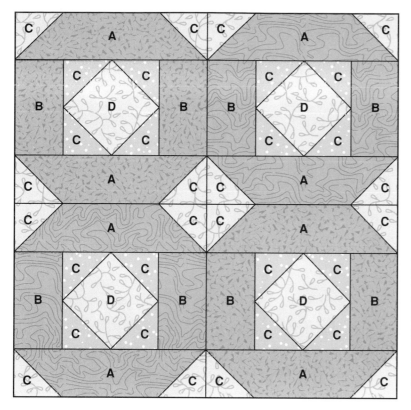

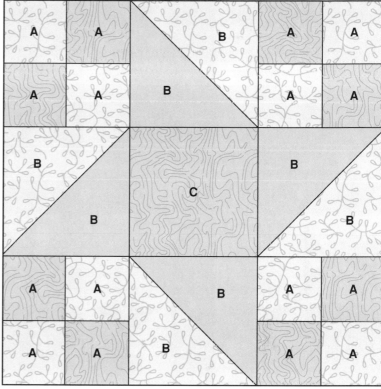

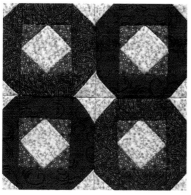

KANSAS DUGOUT

A43 Make DCCCC unit (4 times); add B pieces to 2 opposite sides of DCCCC unit (4 times). Make CAC unit (8 times); add to 2 remaining sides of each DCCCC unit to make 4 sections. Join the sections as a four-patch to complete the block.

FRIENDSHIP STAR VARIATION

A44 Use A pieces to make four-patch (4 times). (See page 309 for help in making four-patches.) Make BB unit (4 times). Combine AAAA units, BB units and C piece into rows, then join the rows to make the block.

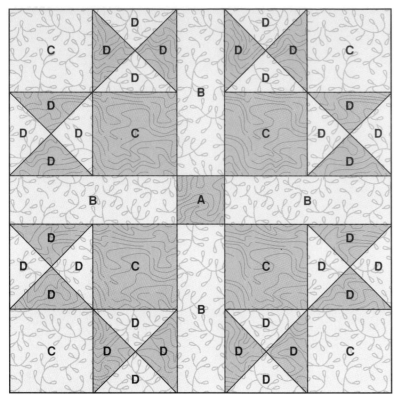

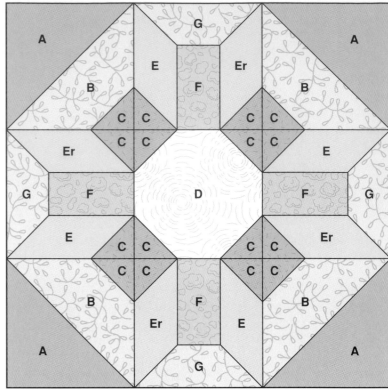

A45 Make DDDD unit (8 times); join with C pieces to make 4 four-patch units. (See page 309 for help in making four-patches.) Join 2 CD units with B piece to make a row (2 times); make BAB unit and join with the CDB units to complete the block.

VARIABLE STAR

A46 Make ABC unit (4 times). Make EC unit and ErC unit, join with F piece, then miter with G (4 times). (See page 309 for information on mitering.) Make CCCCD unit and combine with other units to make nine-patch. (See page 309 for help in making nine-patches.)

PROSPERITY

PATCHWORK

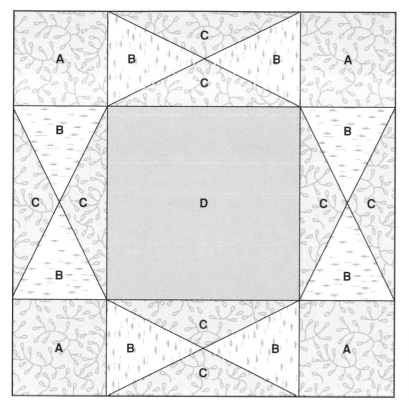

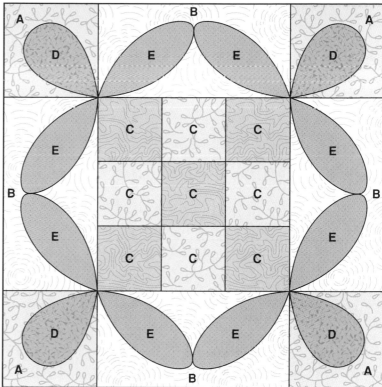

**PULLMAN'S
PUZZLE**

A47 Sew B to C (8 times), then join 2 BC units (4 times). Combine the BCBC units with A pieces and D piece into rows, then join the rows to form the block.

HONEY BEE

A48 Using C pieces, make a nine-patch for the center. (See page 309 for help in making nine-patches.) Add B pieces to 2 opposite sides of C section. Sew A pieces to each end of remaining B pieces, and join to top and bottom of BC section. Appliqué the D and E pieces in place. (See page 308 for appliqué information.)

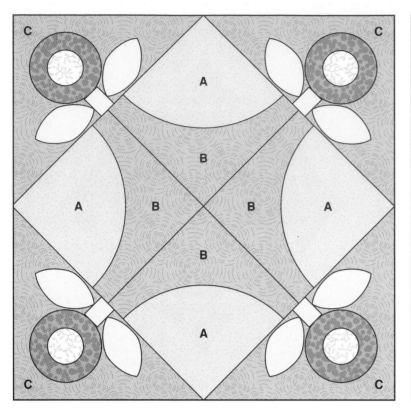

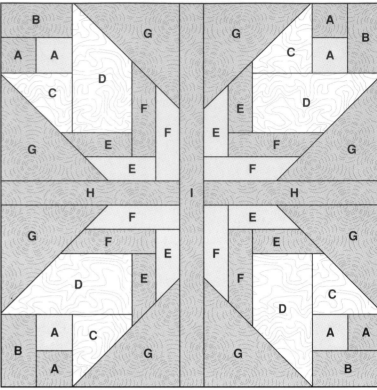

SPICED PINKS

A49 Sew A to B (4 times). (See page 309 for help with sewing curved seams.) Sew the 4 AB units together to form the square in the center of block. Appliqué flower, stem, and leaves to each C piece. (See page 308 for appliqué help.) Add C to AB unit (4 times).

NAVAJO TULIPS

A50 Sew A to A, add B. Sew C to AA side, add D. Sew E to CD side, add F. Sew E to EF side, add F. Add G pieces to each side to make a square. Make this unit 4 times. Join 2 units with H (2 times), then join the 2 halves with I piece.

PATCHWORK

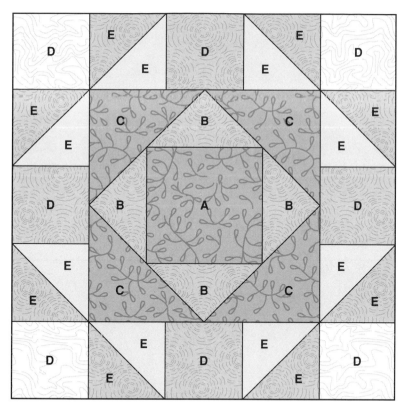

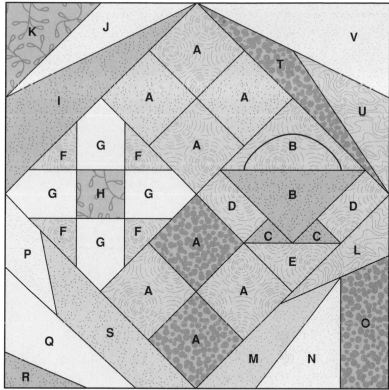

TEA PARTY

A51 Sew B pieces to 2 opposite sides of A, then to 2 remaining sides. Add C to all 4 sides of AB unit in the same manner (opposite sides). Make EE unit (8 times). Make EE/D/EE section (4 times); join 2 sections to opposite sides of ABC unit. Add D pieces to each end of remaining EDE units and sew to top and bottom of first section to make the block.

CRAZY SAMPLER

A52 Using A pieces, make a four-patch (2 times). Make BB unit. Make 2 CD units (1 and 1r); add to BB unit. Sew E piece to CC edge. Embroider basket handle as shown. Make GHG unit. Make FGF unit (2 times). Sew FGF units to 2 sides of GHG. Now you have 4 small squares made; sew them together as a four-patch. Sew I to J, add K. Sew to one side of center square. Sew M to N, add O, then add L and sew to side of center square. Make PS unit, add Q, add R; sew to side of center square. Join T and U, add V. Sew to last side of center square.

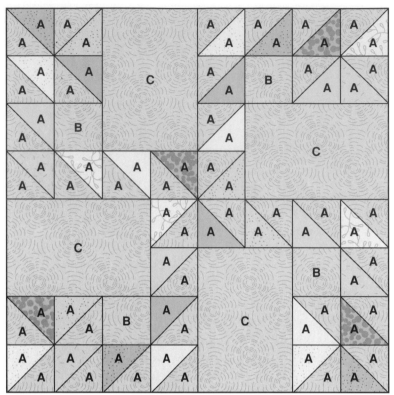

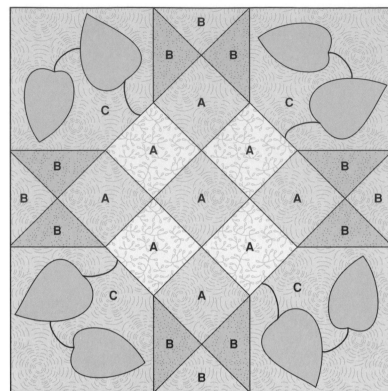

A53 Make AA unit (36 times). Combine 2 AA units and add C (4 times). Referring to diagram, join AA units and B pieces to make four-patches. Join the four-patches to form sections that fit next to AA/C section (4 times). Sew ABC sections to make four-patch.

SAWTOOTH PINWHEEL

A54 Make center nine-patch using A pieces. Add 2 B pieces to C piece (4 times); sew BC units to 2 opposite sides of A section. Sew B pieces to each B edge of remaining BC units; sew to remaining sides of first section. Appliqué leaves to C pieces, then embroider stems.

ARROWROOT

PATCHWORK

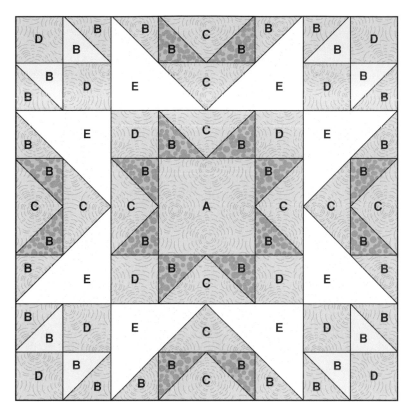

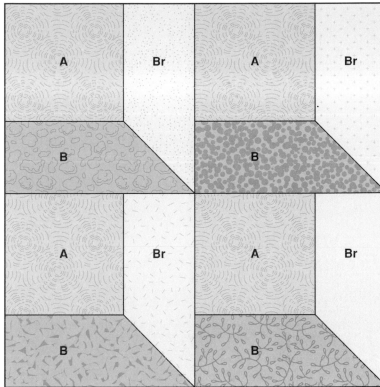

ODD FELLOW'S CHAIN

A55 Make BB unit (8 times), combine with D pieces to make four-patch (4 times). Make BCB unit (8 times); sew to 2 opposite sides of A. Add D pieces to each side of BCB unit (2 times); sew to ABC section. Sew B pieces to 2 sides of BCB unit, add C, then add 2 E pieces (4 times). Sew 2 BCE sections to opposite sides of center section. Sew 2 BD units to each end of BCE section (2 times), add to center section to make the block.

ATTIC WINDOWS

A56 Sew B and Br to A (4 times). (Refer to information on mitering on page 309.) Sew the AB units to make a four-patch.

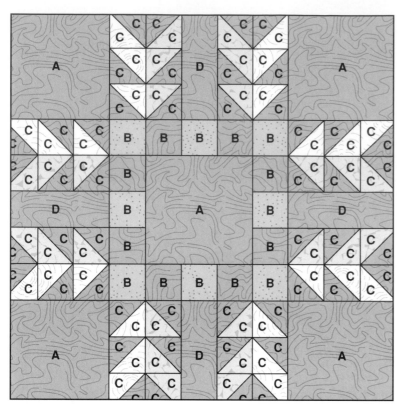

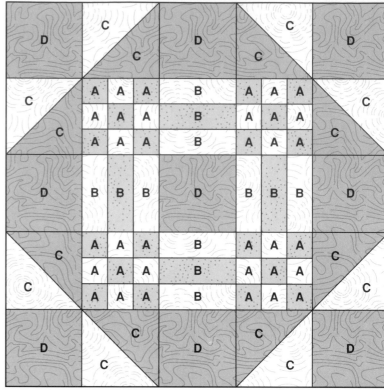

TEXAS TREASURES

A57 Make BBB unit (4 times); sew to opposite sides of center A piece. Add B pieces to each end of BBB unit (2 times); add to remaining sides of first section. Make CC units (48 times). Join 6 CC units in larger units of 2 across and 3 down (4 times and 4r times). Join 1 of these sections to D, then add the reverse section to D (4 times). Join a CDC section to each side of the center section. Add A pieces to 2 opposite sides of CDC section (2 times); join to center section to complete the block.

GOOSE IN THE POND

A58 Using A pieces, make nine-patch (4 times). Make BBB unit (4 times); add to 2 sides of center D piece. Add A units to each end of B unit (2 times); join to remaining sides of center section. Make CC unit (8 times). Join 2 CC units with D (4 times), add CDC sections to 2 opposite sides of center section. Sew D unit to each end of CDC section (2 times); sew to remaining sides of center section.

PATCHWORK

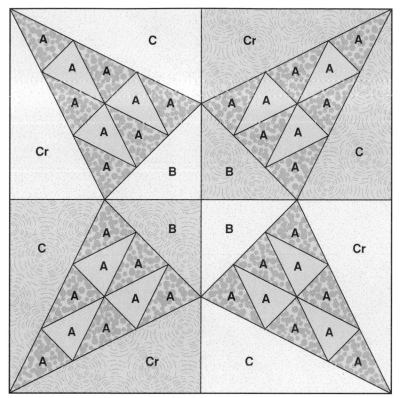

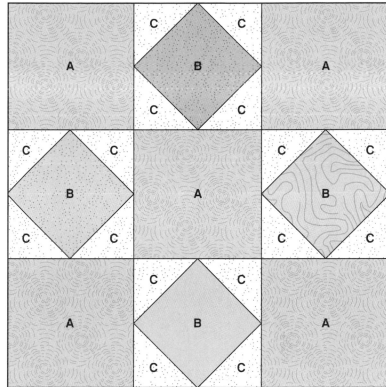

A59 Referring to diagram, sew 5 A pieces together to form a row, add a row of 3 A pieces, then add a single A piece. Sew B piece to wide end of A section, then add C and Cr to make a square. Make this square 4 times, then join the squares in a four-patch to make the block.

ROCKINGHAM'S BEAUTY

A60 Sew C pieces to opposite sides of B, then to 2 remaining sides (4 times). Combine the CB units with the A pieces to make a nine-patch.

STAR CROSS

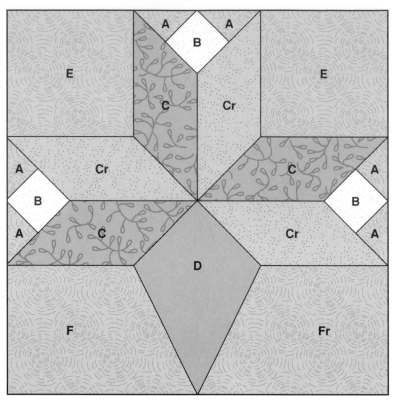

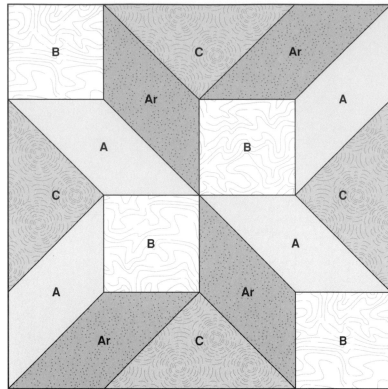

A61 Sew A pieces to 2 adjoining sides of B (3 times). Sew C to Cr; set in ABA unit (3 times). Join 2 units together, join the third unit with D piece, then sew the 2 sections together. Miter the E pieces in place, then the F and Fr pieces. (See page 309 for mitering information.)

CORNUCOPIA

A62 Join A and Ar; miter with B piece (4 times). Join the AArB units as shown, then miter the C pieces into place. (See page 309 for mitering information.)

CUBE LATTICE

PATCHWORK

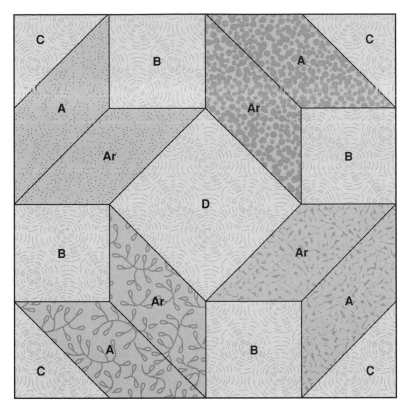

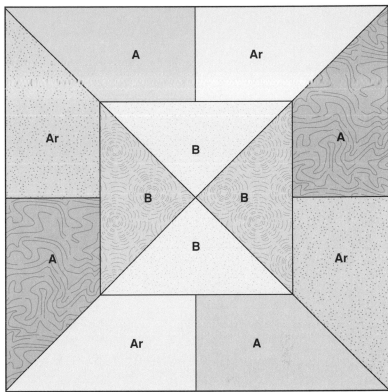

A63 Join A and Ar; miter with B piece (4 times). Add C pieces to A edges. Join the AArBC units to D, then miter the ArB seams. (See page 309 for help with mitering.)

BACHELOR'S PUZZLE

A64 Join A and Ar; add B (4 times). Join the AArB units into pairs, then sew together along the diagonal to complete the block.

GEOMETRY

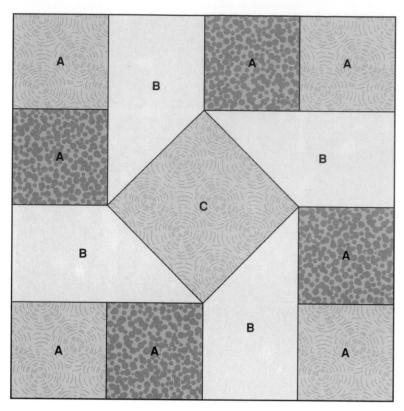

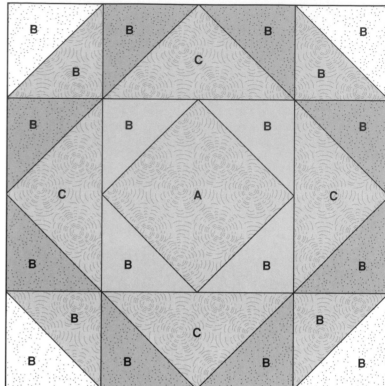

A65 Make AA unit and add B piece (4 times). Miter AAB units to C piece. (For information on mitering, see page 309.)

SUSANNAH

A66 Sew B pieces to 2 opposite sides of A, then to 2 remaining sides. Make BB unit (4 times), and BCB unit (4 times). Join units into rows, then join rows to complete the block.

MOSAIC

PATCHWORK

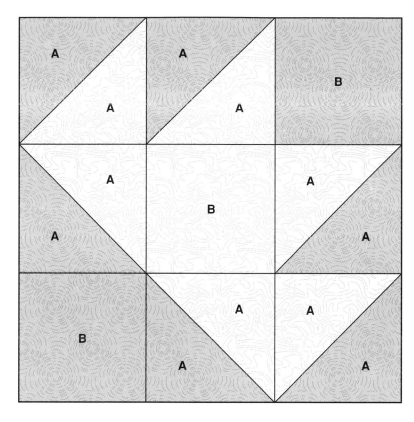

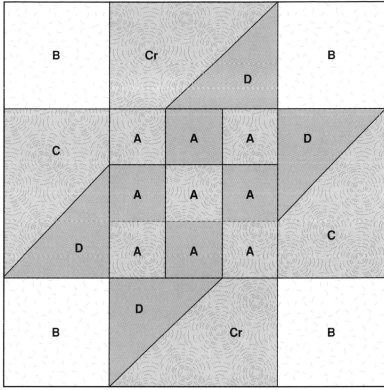

MAPLE LEAF VARIATION

A67 Make AA unit (6 times). Join units with B pieces into rows, then join the rows to make the block.

SHORTCUT TO SCHOOL

A68 Use A pieces to make center nine-patch (see page 309 for information on nine-patches). Make CD unit (2 times) and sew to opposite sides of center unit. Make CrD unit; add B piece to each end (2 times). Join the three rows to complete the block.

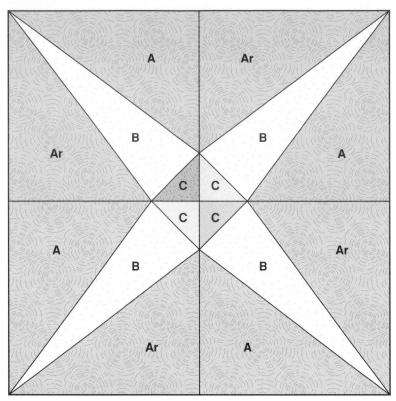

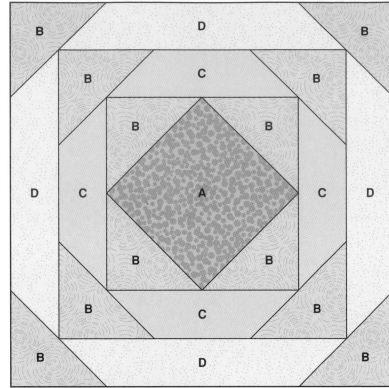

A69 Sew C to B, then add A and Ar (4 times). Sew the 4 units as a four-patch. (See page 309 for information on four-patches.)

TIPPECANOE

A70 Sew B pieces to 2 opposite sides of A, then to 2 remaining sides. Add C pieces to all sides of first unit, then add B pieces to corners. Add D pieces to all sides of main section, then add B pieces to corners to complete the block.

AMISH PINEAPPLE

PATCHWORK

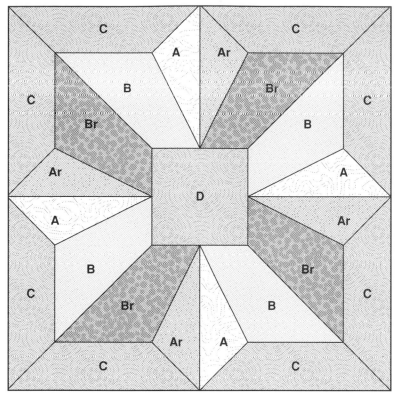

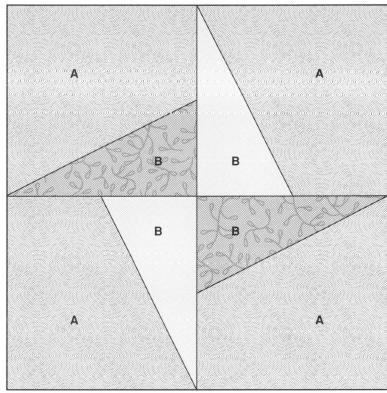

A71 Sew B and C pieces together, then miter with A (4 times); sew Br and C pieces together, then miter with Ar (4 times). Join units in pairs along the AAr seams (4 times). Sew each resulting unit to D piece, then miter along the BC and BrC seams. (For help with mitering, see page 309.)

FACETS

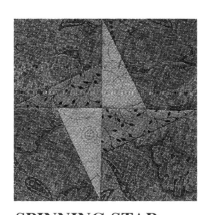

A72 Sew AB unit (4 times). Join the units into 2 rows, then join the rows to make the block.

SPINNING STAR

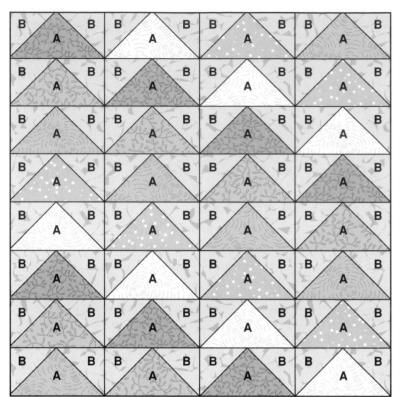

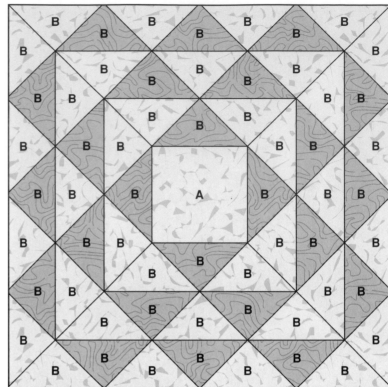

A73 Make BAB unit (32 times). Join into vertical rows of 8 units.

Note: Congratulations on joining 96 pieces of fabric into a 4-inch square!

FLYING GEESE

A74 Make BB squares 20 times. Sew 2 B pieces to opposite sides of A, then to 2 remaining sides. Put block together in diagonal rows, joining BB squares and B pieces as shown.

OCEAN WAVES

PATCHWORK

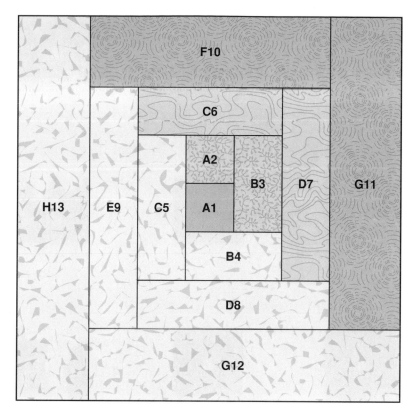

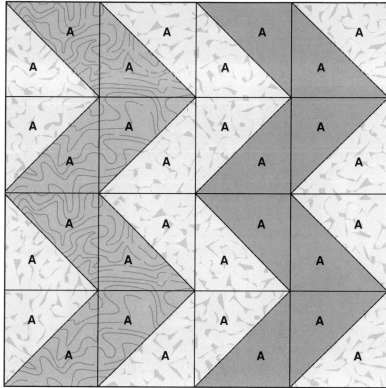

LOG CABIN

A75 In this block the letters refer to the template, and the numbers refer to the order in which the pieces are added. Begin in the center (A1); add A2, then B3. Keep adding pieces in this manner through H13.

STREAK OF LIGHTNING

A76 Make AA unit (16 times). Join the units into rows, then join the rows to make the block.

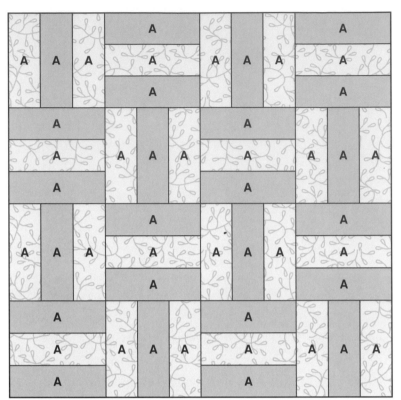

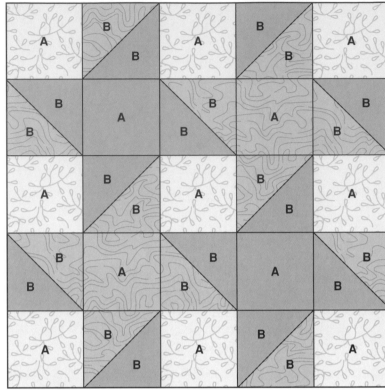

A77 This block can be made by sewing strips together, then cutting them apart in squares, and putting the squares together. Or, each unit can be sewn individually, using the A template: Make AAA unit (16 times). Sew units together into rows, then sew rows together to make the block.

BASKET WEAVE

A78 Make BB unit (12 times). Combine the BB units with the A pieces to form 5 rows. Join the rows to make the block.

MILKY WAY

PATCHWORK

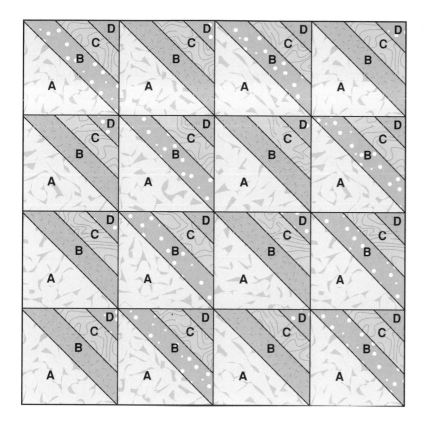

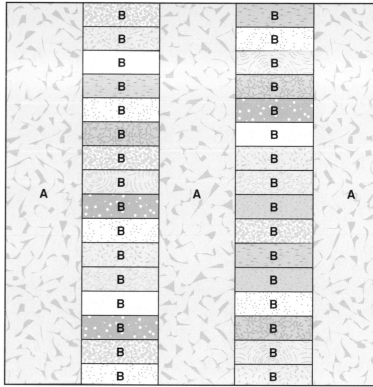

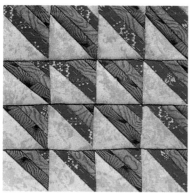

A79 This block can be made using the 4 templates required. But it is easier to sew four strips together, then cut out 16 squares by laying the square template on the sewn strip. Once you have the 16 squares sewn, join them into rows, then join the rows to make the block.

ROMAN STRIPE

A80 This block, too, can be made with cither templates or strips of fabric. Make 2 vertical rows of 16 B pieces each. Join them with A pieces to make the block.

CHINESE COINS

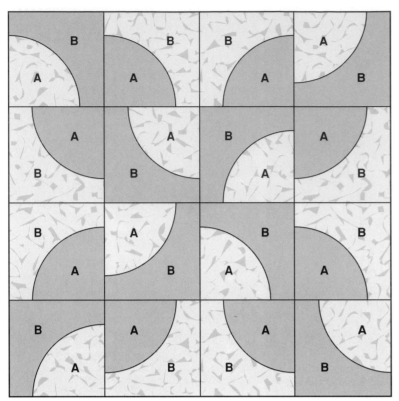

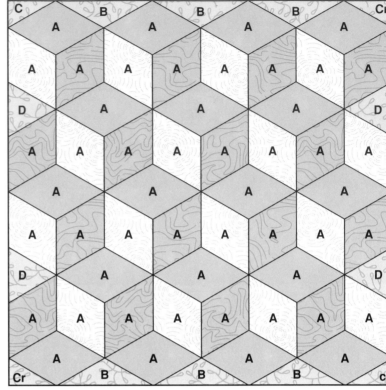

DRUNKARD'S PATH

A81 Make 16 AB units. (See page 309 for help with sewing curved seams.) Sew the AB units into rows, then sew the rows together to make the block.

TUMBLING BLOCKS

A82 This block is assembled in horizontal rows. Begin by making whole cubes (AAA units), using the illustration as guide (14 times). (See directions for mitering on page 309.) Also make the partial cubes to sew to the ends of the rows. Sew units into rows, then sew rows together, pivoting at each point where one cube fits between the others.

PATCHWORK

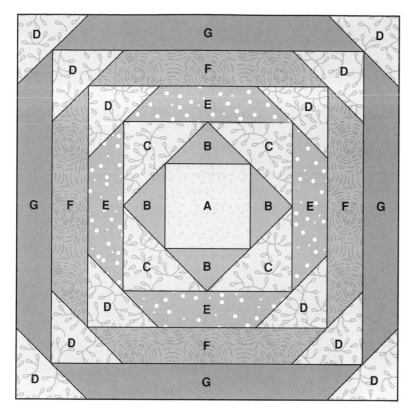

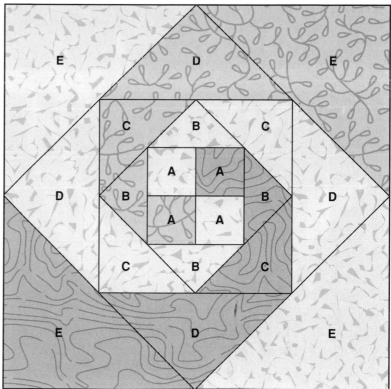

PINEAPPLE

A83 Begin in the center, attaching B pieces to 2 opposite sides of A piece, then to 2 remaining sides. Add C pieces to AB unit in the same manner. Add E pieces to ABC unit, then add D corner pieces. Add F pieces, then D corners. Finally, add G pieces and the last 4 D corners.

SNAIL'S TRAIL

A84 Begin in the center by making the four-patch, using A pieces. (See page 309 for help in making four-patches.) Add B pieces to 2 opposite sides of four-patch, then to 2 remaining sides. Add C pieces in this manner, then D pieces, and, finally, the E pieces.

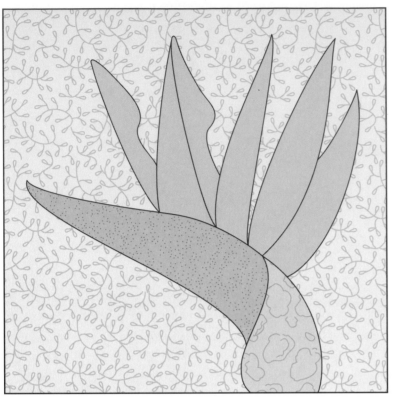

BIRD OF PARADISE

DAFFODIL

B1 Cut a 4-inch square (plus seam allowances) of background fabric. Appliqué the flower on the background square. (See page 308 for appliqué information.)

B2 Appliqué daffodil on background fabric. Embroider lines on flower's trumpet with stem stitch.

APPLIQUÉ

96

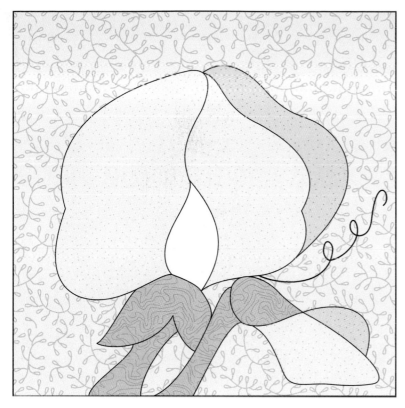

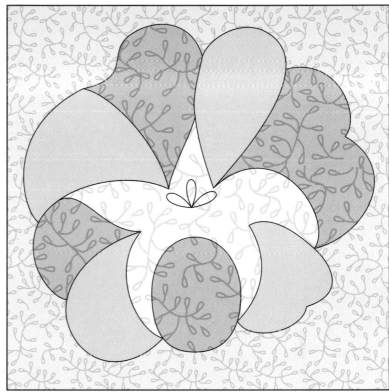

B3 Appliqué flower and stems on background fabric. Use a stem stitch or backstitch for the little vine.

SWEET PEA

B4 The easiest way to make this flower is to apply the petals to the center star. The tiny yellow centers are embroidered.

MORNING GLORY

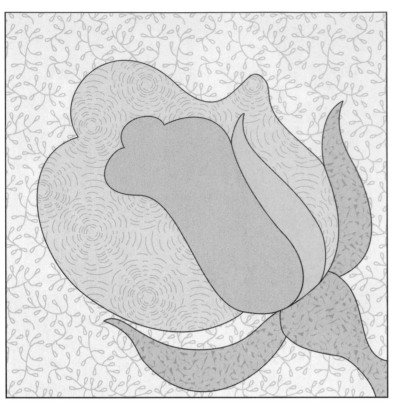

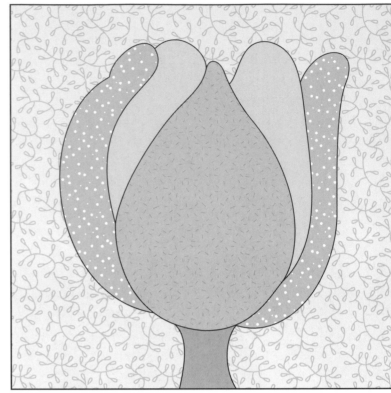

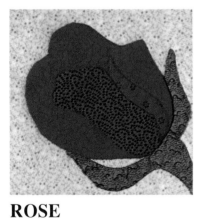

ROSE

B5 Cut a 4-inch square (plus seam allowances) of background fabric. Appliqué the rose on the background square. (See page 308 for appliqué information.)

TULIP

B6 Appliqué the stem and tulip petals to background square.

APPLIQUÉ

B7 Appliqué the pansy petals to the background fabric. Use stem stitch to embroider the lines on the petals.

PANSY

B8 Appliqué leaf and blossoms on background fabric. Embroider lines on leaf with stem stitch; use French knots for centers of flowers.

GERANIUM

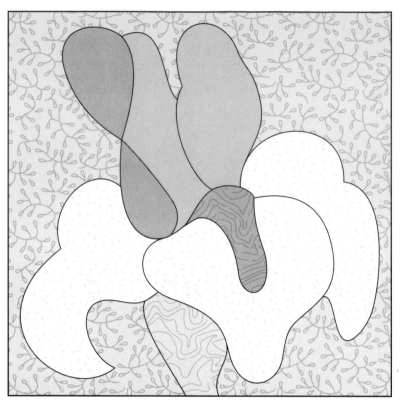

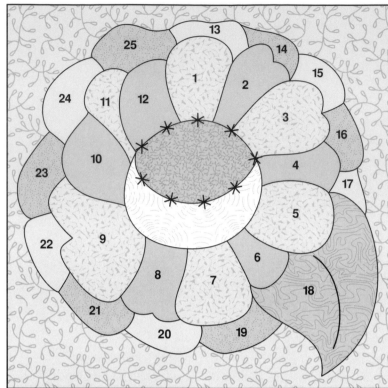

IRIS

B9 Cut a 4-inch square (plus seam allowances) of background fabric. Appliqué the iris on the background square. (See page 308 for appliqué information.)

ZINNIA

B10 To make this flower easier to appliqué, we have numbered the templates in the order they were sewn to each other. First, join the 2 center pieces and set aside. Appliqué the inner row of petals (1–12) to each other, then apply the center unit. Appliqué the outer row of the leaf and petals (13–25) to the background fabric, then apply the center and inner petals on top. Embroider the little stars around the center using straight stitches.

APPLIQUÉ

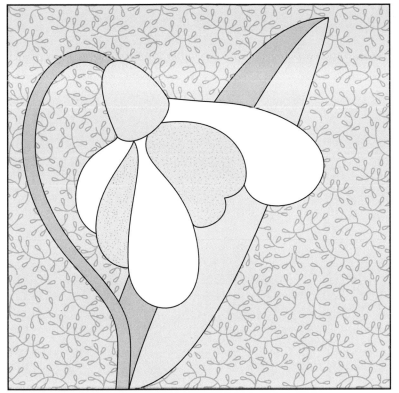

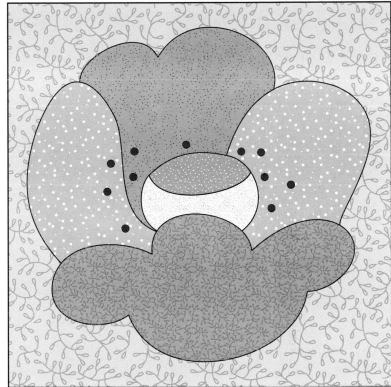

B11 The stem for this flower can be made using a bias tube. (See page 309 for information on bias tubing and page 308 for help with appliqué.)

SNOWDROP

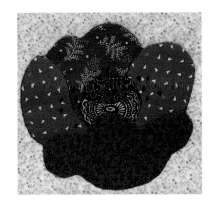

B12 Appliqué the petals and center onto the background fabric. Make the little dots with French knots.

POPPY

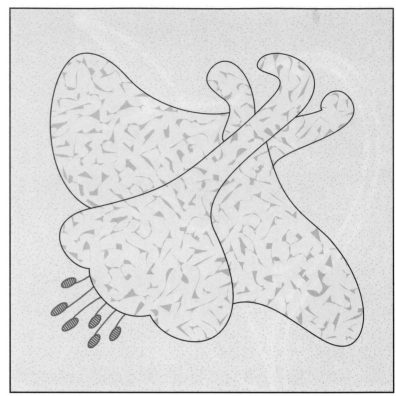

B13 Cut a 4-inch square (plus seam allowances) of background fabric. Appliqué the daisy petals and center onto the block. The tiny dots around the center are made with French knots.

DAISY

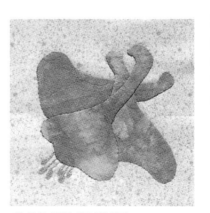

B14 Appliqué flower onto background fabric. (See page 308 for appliqué information.) Embellish with stem stitch or backstitch and satin stitch.

COLUMBINE

APPLIQUÉ

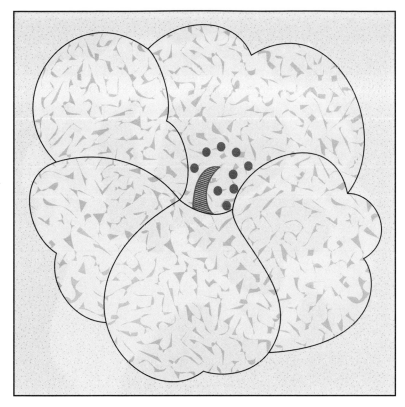

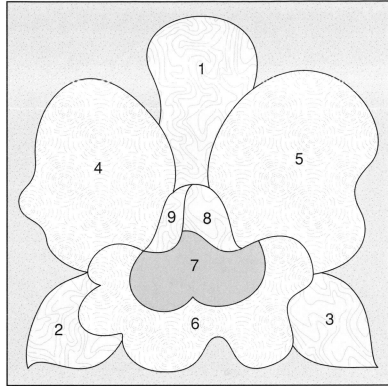

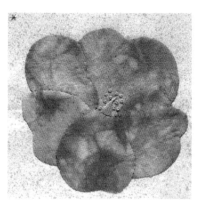

B15 Appliqué petals in place. The center is embroidered using satin stitch; add French knots around the center.

B16 Appliqué this delicate orchid to the background in numbered sequence, beginning with piece number 1.

HIBISCUS

ORCHID

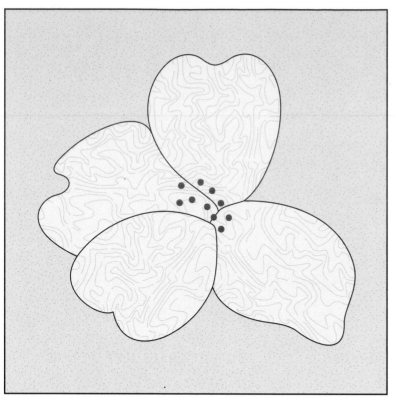

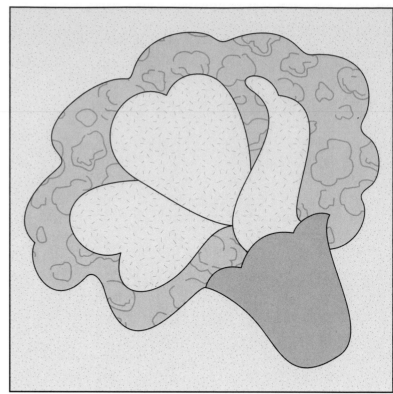

B17 Cut a 4-inch square (plus seam allowances) of background fabric. Appliqué the dogwood petals on the background square. (See page 308 for appliqué information.) Make the little dots in the center with French knots.

DOGWOOD

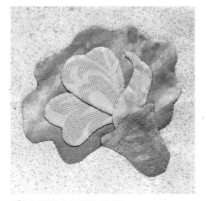

B18 Appliqué flower to background fabric. Choose 2 close shades of one color of fabric for the petals to get the best effect.

CARNATION

APPLIQUÉ

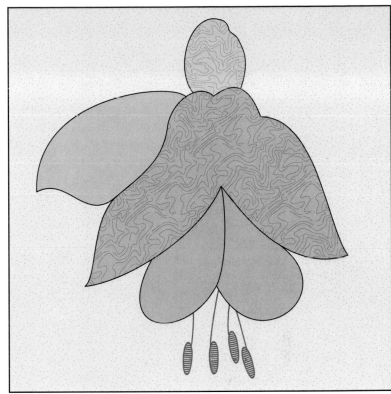

B19 Appliqué to background fabric. It is important to cut the individual pieces (even though the same fabric is used) to achieve the dimension of the foliage.

ANTHURIUM

B20 Appliqué flower to background fabric; complete with embroidery.

FUCHSIA

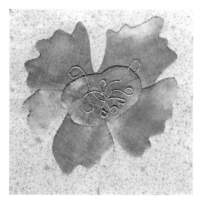

B21 Appliqué petals, then center to the background fabric. The center of the flower is embroidered with stem stitch.

PINKS

B22 Appliqué the petals and center to the block. Make a double outline around the center with French knots.

ASTER

APPLIQUÉ

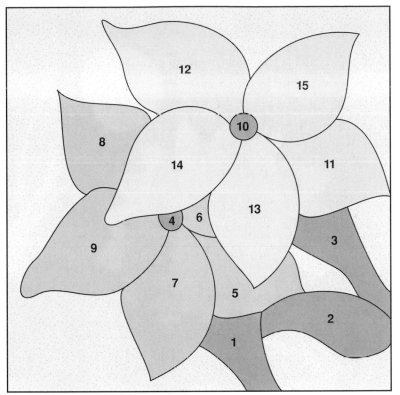

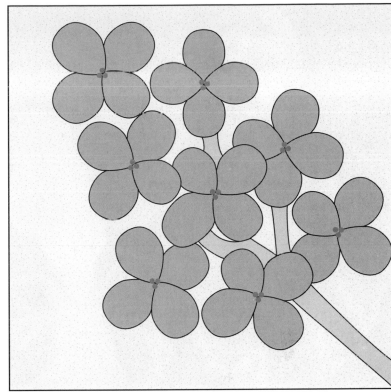

JASMINE

B23 Appliqué to background in sequence, beginning with number 1; continue through piece 15.

LILAC

B24 Cut a 4-inch square (plus seam allowances) of background fabric. Appliqué stem and blossoms in place. Make tiny centers with French knots.

B25 Appliqué leaves and blossom in place. Embroider the leaves and bloom as shown.

FLETT'S VIOLETS

B26 Appliqué pieces in place. Use a satin stitch to embellish the tip of every petal; use lazy daisy stitches for the center and bud.

INDIAN BLANKET

APPLIQUÉ

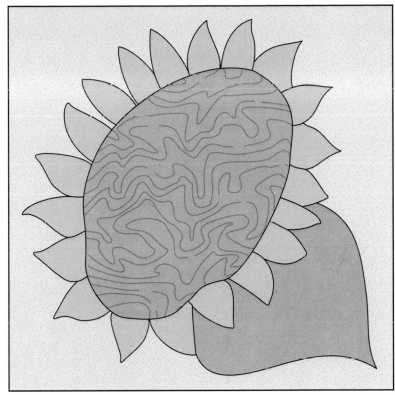

**INDIAN
PAINTBRUSH**

B27 Appliqué the pieces onto the background fabric. (See page 308 for appliqué information.)

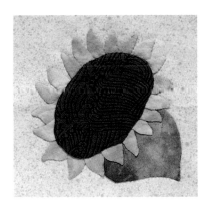

SUNFLOWER

B28 If you use a plain fabric for the center section, cover it with embroidered lazy daisy stitches to get the seed effect.

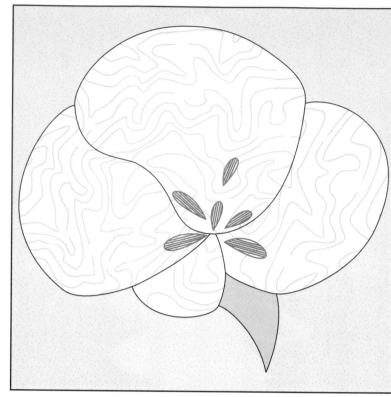

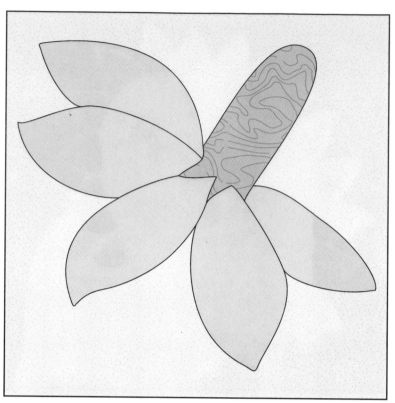

B29 Cut a 4-inch square (plus seam allowances) of background fabric. Appliqué pieces in place.

CONEFLOWER

B30 Appliqué the leaf and petals in place. Use satin stitch to embroider the center.

EVENING PRIMROSE

APPLIQUÉ

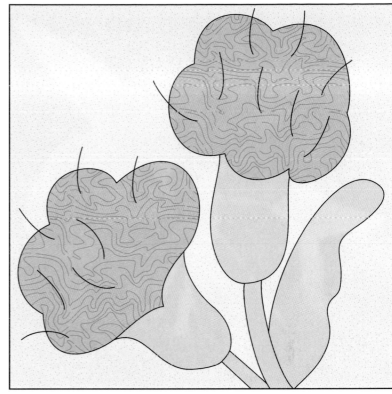

B31 Choose shades of clear, bright blues to make this Texas state flower.

BLUEBONNET

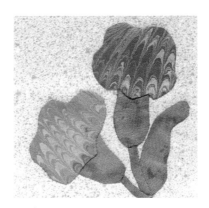

B32 The unique fabric we used for the thistle bloom really didn't need embellishment. If you select a plain fabric; embroider lines (as shown in pattern) using stem stitch.

THISTLE

SPIDERWORT

B33 Cut a 4-inch square (plus seam allowances) of background fabric. Appliqué leaves and flower in place. Use French knots in center.

**BIRDCAGE
EVENING
PRIMROSE**

B34 Appliqué this delicate bloom. Use stem stitch to embroider the centers, with a French knot at the end of each.

APPLIQUÉ

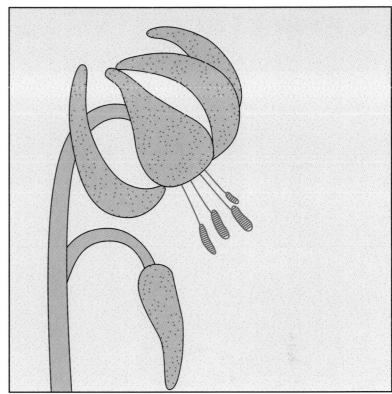

BLUE PHLOX

B35 Use bias tubing for the stems. (For bias tubing information, see page 309.) Appliqué all pieces in place.

GLACIER LILY

B36 Cut a 4-inch square (plus seam allowances) of background fabric. Use bias tubing for stems. Appliqué the flower in place. Make the stamens with stem stitch and satin stitch.

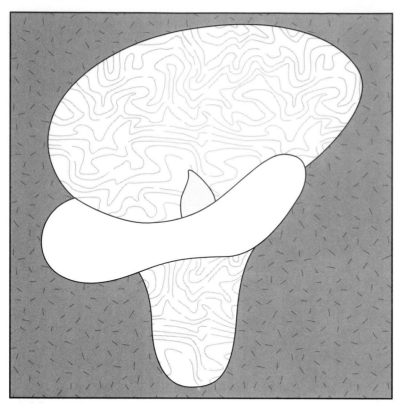

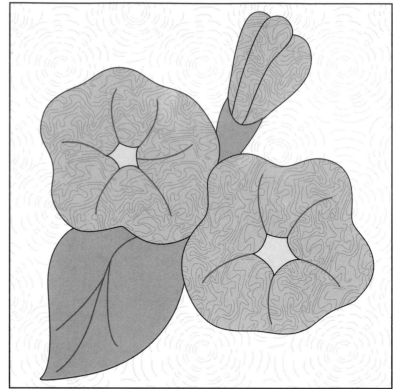

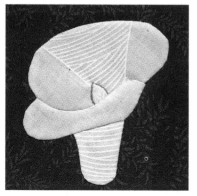

B37 Appliqué flower in place on background fabric.

CALLA LILY

B38 Appliqué all pieces in place on background fabric. Embroider the details on leaves and petals with stem stitch.

PETUNIA

APPLIQUÉ

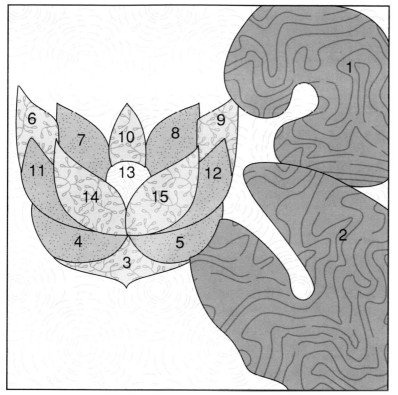

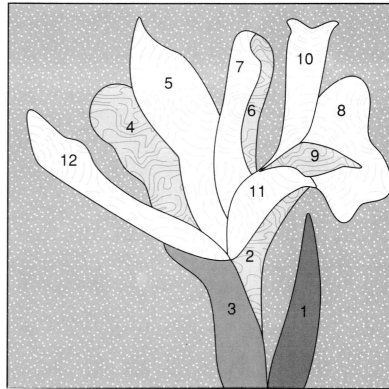

B39 Appliqué pieces to background in sequence, beginning with number 1; continue through piece 15.

WATER LILY

B40 Appliqué the iris by following the number sequence, beginning with piece 1; continue through piece 12.

DUTCH IRIS

115

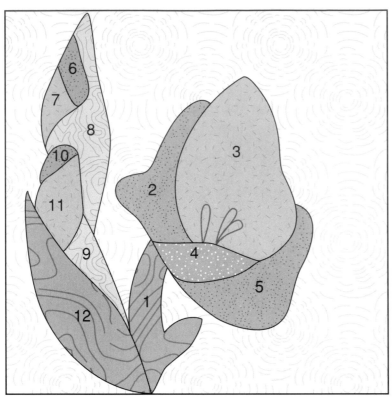

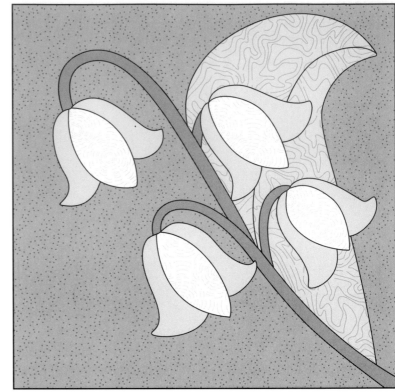

GLADIOLUS

B41 Appliqué this bright bloom and tender buds by following the number sequence, beginning with stem piece 1 and continuing through piece 12. Use lazy daisy stitches to make center.

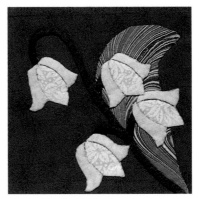

LILY OF THE VALLEY

B42 Cut a 4-inch square (plus seam allowances) of background fabric. The stems can be done with bias tubing. (See page 309 for information on bias tubing.) Appliqué pieces in place.

APPLIQUÉ

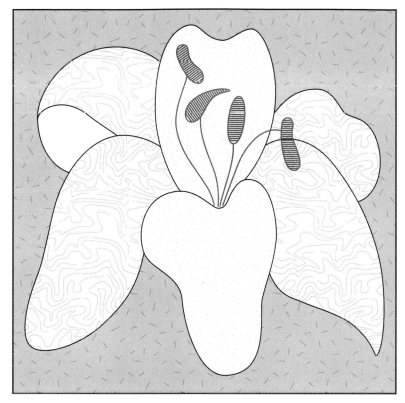

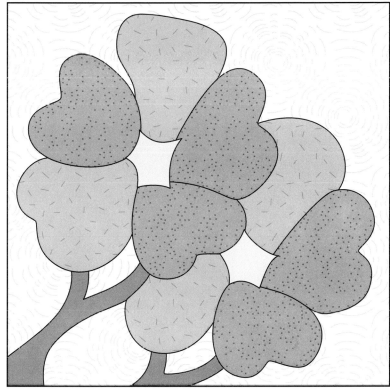

B43 Appliqué the petal pieces in place. The stamens in the center of the flower are made with stem stitch and satin stitch.

LILY

B44 Cut a 4-inch square (plus seam allowances) of background fabric. Appliqué pieces in place.

PRIMROSE

117

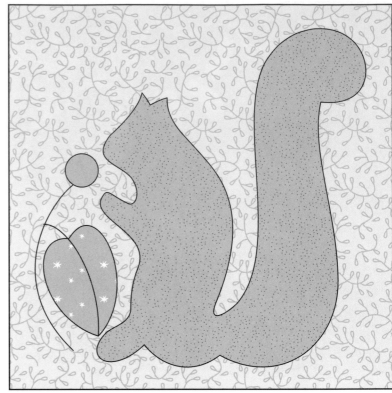

B45 Appliqué all pieces onto the background fabric. Embroider lines with stem stitch; use a French knot or a tiny bead for the bird's eye.

BIRD II

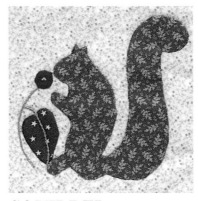

B46 Appliqué pieces onto background fabric. Use stem stitch to embroider the stem and leaf.

SQUIRREL

APPLIQUÉ Folk Art

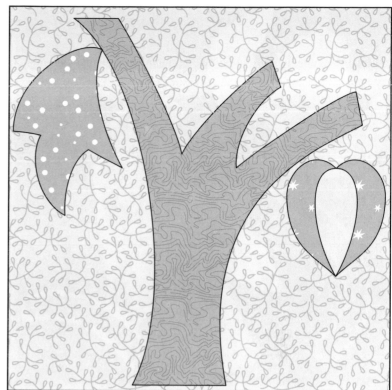

B47 Cut a 4-inch square (plus seam allowances) of background fabric. Appliqué the 4 pieces in place.

B48 Today's marbleized fabrics make a wonderful tree trunk; but other fabrics will also work well to appliqué this folk art design.

MOON AND STARS

TREE

BIRD I

B49 Appliqué the pieces in place. Use a French knot for the bird's eye, or use a small bead.

EAGLE

B50 This eagle offers a great opportunity for creative fabric selection. Use a French knot or bead for the eye.

APPLIQUÉ Folk Art

B51 Cut a 4-inch square (plus seam allowances) of background fabric. Appliqué the church onto the block.

CHURCH

B52 The horse is appliquéd from a single piece of fabric.

HORSE

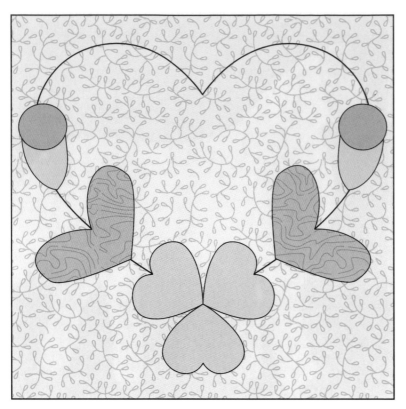

B53 Appliqué hearts and flowers. Embroider the line that forms the heart with stem stitch.

FLORAL HEART

B54 Appliqué flower pot and flowers. Use stem stitch to embroider the flower stems and handles on the flower pot.

FLOWER POT

APPLIQUÉ Folk Art

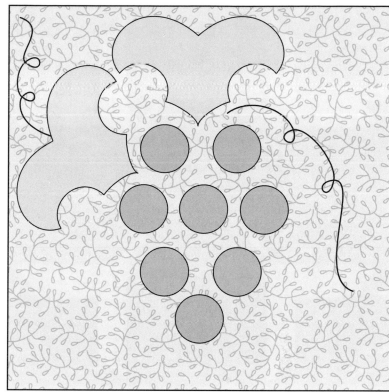

B55 Cut a 4-inch square (plus seam allowances) of background fabric. Appliqué the fruits and leaves in place. Embroider the stems and leaves using a stem stitch.

APPLE AND ORANGE

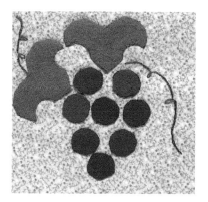

B56 Appliqué the grapes and leaves in place. Embroider the vines with stem stitch.

GRAPES

123

B57 Cut a 4-inch square (plus seam allowances) of background fabric. Appliqué pieces in place on the block.

CAROLINE LILY

B58 Appliqué flowers and leaves in place, then use stem stitch to outline the circle.

ROSE OF SHARON

APPLIQUÉ Baltimore Album

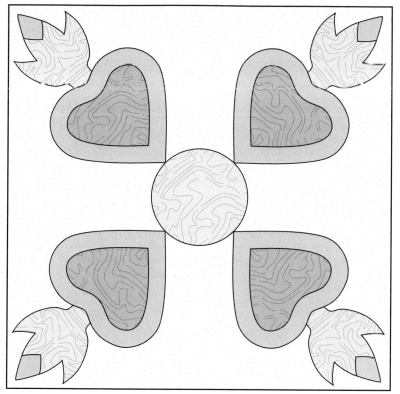

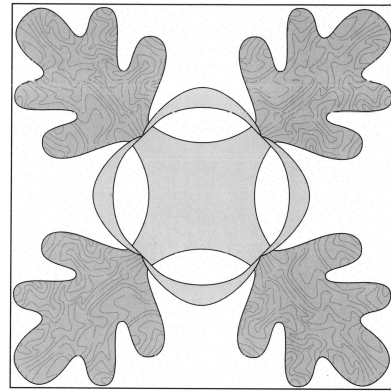

B59 Cut a 4-inch square (plus seam allowances) of background fabric. Appliqué the pieces in place.

HEART BLOSSOMS

B60 Appliqué the pieces onto the background fabric. (See page 308 for appliqué information.)

OAK LEAVES

B61 Appliqué leaves and flower for each pansy in place on the background fabric.

B62 Special fabrics highlight this traditional appliqué design.

PANSIES

WHIG ROSE

APPLIQUÉ Baltimore Album

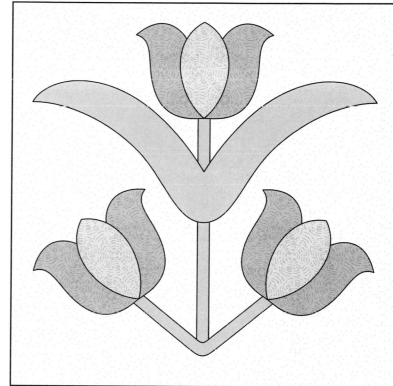

B63 Cut a 4-inch square (plus seam allowances) of background fabric. Appliqué the design in place.

B64 Appliqué the pieces in place on background fabric. (See page 308 for appliqué information.)

POMEGRANATE

TULIPS

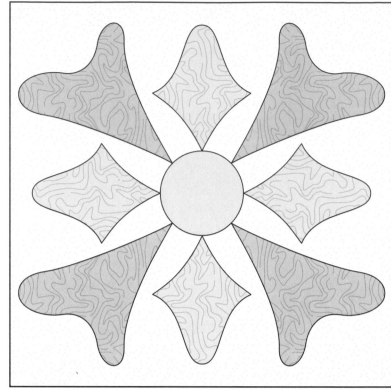

B65 Appliqué the pieces in place on the square of background fabric. Use stem stitch to embroider the leaf stem.

THISTLE

B66 Appliqué all pieces in place on the square of background fabric.

GEOMETRIC POSY

APPLIQUÉ Baltimore Album

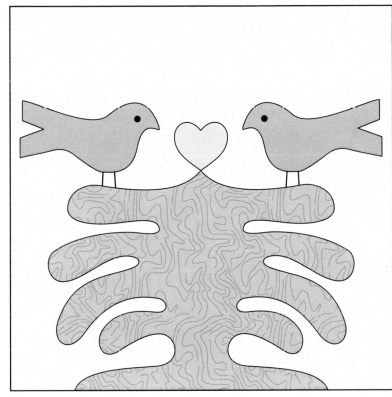

B67 Appliqué pieces in place. Traditional patterns take on a new look with today's fabrics.

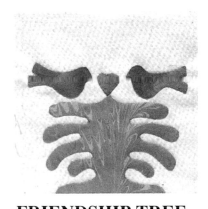

B68 Appliqué pieces in place; embroider birds' legs with straight stitches; make eyes with French knots or tiny beads.

BALTIMORE DAISY

FRIENDSHIP TREE

**SUNBONNET WITH
FLOWER BASKET**

B69 After you appliqué all
pieces in place, embroider folds
in the hat and dress with stem
stitch. Embroider flowers in the
basket or use tiny buttons.

**UMBRELLA
SUNBONNET**

B70 Appliqué pieces on background fabric; embroider umbrella handle using stem stitch.

APPLIQUÉ Sunbonnets

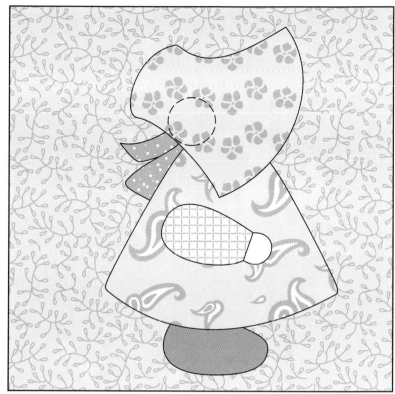

B71 Appliqué figure onto background fabric. We used a ceramic duck button; however, the duck can be appliquéd. (See page 320 for ceramic button source.) Embroider some grass with small straight stitches.

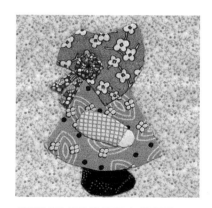

B72 Appliqué pieces on background fabric. Be creative with fabric combinations for the sunbonnet girl.

SUNBONNET FEEDING DUCK

SUNBONNET SUE

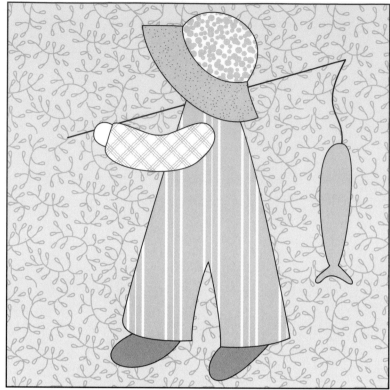

B73 Appliqué figure onto background fabric. Again, we used a ceramic button instead of appliquéing the duck. Embroider some grass with small straight stitches.

BOY FEEDING DUCK

B74 Appliqué figures onto background fabric. We found some fabric printed with a small fish design and used it for the fish appliqué. Plain fabric, of course, will also work well. Embroider the pole and the fishing line with stem stitch.

FISHERMAN

APPLIQUÉ Sunbonnets

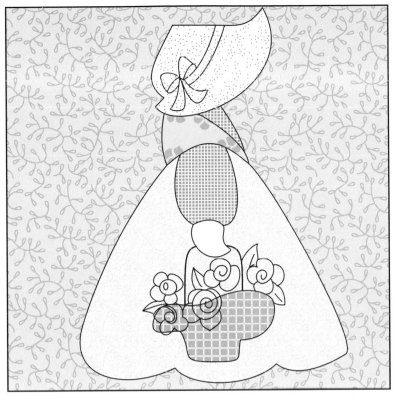

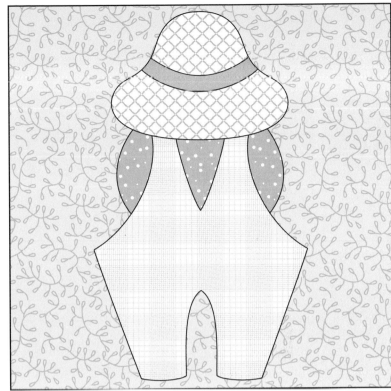

B75 Appliqué figure onto background fabric. Embroider the ribbon on her hat, or make a bow with 1/16-inch satin ribbon. Embroider the flowers in the basket, or use tiny buttons.

SOUTHERN BELLE

B76 Cut a 4-inch square (plus seam allowances) of background fabric. Appliqué pieces in place on the block.

OVERALL BILL

B77 Appliqué all pieces to background square. Embroider apron strings, flower stem, and flower petals, using stem stitch.

SUNBONNET WITH FLOWER

B78 All pieces are appliquéd onto background fabric. (For additional appliqué information, turn to page 308.)

SUNBONNETS HUGGING

APPLIQUÉ Sunbonnets

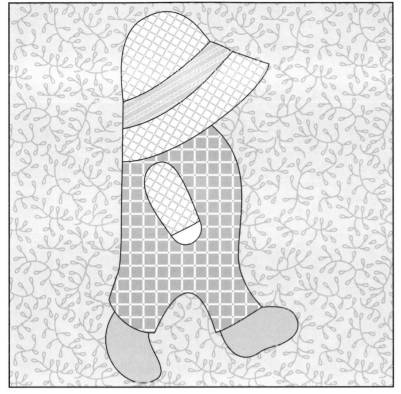

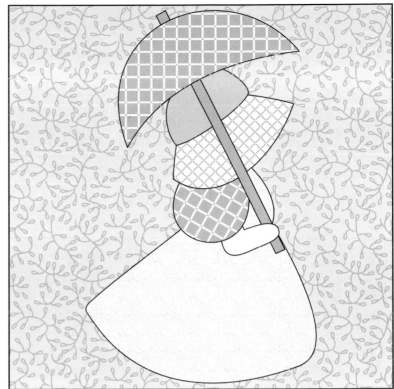

B79 Appliqué all pieces onto background square.

OVERALL ANDY

B80 Appliqué all pieces onto background square.

SINGING IN THE RAIN

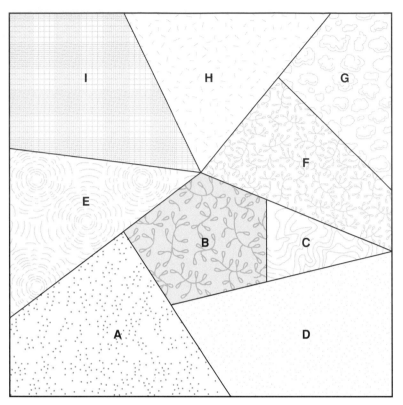

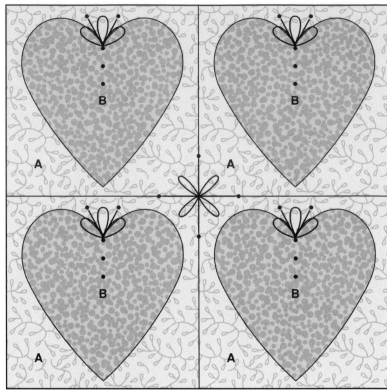

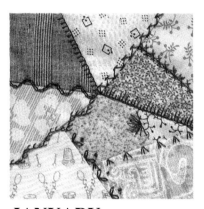

C1 Sew C piece to B piece, add D piece, then A piece. Join F piece to G piece, then add to first unit. Make EIH unit; miter it with the first unit. (See page 309 for mitering information.) Embellish with fancy embroidery stitches, beads, or buttons.

**JANUARY
ICE CRYSTALS
CRAZY QUILT**

C2 Appliqué heart to A piece (4 times). (See page 308 for appliqué information.) Sew the squares into rows, then sew the rows together to make the block. Use French knots and lazy daisy stitches to embellish.

**FEBRUARY
HEARTS**

HOLIDAYS Calendar

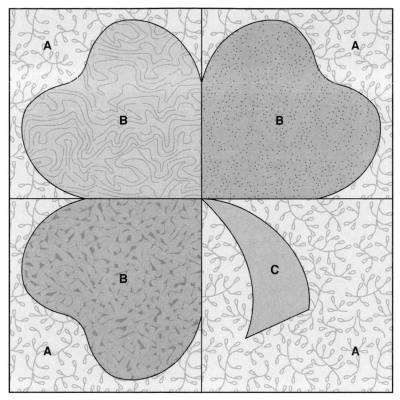

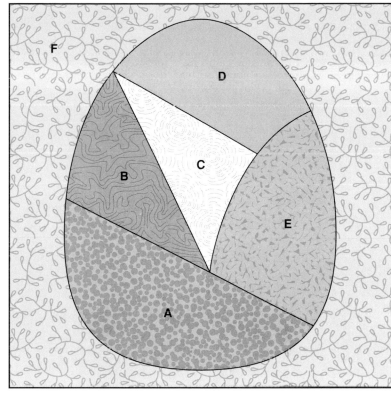

C3 For A pieces, cut four 2-inch squares (add seam allowances). Appliqué B piece to 3 squares and C piece to the fourth square. Join the squares into rows, then join the rows to complete the block.

**MARCH
SHAMROCK**

C4 Cut a 4-inch square (plus seam allowances) for background (F). Appliqué C piece to D piece, and B piece to C; add E piece, then A piece. Finally, appliqué the whole egg to the background. Embroider or embellish as you wish.

**APRIL
EASTER EGG**

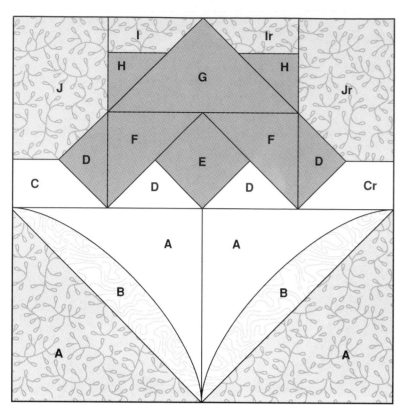

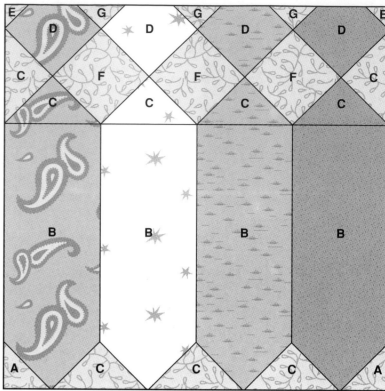

**MAY
MOM'S
NOSEGAY**

C5 Sew C and D pieces to J; miter CD seam. Sew Cr and D pieces to Jr; miter CrD seam. (See page 309 for information on mitering.) Make IH and IrH units and sew to G. Make DED unit, then add F pieces to adjoining sides. Join DEF unit with GHI unit; add JCD to left side and JrCrD to right side. Appliqué B piece to A piece (2 times). Join A to AB (2 times), then join the 2 ABA units and add to top section to complete the block.

**JUNE
DAD'S SILK
TIES**

C6 Piece the top section diagonally: Make CDG, CFDG (2 times), CFDE, and CC. Sew the units together; add E piece to upper left corner. Make BBBB unit; miter with C (3 times), and add A pieces. Join top and bottom sections to complete the block.

HOLIDAYS Calendar

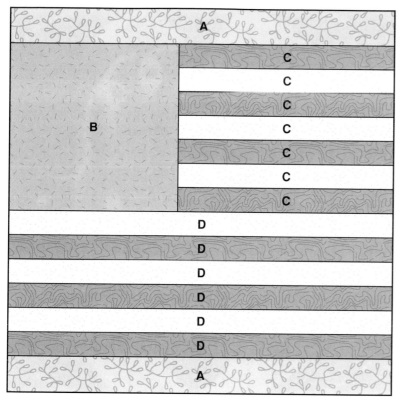

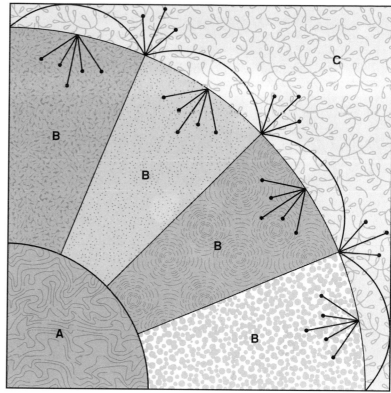

C7 Sew all C pieces together and add B piece, then A piece. Sew all D pieces together, then add A piece. Join top and bottom sections to make block.

JULY
AMERICAN
FLAG

C8 Cut a 4-inch square (plus seam allowances) for background (C). Sew B pieces together in pairs, then join pairs; appliqué to the background block. Appliqué A piece into place. Embroider the scallop and embellish.

AUGUST
FAN WITH
EMBROIDERY

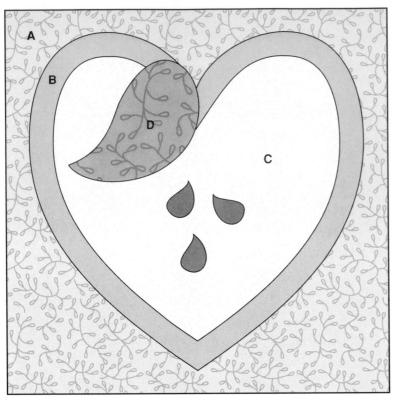

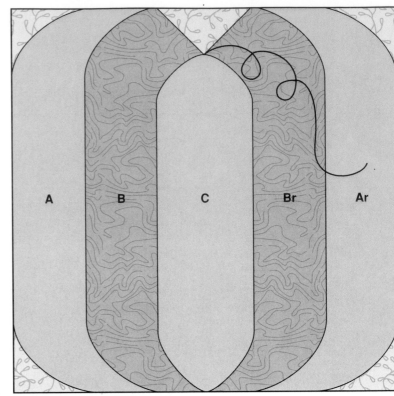

C9 Cut a 4-inch square (plus seam allowances) for background (A). The B piece is cut as a whole heart, as is the C piece. Appliqué C to B, then D to CB; appliqué entire unit to background. Embroider the seeds, or use little tear-drop buttons.

SEPTEMBER APPLE

C10 Cut a 4-inch square (plus seam allowances) of background fabric. Appliqué the 5 pumpkin pieces to the background. Embroider the vine.

OCTOBER PUMPKIN

HOLIDAYS Calendar

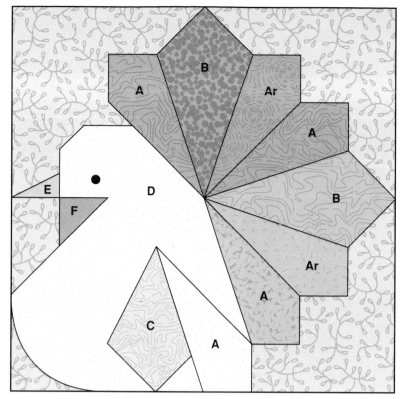

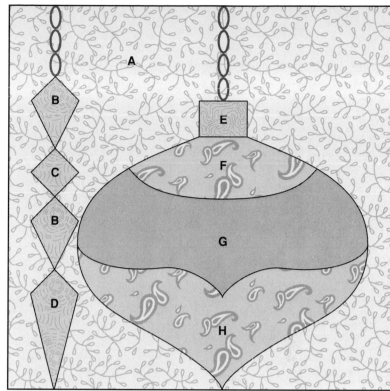

C11 Cut a 4-inch square (plus seam allowances) of background fabric. Make ABAr unit (2 times), join the units, and add A piece. Make CA unit. Appliqué turkey body (D), which fits under the CA unit, and the E and F pieces into place. Apply the CA unit and the ABAr unit to complete the block.

NOVEMBER TURKEY

C12 Cut a 4-inch square (plus seam allowances) of background fabric (A). Appliqué the BCBD section to the background. Apply G to H and F to G; add E, then appliqué to background. Use chain stitch for the hangers.

DECEMBER ORNAMENTS

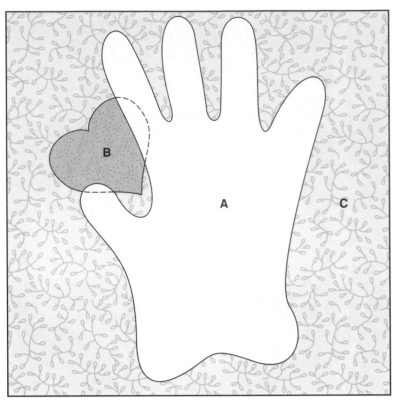

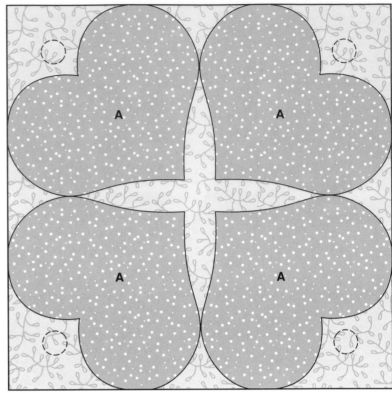

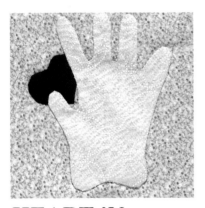

HEART 'N HAND

C13 Cut a 4-inch square (plus seam allowances) of background fabric (C). Appliqué the heart and then the hand in place.

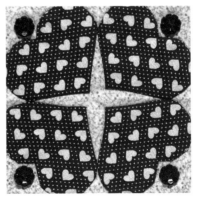

HEART CUTOUT

C14 Cut a 4-inch square (plus seam allowances) of background fabric. Appliqué the A pieces in place. The little circles can be appliquéd or embroidered, or you can use buttons for embellishment.

HOLIDAYS Hearts

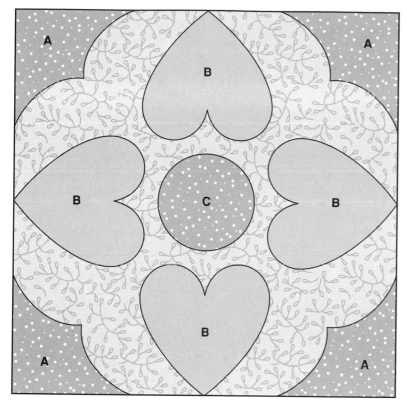

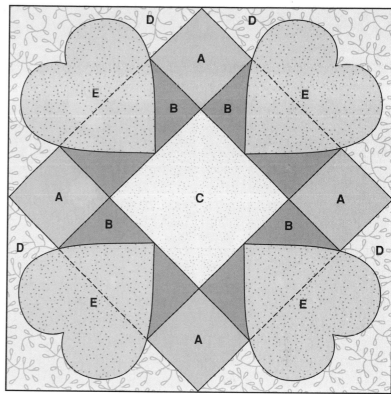

C15 Cut a 4-inch square (plus seam allowances) of background fabric. Appliqué A, B, and C pieces in place.

HEART SNOWFLAKE

C16 This block is pieced, then the hearts are appliquéd in place. Sew B pieces to 2 opposite sides of C. Make ABA unit (2 times); sew units to 2 remaining sides of C piece. Add D pieces to all sides of ABC section. Appliqué hearts (E) in place.

AMISH HEARTS

143

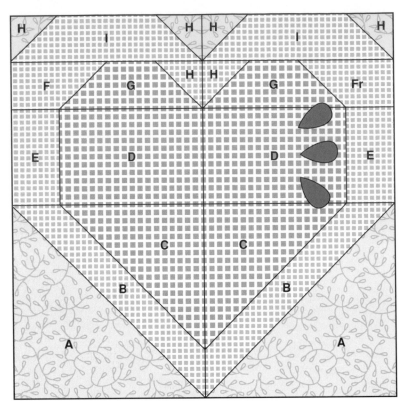

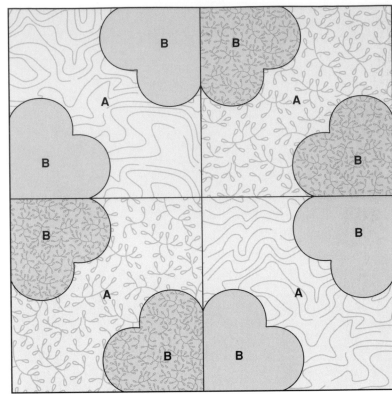

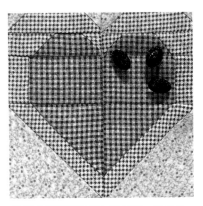

WATERMELON HEART

C17 Make HIH unit (2 times). Make FGH and HGFr units, and add each to an HIH unit. Make DE unit (2 times), and add each to a top section. Make ABC unit (2 times), adding each to top section. Join the 2 vertical sections to complete the block. Embroider seeds or use tear-drop buttons for embellishment.

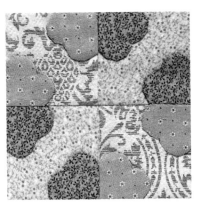

HEARTS TOUCHING

C18 For A pieces, cut four 2-inch squares (plus seam allowances). Appliqué the B pieces in place, then piece the squares into rows. Join the rows to make the block.

HOLIDAYS Hearts

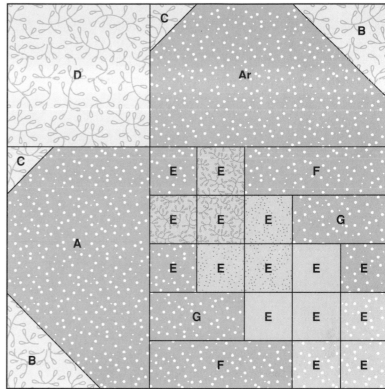

C19 Make FEF unit (4 times). Add FEF units to 2 sides of C. Add D pieces to each end of FEF (2 times); join these units to 2 remaining sides of C. Add B pieces to 2 sides of center section, then add A pieces to form square. Appliqué the hearts in place.

HEARTS AND STARS

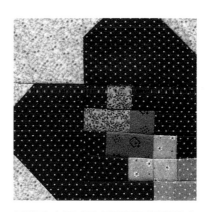

C20 Make ABC unit and ArBC unit. Following diagram, make the EFG unit by forming rows, then joining rows to form a square. Join ArBC to D, and ABC to EFG section. Join the 2 sections to make the block.

HEART WITHIN A HEART

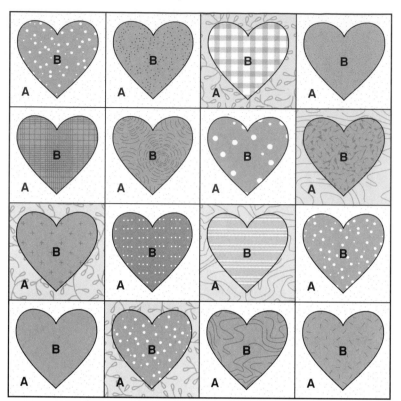

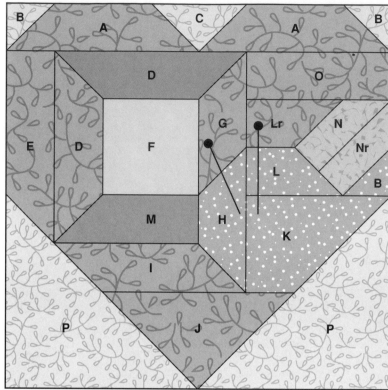

HEART SAMPLER

C21 Join A pieces into rows, then join rows to form block. Appliqué the hearts (B) in place.

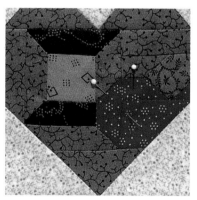

SEWING HEART

C22 Make NNrB unit; join L and Lr, and miter with NNrB. Add O and K pieces to unit. Sew M and D pieces to three sides of F piece, and miter MD and DD seams. Make GH unit and add to DFM; add I piece to M and miter GD and HI seams. Add E to D. Join DEFGHIM section with OLNBK section. Make BACAB unit and add to top of previous section; add J piece to bottom of section. Now add P pieces to complete block. Decorate with quilter's pins if desired.

HOLIDAYS Hearts

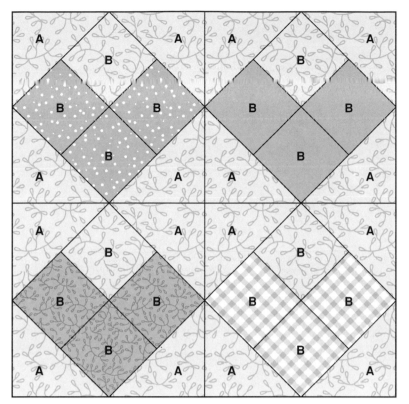

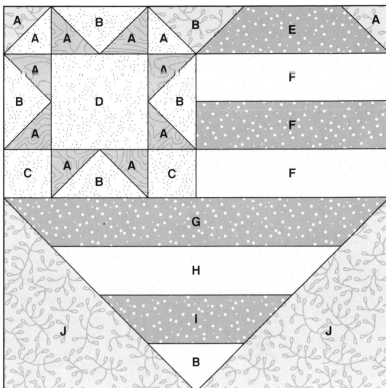

PIECED HEART

C23 Use B pieces to make a four-patch, add A pieces to all sides (4 times). Join 2 sections to make a row (2 times), then join the rows to make the block.

FLAG HEART

C24 Make ABA unit (4 times). Make AA unit; join with ABA, A, B, E, and A to form top row. Sew ABA to 2 opposite sides of D; make C/ABA/C unit and add to ABD unit. Make FFF unit and add to ABCD unit; join this section to top row. Make GHIB unit, add J pieces to 2 sides, and attach GHIBJ to first section to complete the block.

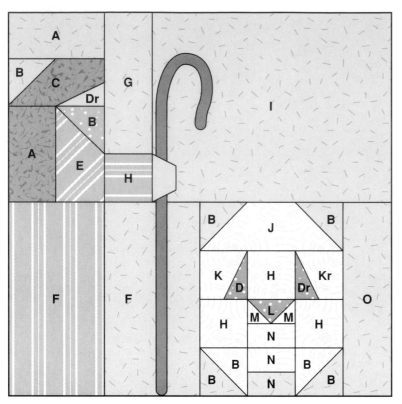

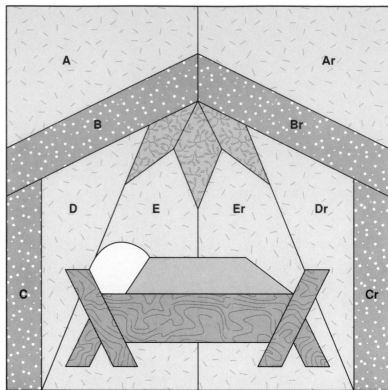

SHEPHERD TENDING FLOCK

C25 Make MLM and add 3 N pieces. Make BB unit (2 times), add H pieces, then add these units to LMN section. Make KD and KrDr units, join with H piece, and sew to HLH edge. Make BJB unit and sew to KHKr edge. Sew O piece to right side of section and F pieces to left side. Make and join BCDr and AEB units; sew A piece to BC edge; make GH unit and add to this section, then add I piece. Join the top and bottom sections. Finally, appliqué staff and hand.

MANGER

C26 The star and manger are appliquéd. Extend E and Er pieces to meet B and Br. Piece the block by making CDE unit and adding B and A pieces. Make ErDrCr unit and add Br and Ar pieces. Join the 2 sections. Appliqué star and manger.

HOLIDAYS Christmas

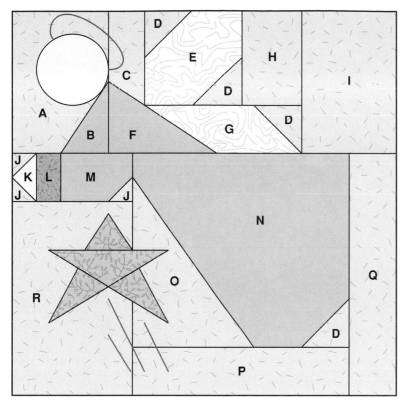

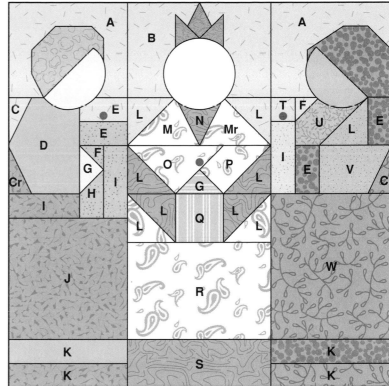

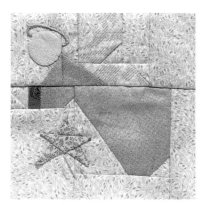

ANGEL ON HIGH

C27 Make DED unit; then add H and C pieces. Make GD unit and add to first unit, then add F piece. Make AB unit and add to left side of first section; add I piece to right side. Make JKJ and MJ units; join together with L piece, then add R piece. Make OND unit, add P then Q pieces, and attach to RJM edge. Join the 2 sections. Appliqué the angel's head and the star. Embroider the halo and star's rays with stem stitch.

WE THREE KINGS

C28 Make this block in 3 sections, beginning with the center section. Make LMNMrL unit; add B piece. Make and join LO and GP units, then add L and attach to first section. Make LL unit (2 times) and join with Q piece; add R and S pieces; join with top section. Begin right section by making and joining FULE and EVC units; make and attach TI unit. Add A piece to top edge of section; add W and K pieces to bottom of section and sew to center section. Make left section by making FGH unit, adding I piece, then EE unit. Make CDCr unit, add I piece, and join with first unit. Sew A piece to top of unit, then add J and K pieces and sew to left side of center section. Appliqué heads, crowns, and turbans. Embroider the handles or use beads or tiny

149

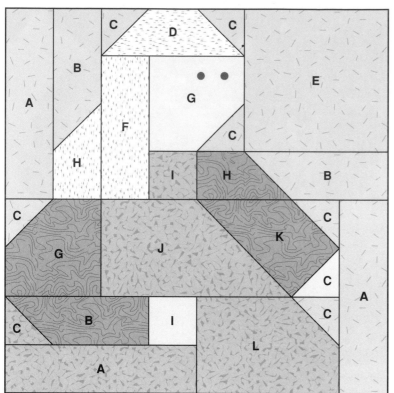

JOSEPH

C29 Make and join GC and HI units, add F piece. Make CDC unit and add to FG edge. Make EB unit and miter with first section. (See page 309 for mitering information.) Make BH unit, add A piece, and join to left side of first section. Make and join CG and JKCC units. Make CBI unit and add A piece, then LC unit. Join ABCILC unit with previous unit; add A piece, then join to top section. Use French knots or beads for eyes.

SNOWMAN

C30 This block is appliquéd. Cut a 4-inch square (plus seam allowances) of background fabric. Appliqué the snowman pieces onto the background square. Use buttons for eyes and embroider mouth.

HOLIDAYS Christmas

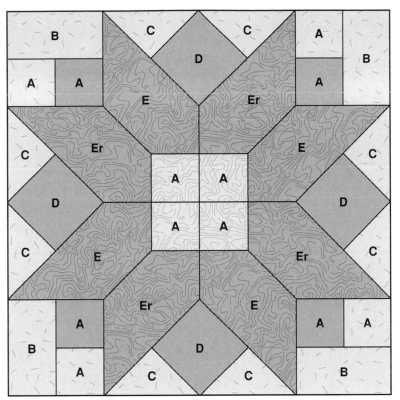

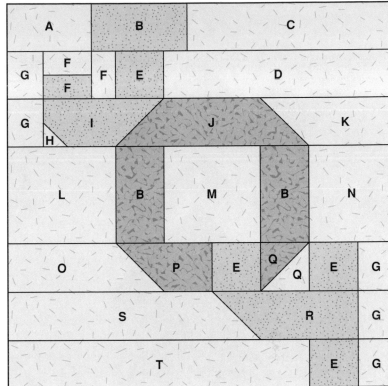

PIECED POINSETTIA

C31 Miter ErEA unit (4 times). Make AAB unit (4 times), and CDC unit (4 times). Join the ErEA units together; set in CDC units, then AAB units. (See page 309 for mitering information.)

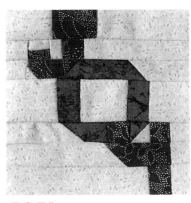

JOY

C32 Make ABC unit. Make FF unit, then join with G, F, E, and D pieces and attach to top row. Make HIJK unit, add G piece, and sew to top section. Make LBMBN unit and sew to top section. Make QQ unit, combine with O, P, E, and G pieces, and add to top section. Make and attach SRG row, then make and join TEG row to top section.

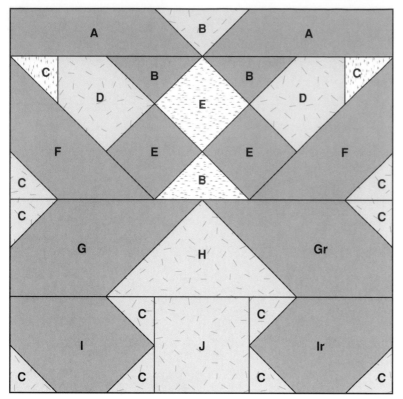

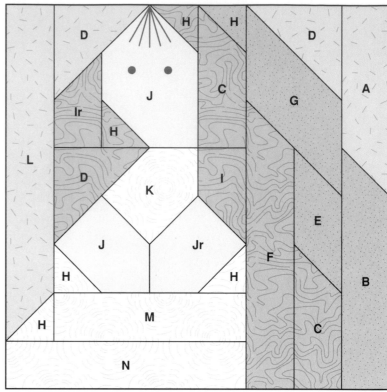

GIFT BOW

C33 Make ABA unit. Make and join CDEB, BEE, and BDC units in diagonal rows. Make FC unit (2 times) and add to diagonal row section, then add to top row. Make CGHGrC unit and add to top section. Make CICC and CCIrC and join with J piece. Add this unit to top section.

MARY

C34 Make and join HJH and and HC units; add Ir, then D pieces. Miter JKJr unit; add H pieces, miter I piece in place, then add D and M pieces and sew to top section. (See page 309 for mitering information.) Make and attach LH unit to main section, then add N piece Make ECF unit, add G and D pieces; attach to main section. Make AB unit and sew to main section. Embroider hair and use French knots or beads for eyes.

HOLIDAYS Christmas

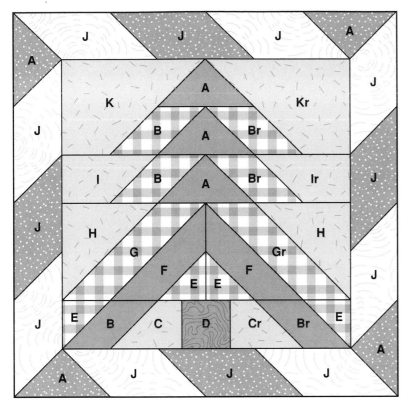

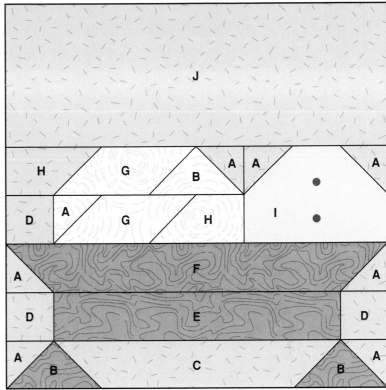

CANDY CANE TREE

C35 Make BABr unit (2 times), add A piece to top of one BABr unit, then sew K and Kr pieces to sides. Join I and Ir pieces to second BABr unit and join to first section. Make and join GHFE and EFGrH units; attach to top section. Make EBC and DCrBrE units; join and then attach to top section. Make JJJA unit (4 times); join to all sides of block and miter. (See page 309 for mitering information.)

BABY JESUS

C36 Make and join HGBA and DAGH units; make AIA unit and join with first unit. Make and join AFA, DED, and ABCBA units, and attach to first section. Sew J piece to top to complete the block. Use embroidery and/or buttons to complete face.

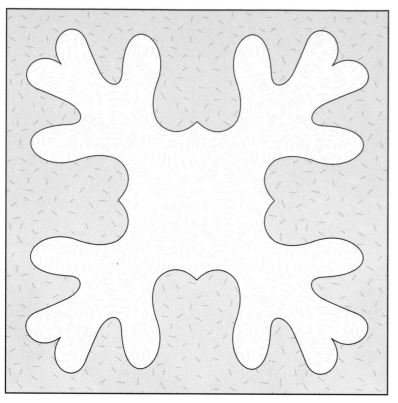

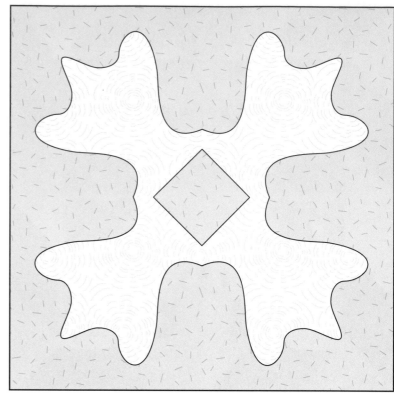

C37 This block is appliquéd. Cut a 4-inch square (plus seam allowances) of background fabric. Appliqué snowflake.

SNOWFLAKE I

C38 This block is appliquéd. Cut a 4-inch square (plus seam allowances) of background fabric. Appliqué snowflake.

SNOWFLAKE II

HOLIDAYS Christmas

C39 This block is appliquéd. Cut a 4-inch square (plus seam allowances) of background fabric. Appliqué snowflake.

SNOWFLAKE III

C40 This block is appliquéd. Cut a 4-inch square (plus seam allowances) of background fabric. Appliqué snowflake.

SNOWFLAKE IV

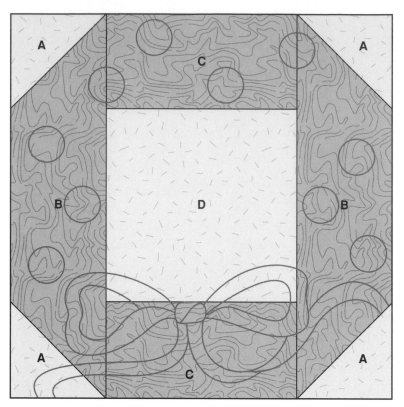

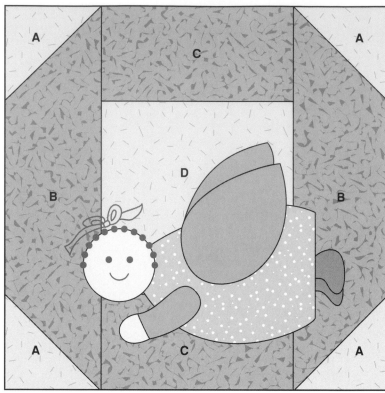

C41 Make ABA unit (2 times) and CDC unit. Join the 3 units. Sew buttons on the wreath. The ribbon can be appliquéd; or you can use real ribbon, tied in a bow and tacked in place.

RIBBON & BUTTON WREATH

C42 Make ABA unit (2 times) and CDC unit. Join the 3 units. Appliqué the angel. Embroider the face details and hair ribbon. Use French knots or beads for hair.

ANGEL WREATH

HOLIDAYS Christmas

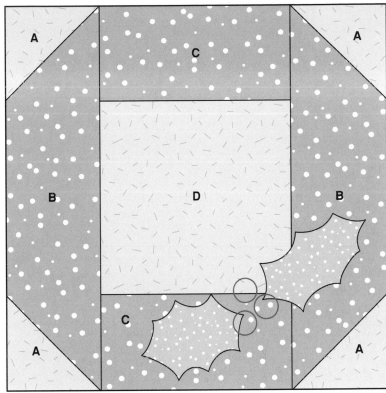

C43 Make ABA unit (2 times) and CDC unit. Join the 3 units. Appliqué the partridge and the pear leaves. Embroider beak and eye, or use a tiny bead or button for the eye.

PARTRIDGE WREATH

C44 Make ABA unit (2 times) and CDC unit. Join the 3 units. Appliqué the holly leaves. You can appliqué the berries as well, or use beads or buttons.

HOLLY WREATH

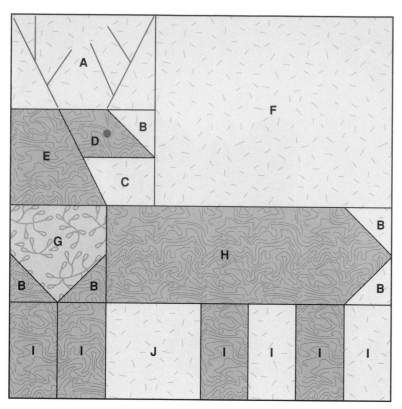

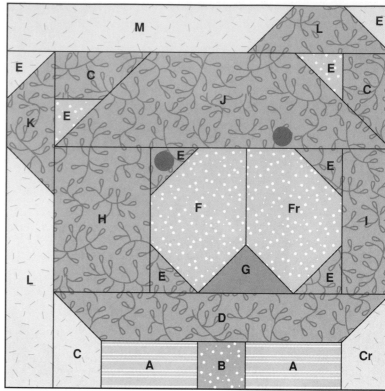

REINDEER

C45 Make BCD unit, add E piece, then A piece; join unit to F piece. Make and join BGB and HBB units; attach to top section. Make IIJIIII unit and add to top section. Embroider antlers, using stem stitch.

TEDDY BEAR

C46 Make and miter EFE and EFrE units with G piece (see page 309 for mitering information); add I and H pieces. Make ABA unit; join and miter with C, D, and Cr pieces; add to center section. Make EC unit (2 times) and add to J piece; join with center section. Make EKL unit; attach to left side of center section. Make and attach MLE unit. Use buttons for eyes.

HOLIDAYS Christmas

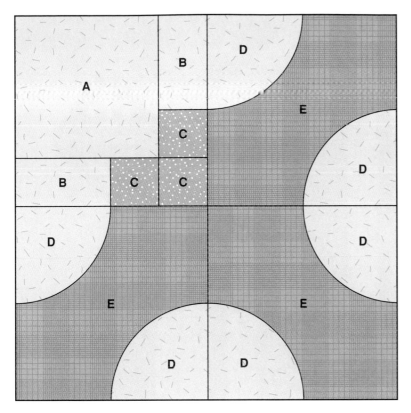

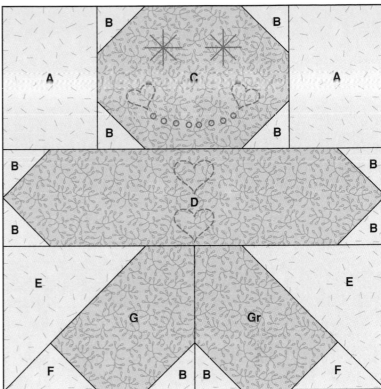

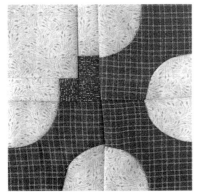

HOLLY LEAF

C47 Make DED unit (3 times). (See page 309 for help in working with curved seams.) Make BC and BCC units and attach to A piece. Combine the 4 units as a four-patch. (See page 309 for help in making four-patches.)

GINGERBREAD BOY

C48 Make BBBBC unit; add A piece to each side. Make BBBBD unit and join with top section. Make and join EFGB and EFGrB units; attach to top section. Embroider details, using stratight stitch, stem stitch, and satin stitch, or accent with buttons.

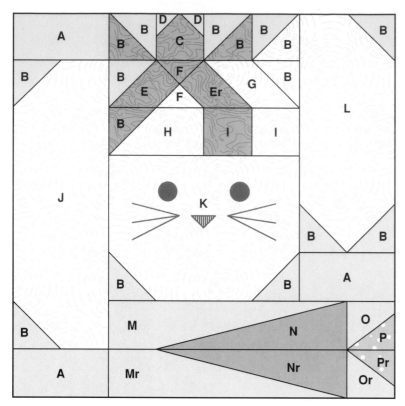

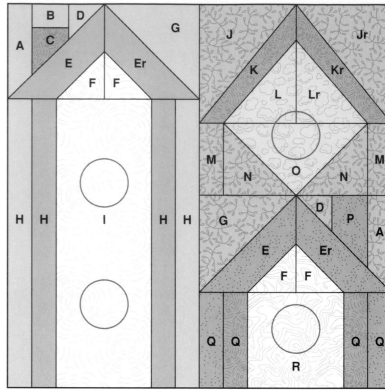

BUNNY WITH CARROT

C49 Make BB unit (3 times) and DCD unit; join units for center top row. Make BEF and FEr units; join and add G and B pieces and add to first section. Make BHII and BKB units; join, and add to first section. Make BLBB unit; add A piece and attach this section to right side of first section. Make MN and MrNr units and join; make OP and OrPr units, join, and add to NNr edge. Join this section to main section. Make BJB unit; add A pieces to top and bottom and sew to main section. Embroider face details with satin stitch and straight stitch. Use buttons for eyes.

BIRDHOUSES

C50 Make BC unit, add A and D pieces; make EF unit and join with ABCD unit. Make FErG unit and attach to first section. · Make HHIHH unit and join to first section. Make and join JKL and LrKrJr units. Make MNONM unit and join to JKL unit. Make DPA unit and add Er and F pieces. Make GEF unit, join with previous unit, and attach to MNNM edge Make QQRQQ unit, sew to bottom of previous section, then sew the left and right sides together. Appliqué the 4 birdhouse openings.

HOLIDAYS Easter

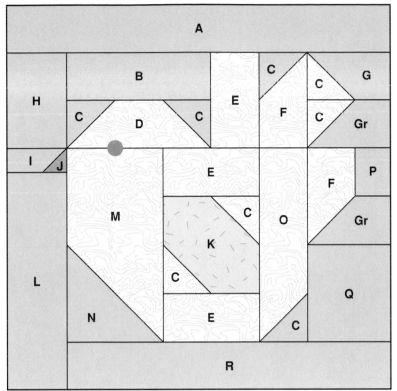

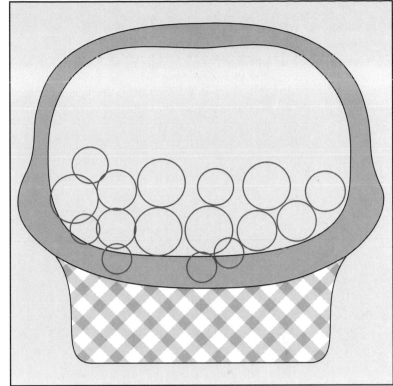

CHICK

C51 Make top section as follows: Make CDC unit, add B to top, H to left side, and E to right side. Make CF unit and add to E edge. Make and join CG and CGr and add to right side. Add A to top edge. Make bottom section as follows: Make CKC unit, add E to top and bottom; add MN to left side and OC to right side. Miter F and Gr with P, add Q, and attach to right side. Add R to bottom edge. Make IJ unit, add L, and join on left side. Join top and bottom sections. Use a small black bead or a French knot for the chick's eye.

BASKET

C52 Cut a 4-inch square (plus seam allowances) of background fabric. Appliqué the basket to the background, then fill with yo-yos and buttons. (See page 308 for yo-yo directions.)

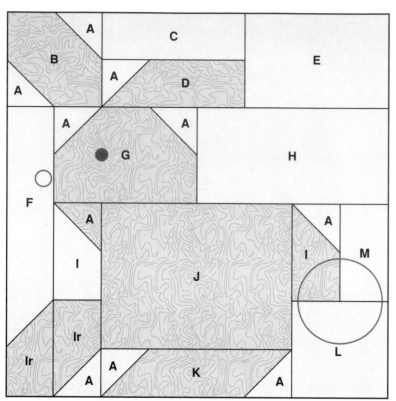

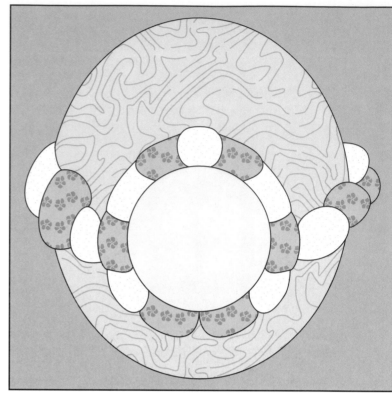

HIPPITY HOP

C53 Make AD unit and join with C piece. Make ABA unit and add to CA edge, sew E piece to CD edge. Make AGA unit and add H piece. Make AI unit (2 times;, sew M and L pieces to one AI unit. Make AKA unit and join with J piece; sew this section to AIML section. Make IrA unit and join with remaining AI unit; attach to JA edge, then sew to AGAH section. Make FIr unit and sew to left side of lower section, then join unit to top section. Add a yo-yo tail (see page 308 for yo-yo instructions). Embroider or use buttons or beads for eye and nose.

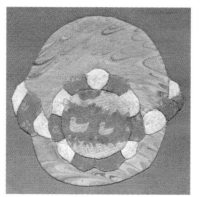

EASTER EGG

C54 Cut a 4-inch square (plus seam allowances) of background fabric. Appliqué egg, adding detail with embroidery (lazy daisy stitch, stem stitch, and French knots). Use a print with a tiny scene or pretty motif for the opening into the egg.

HOLIDAYS Easter

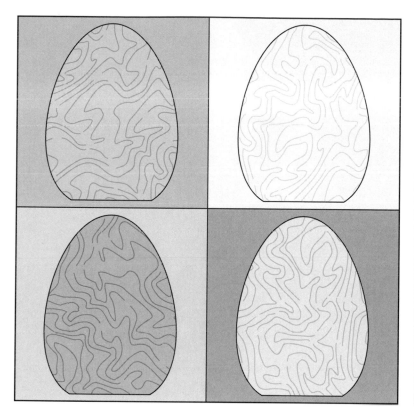

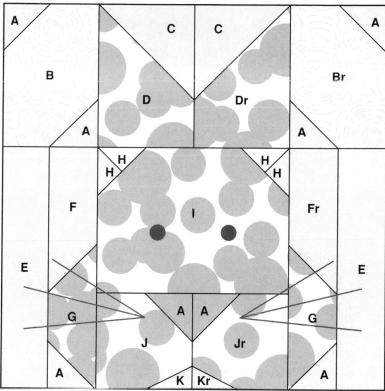

EASTER EGG SAMPLER

C55 Cut four 2-inch squares (plus seam allowances) and piece as a four-patch (see page 309 for help in making four-patches). Appliqué the eggs and add lavish embroidery and embellishment. Use ribbon, lace, beads, buttons, and your imagination.

RABBIT

C56 Make and then join ABA, CD, CDr, and ABrA units. Make HH unit (2 times), and sew to I piece. Make and join AJK and AJrKr units; join to HI unit. Make FGA and FrGA units and sew to sides of center section, then add E pieces to sides and sew to top section. Embroider face details, using satin stitch for eyes and straight stitch for whiskers.

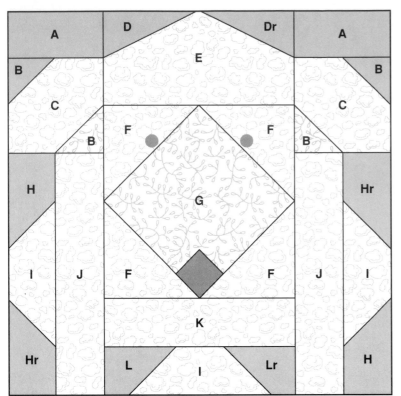

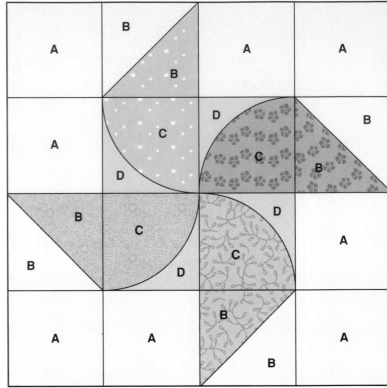

LAMB

C57 Appliqué nose piece to G piece, then add F pieces to all sides of G. Make DEDr unit and sew to top of FG unit. Make LILr unit, add K piece and sew to bottom of FG unit. Make BCB unit (2 times) and add A piece to each unit. Make HIHr and HrIH units, add J pieces to each unit, then sew these units to ABC units. Sew these sections to center section. Embroider or use beads for eyes.

CURVED PINWHEEL

C58 Make CD unit (4 times). (See page 309 for help with sewing curved seams.) Make BB unit (4 times). Combine the BB, CD and A units in rows, then join the rows to complete the block.

HOLIDAYS Easter

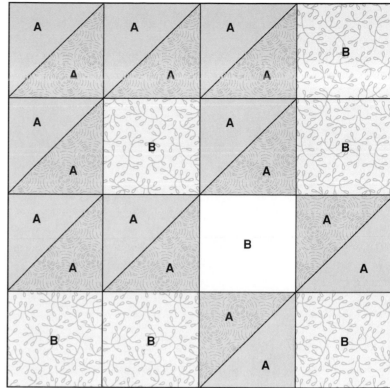

EASTER EGG II

C59 Cut a 4-inch square (plus seam allowances) of background fabric. Appliqué the egg and ribbon, or use a real ribbon.

PIECED BASKET

C60 Make AA unit (9 times). Combine AA units with B pieces to make rows, then join the rows to complete the block.

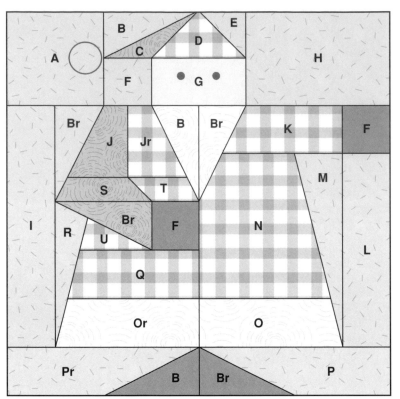

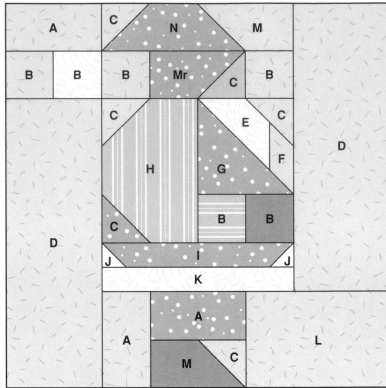

SANTA

C61 Make ST and JJr units and join; add Br and B to sides. Make UQOr unit and add R piece to side. Make BrF unit and miter into RUQ. Join this section to the first section and add I piece to left side. Make PrB unit and sew to bottom of left section. Make NO unit; add M, then K, then Br pieces. Make FL unit and sew to KM edge; make BrP unit and sew to bottom of this section. Join the right and left sections. Make BCDE and FG units and join; add A and H pieces to sides and sew to bottom section. Use beads or French knots for eyes. Appliqué the pompom on Santa's hat or use a tiny yo-yo (page 308) or button.

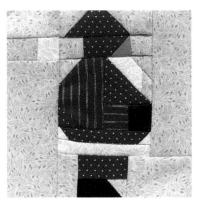

PROFILE SANTA

C62 Make BB unit; add A and D pieces. Make CNM and BMrCB units; join the units. Sew 2 C pieces to H piece. Make EF unit; add G and C pieces, then make and attach BB unit. Add CHC unit to this section. Make JIJ unit, add K piece, then attach to bottom of center section and add D piece to right side. Make MC unit, add A piece to top; add A piece to left side and L piece to right side. Attach this unit to KD edge; then join the 2 sections.

HOLIDAYS Santas

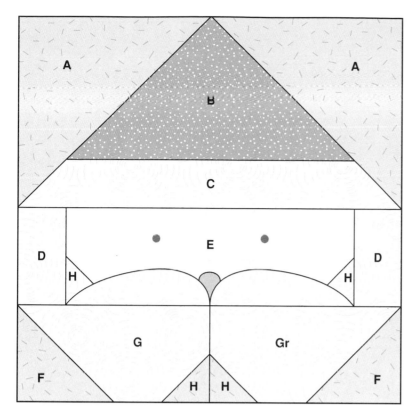

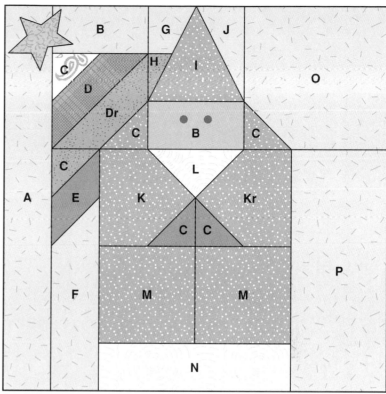

HEART SANTA

C63 This block is a combination of piecing and appliqué. Cut E and H pieces full size; Santa's nose and moustache are appliquéd over them. Make BC unit and add A pieces to each side. Sew H pieces to E, add D pieces and join with top section. Make and join FGH and HGrF units, and add to top section. Then appliqué nose and mustache. Use beads or buttons for eyes.

SANTA WITH TREE

C64 Make KCC and LKr units and join. Make MM unit and join to CKL, then add N piece. Make CEF unit and add to left side of center section; add P piece to right side of center section. Make CDDrC unit and add B piece. Make GH unit, add to I piece, then add J piece; attach B piece to GHIJ, then add to BCD section. Make CO unit and sew to right side of top section; add this section to the bottom section. Sew A piece to left side to complete the block. Appliqué the star; use French knots, buttons, or beads for eyes.

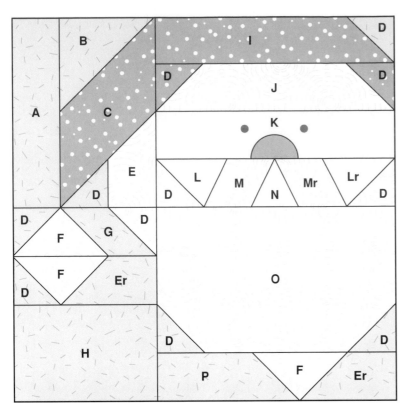

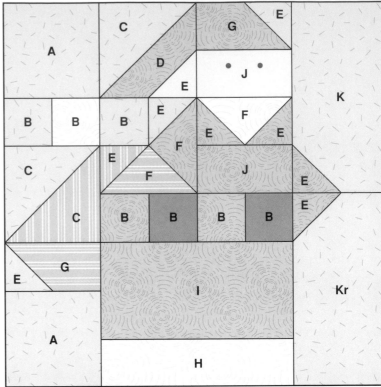

SANTA FACE

C65 Make ID and DJD units and join, then add K piece. Make DLMNMrLrD unit and add to K edge; make DOD unit and add to bottom of first section, then make PFEr and add to DOD. Make DE unit and add C, then B pieces; add A piece to left side. Make and add DFGD unit; then make DFEr and add to DFGD. Add H piece to bottom of this section and join with right section. Appliqué nose and add bead or French knot eyes.

SANTA WITH BAG

C66 Make CDE and EGJ units. Make and join EBE and FF units; make EFE unit and add J piece, then join this unit with BEF unit. Add this section to first section. Make BBBB unit and add to first section, then add I and H pieces. Make and join KE and KrE units; add to right side of center section. Make BB, CC, and EG units and join, then add A pieces to top and bottom; sew this section to the left side of center section. Use French knots or beads for eyes.

HOLIDAYS Santas

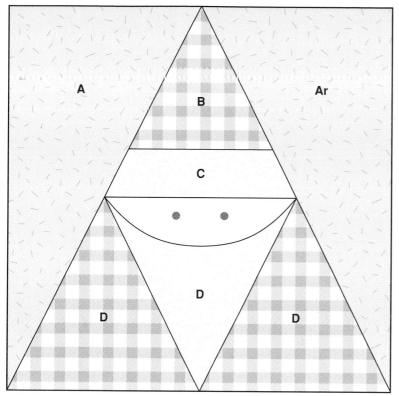

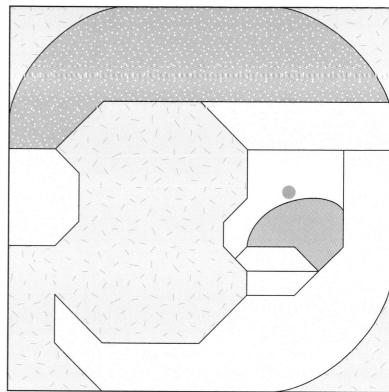

TRIANGLE SANTA

C67 Make DDD unit and appliqué face, then make and add BC unit. Add A and Ar pieces to sides. Use French knots or beads for eyes.

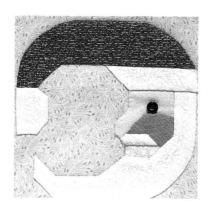

MOON SANTA

C68 This block is appliquéd. Cut a 4-inch square (plus seam allowances) of background fabric. Appliqué Santa onto background. Use satin stitch, bead, or button for eye.

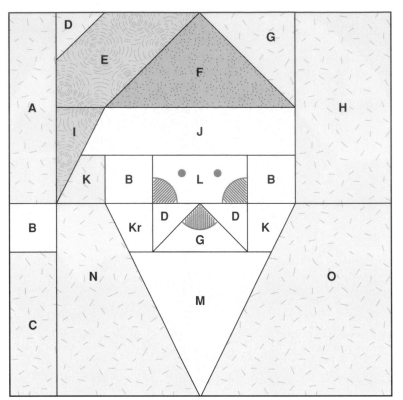

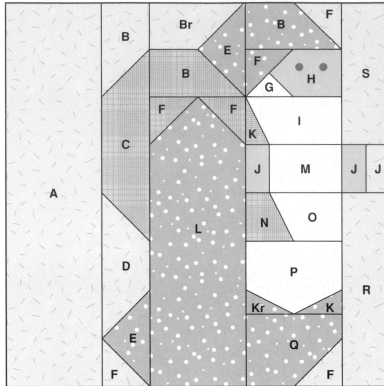

DIAMOND SANTA

C69 Make DEFG unit. Make KBLB unit; add J piece, then I piece. Join to DEFG unit, then add H piece to right side. Make DGD unit, add K and Kr pieces to each side, then M piece to bottom edge. Sew O and N pieces to sides and attach to top section. Make ABC unit and sew to left side of block. Use satin stitch to make cheeks and mouth. Use French knots or beads for eyes.

FATHER CHRISTMAS

C70 Make BF, FGH, KI, JM, NO, KrPK, and QF units and join to form a vertical row. Make SJJR unit and sew to right side of first section. Miter B, Br, and E pieces together (see page 309 for mitering information). Make FFL unit, join with BBrE, and add to left side of previous section. Make BCDEF unit and attach to left side of block, then add A. Use French knots or beads for eyes.

HOLIDAYS Santas

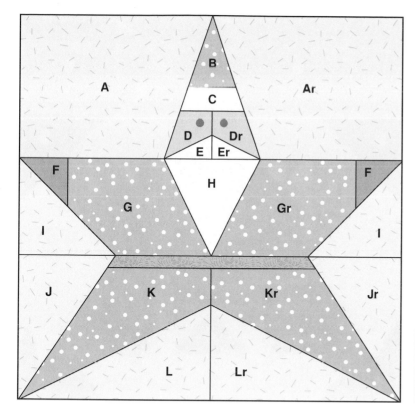

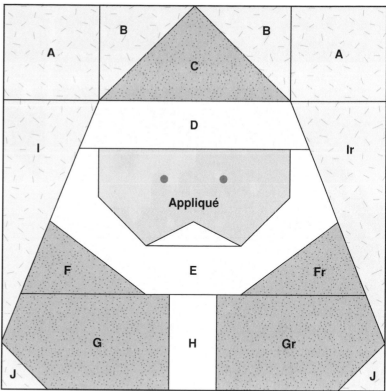

STAR SANTA

C71 Make DE and DrEr units and join; make BC unit and add, then sew A and Ar pieces to sides of this section. Make FGHGrF unit and add I pieces to each end, then sew to top section. Make and join JKL and LrKrJr units; add to top section. Appliqué the belt using ⅛-inch ribbon. Use French knots or beads for eyes. Add a button for a belt buckle.

ROLY-POLY SANTA

C72 Santa's face is appliquéd; cut E as a full piece. Make BCB unit and add A pieces to each side. Appliqué face and mous-tache to E piece, then add D, F, and Fr pieces. Make JGHGrJ unit and sew to FEFr edge; add I and Ir pieces to sides, then add this unit to the first section. Use beads or French knots for eyes.

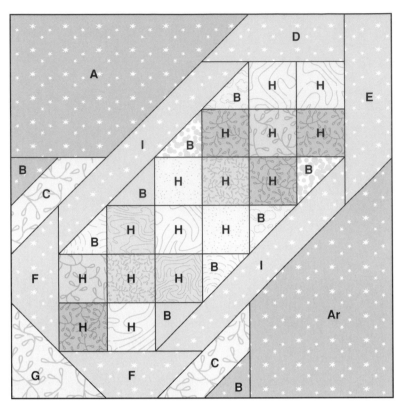

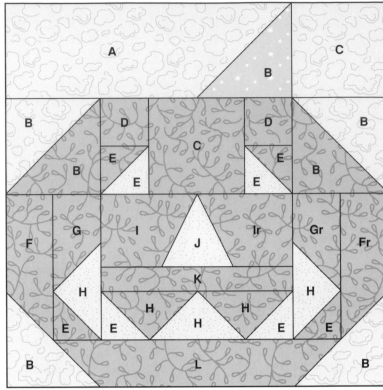

INDIAN CORN

C73 Begin with center of block by making horizontal rows of corn (B and H pieces), then joining the rows. Add I pieces to each side, then D, E, and F pieces. Make BC unit (2 times) and add to A and Ar pieces; join these units with center section, then attach G piece.

JACK-O'-LANTERN

C74 Make ABC unit. Make EE unit (2 times), add D to each unit, then join with C piece. Make BB unit (2 times) and sew to each side of CDE unit. Add BCDE section to ABC section. Make EHHHE, and IJIr units; join with K. Make EHG and EHGr units and sew to EHIJK unit; add F and Fr pieces to sides; add L piece to bottom, then B pieces to corners. Sew this section to top section to complete the block.

HOLIDAYS Halloween

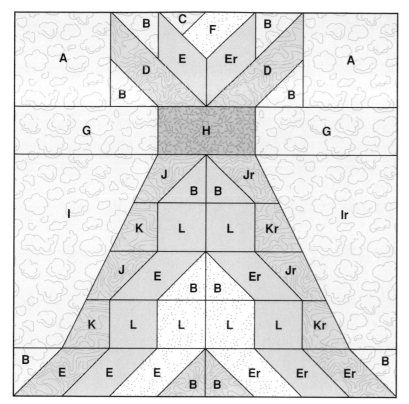

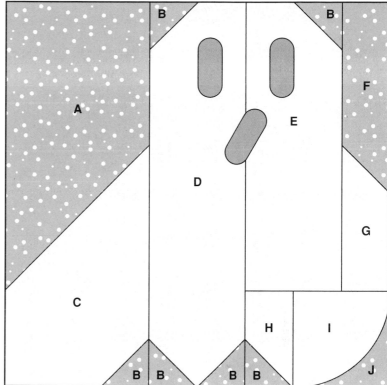

WHEAT

C75 Make BD unit (2 times). Make BE and BEr units and add to BD units; make CF unit and miter with BDEB units. (See page 309 for mitering directions.) Sew A pieces to sides of first section. Make GHG unit and add to top section. Make horizontal rows, beginning with JBBJr and ending with KLLLLKr; join the rows. Join I and Ir to each side. Piece BEEEBBErErErB and add to previous unit. Attach to top.

GHOST

C76 Make and join ACB and DBBB units. Make HB and IJ units (see page 309 for help with sewing curved seams); join the units and add to EBFG section. Join the 2 sections to complete the block. Appliqué the eyes and mouth.

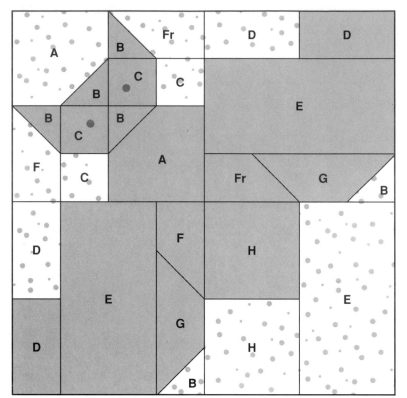

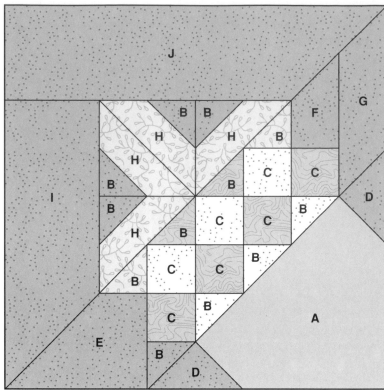

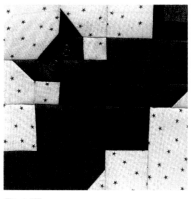

BAT

C77 Make AB unit (2 times); make CC (2 times), and make FB and FrB units. Join FB and CC units, then join the units as a four-patch. (See page 309 for four-patch directions.) Make BGF and BGFr units; join with E pieces and DD units to make 2 squares. Make HH unit and add to E. Join the four sections to complete the block.

ACORN

C78 Make BCCB unit (3 times) and join in rows. Make BE unit and add to left edge of the first section. Make BCF unit and add to right side of section, then add G piece to FC edge. Make DAD unit and attach to first section. Make BH unit (4 times), combine to make triangle unit and add I piece, then add J. Join the 2 sections diagonally to complete the block.

HOLIDAYS Halloween

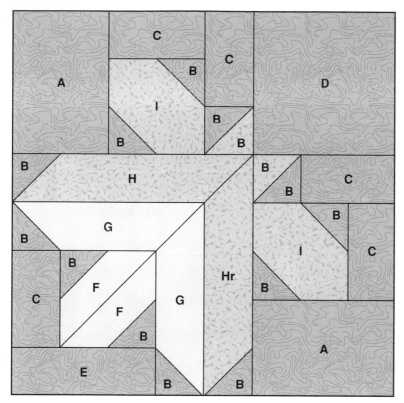

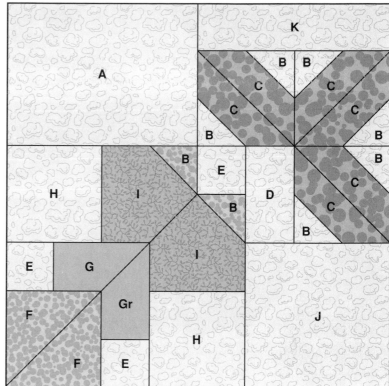

FALL LEAF

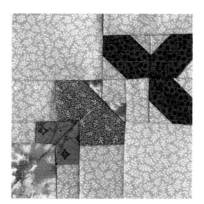

FALL LEAVES

C79 Make BIB unit (2 times); add C piece to each unit. Make BB unit (2 times); add C piece to each unit. Sew BIBC section to BBC section (2 times), then add A piece to each section. Sew B pieces to H, G (2 times), and Hr pieces. Join BH with BG and HrB to GB. Make BFFB unit; add C piece to left side and E piece to bottom. Miter BFCE section with BHG and BHrG units. (See page 309 for mitering directions.) Combine the 3 completed sections with D piece to complete the block.

C80 Make BCCB unit (3 times); add D piece to edge of one BCCB unit, then add J piece. Join remaining 2 BCCB units and add K piece, then A piece. Make EG and EGr units; add F piece to each unit. Make 2 HI units and add to EFG and EFGr units; join the 2 sections. Make BEB unit and add to this section. Sew BCDJ section to right side. Join the 2 sections to complete the block.

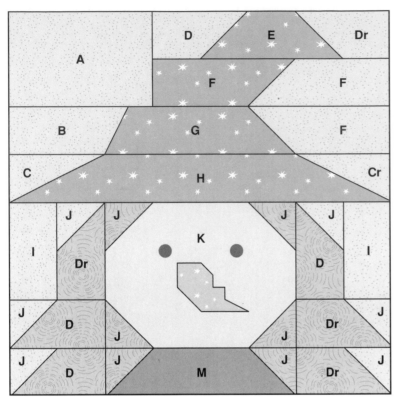

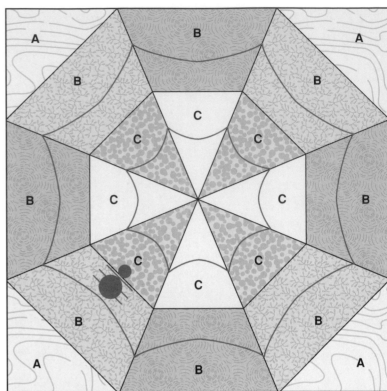

WITCH

C81 Make DEDr and FF units and join, then add A to left side. Make BGF unit and add to top section; make CHCr unit and add to section. Make JD unit (2 times) and join; make JDr unit, add I piece, and sew to JD edge. Make DrJ unit (2 times) and join; make JD unit, add I piece, and sew to DrJ edge. Sew 4 J pieces to K piece; make JMJ unit and attach to JKJ edge. Join 3 units to make bottom section and add to top section. Appliqué the nose and add beads or buttons for eyes.

SPIDER WEB

C82 Make BC unit (8 times); join in pairs (4 times), then join pairs (2 times). Sew the 2 sections together and add A pieces to the 4 corners. Embroider details using stem stitch for the web, satin stitch and straight stitch for the spider.

HOLIDAYS Halloween

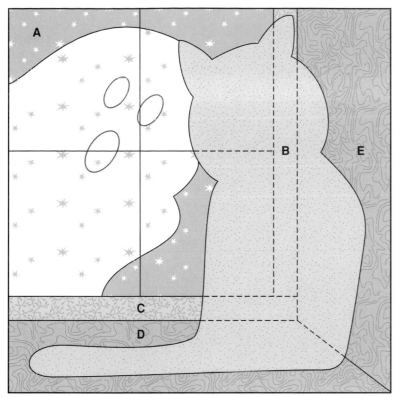

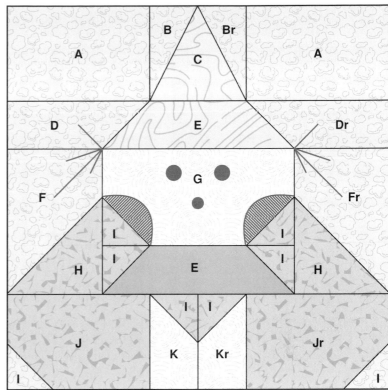

BLACK CAT AND GHOST

C83 Appliqué ghost to A piece, then add B and then C. Attach D and E pieces and miter. (See page 309 for mitering directions.) Use appliqué or embroidery for the ghost's face. Appliqué the cat. Use stem stitch to embroider window panes over the ghost.

SCARECROW

C84 Make BCBr unit and add A pieces to each side. Make DEDr unit and add to top section. Make IGI and IEI units and join. Make FH and FrH units and sew to sides of center section. Attach center section to top section. Make and join JI, KI, KrI, and JrI units; add to main section. Use beads for eyes and mouth. Use satin stitch for hands.

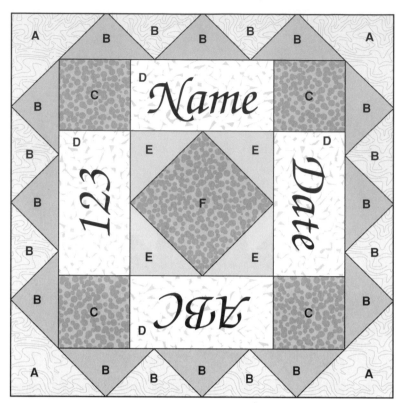

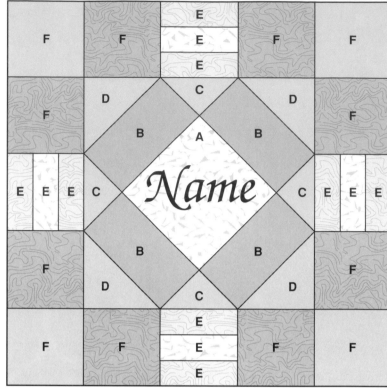

ALBUM BLOCK

D1 Sew E pieces to 2 opposite sides of F, then add E pieces to 2 remaining sides. Join D pieces to 2 opposite sides of EF unit. Make CDC unit (2 times); sew to remaining sides of EF unit. Join 5 B pieces (4 times); add to all sides of center section. Sew A pieces to 4 corners to complete the block. Write or embroider names or dates as desired.

ALBUM BLOCK

D2 Join B pieces to 2 opposite sides of A. Make CBC unit (2 times) and add to AB unit. Sew D pieces to 4 corners. Make EEE unit (4 times), join with F pieces (FEEEF) (4 times), and add to 2 opposite sides of center section. Sew F pieces to each end of remaining FEF units, and sew to 2 remaining sides to complete the block. Add name or date to center of the block.

TRADITIONAL Signature Blocks

ALBUM BLOCK

D3 Make AA unit (16 times). Join 4 AA units to make a pinwheel section (4 times). (See page 309 for help in making four-patches.) Join 2 pinwheel sections with B (2 times). Join the 2 sections with C to complete the block. Embellish C with name, initials, or dates.

ALBUM BLOCK

D4 Make AA unit (8 times), then make BB unit (2 times). Join 4 AA units to form a four-patch (2 times). Join with BB units to form a four-patch to complete the block. Personalize as desired.

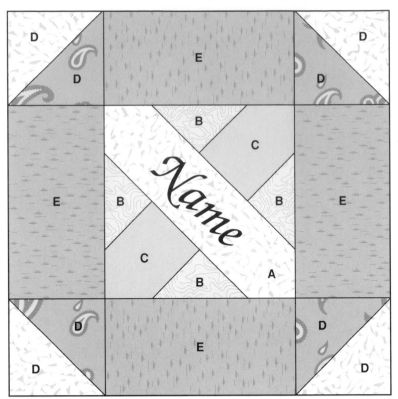

ALBUM BLOCK

D5 Make BCB unit (2 times); join the units with A to make the center section. Make DD unit (4 times). Add E pieces to 2 opposite sides of center section; sew DD units to each end of E (2 times). Add DED units to remaining sides to complete the block. Add name or date to A.

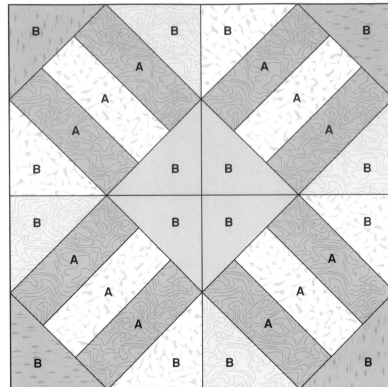

ALBUM BLOCK

D6 Make AAA unit (4 times). Sew B pieces to 2 opposite sides of AAA, then to 2 remaining sides (4 times). Join the 4 sections into a four-patch (see page 309 for help in making four-patches).

TRADITIONAL Signature Blocks

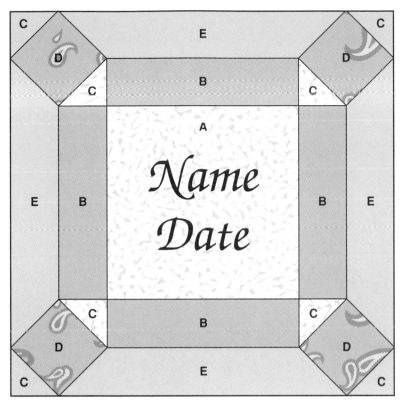

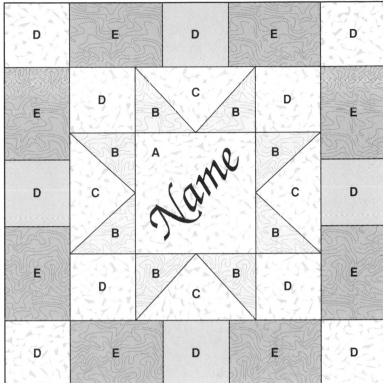

ALBUM BLOCK

D7 Sew B pieces to 2 opposite sides of A. Add C pieces to each end of B (2 times); add these units to remaining 2 sides of A. Sew E pieces to all 4 sides of center section. Make CD unit (4 times) and attach to C edges; miter with E pieces. (See page 309 for mitering directions.) Add name and date to center.

ALBUM BLOCK

D8 Make BCB unit (4 times); add BCB to 2 opposite sides of A piece. Sew D to each end of BCB unit (2 times); join to 2 remaining sides of A. Make EDE unit (4 times); add to 2 opposite sides of center section. Sew D pieces to each end of remaining EDE units and then join the units to main section to complete the block. Personalize the center.

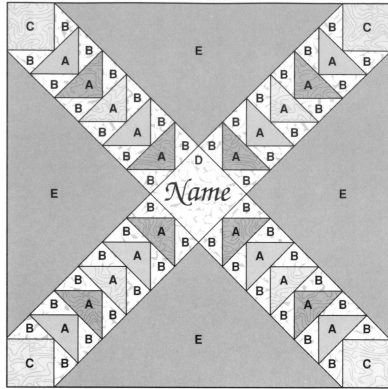

D9 Make BAB unit. Make CBC unit (2 times); add to sides of BAB unit. Add name or date to center of the block.

ALBUM BLOCK

D10 Make BAB unit (20 times). Make BCB unit (4 times). Join 5 ABA units and add BCB unit (4 times). Join 2 ABC units with D piece. Add E pieces to 2 sides of each remaining ABC unit (2 times), then add these sections to the center section to complete the block. The tiny center square is ideal for initials.

ALBUM BLOCK

TRADITIONAL Signature Blocks

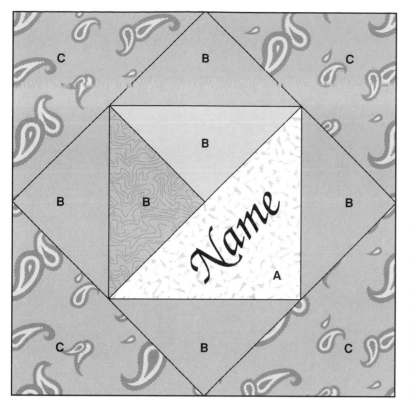

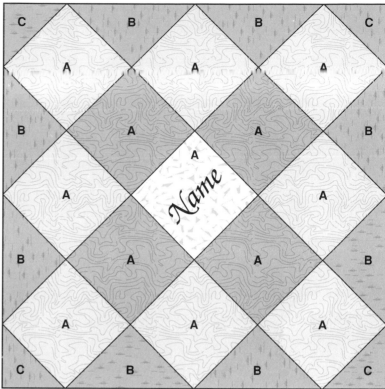

ALBUM BLOCK

ALBUM BLOCK

D11 Make BB unit (2 times); join the units. Make BAB unit and add to BBBB. Sew C pieces to all 4 sides of center section to complete the block. Embellish with name and/or dates.

D12 This block is pieced in diagonal rows. Make 2 rows of 3 A pieces; add B pieces to each end. Make 1 row of 5 A pieces and add C to each end. Join the 3 rows. Make ABBC unit (2 times); add to each side of center section to complete the block. Personalize the center block.

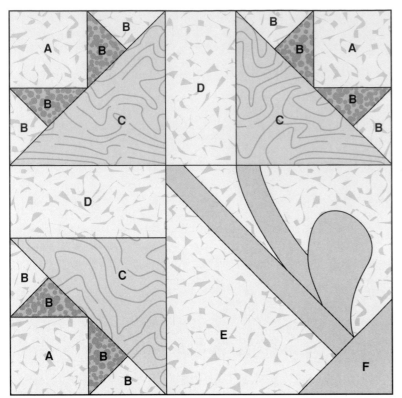

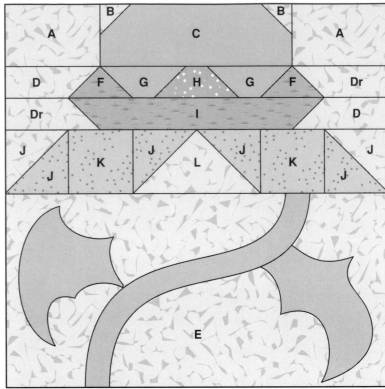

DIAMOND LILY

D13 Appliqué stems and leaf onto E piece; add F. Make BB unit (6 times). Join A with 2 BB units, add C (3 times). Make top row of ABC/D/ABC units. For bottom row, join remaining ABC unit to D and add to EF unit. Join the 2 sections to complete the block.

ORIENTAL POPPY

D14 This block is made in horizontal rows. Beginning with the bottom row, appliqué leaves and stem onto E. (See page 309 for directions for using bias tubing to make stem.) Construct the next row by making JJ unit (2 times) and JLJ unit, then combine these units with K to form the row; join to bottom piece. Make DrID row and add to previous section. Make and join the next row: DFGHGFDr. For top row, add B pieces to C, sew A to each end, and join to main section.

TRADITIONAL Pieced Flowers

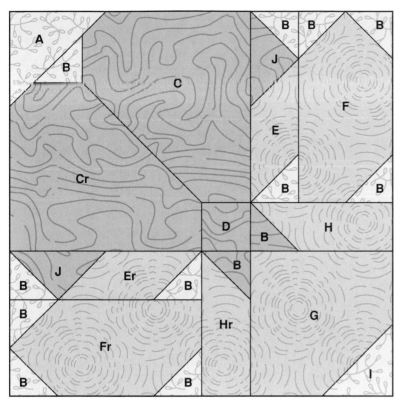

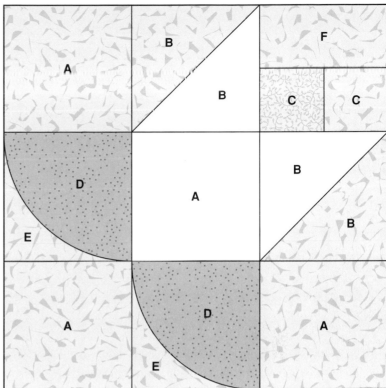

PANSY

D15 Join C and Cr, miter with B and D (see page 309 for mitering directions), and add A. Make BJEB unit (1 time and 1 time reversed). Make FBBB unit and join to BJEB (1 time and 1 time reversed). Make HB unit and add to JEFB (1 time and 1 time reversed). Add I to G. Join the 4 units in a four-patch to complete the block (see page309 for help in making four-patches).

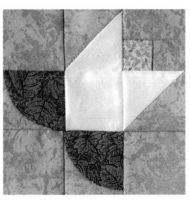

MAGNOLIA

D16 Piece D with E (2 times). (See page 309 for help with sewing curved seams.) Make BB unit (2 times). Join 2 C pieces, add to F; join with BB unit and A to form top row. For center row, combine DE with A and BB. For bottom row join A with DE and A. Join rows to complete the block.

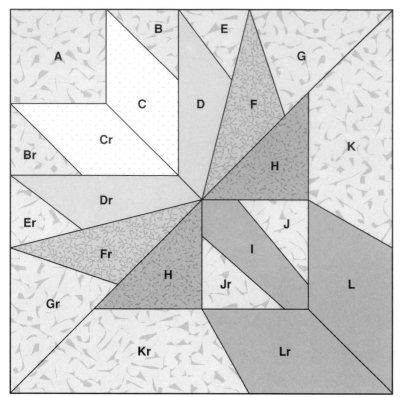

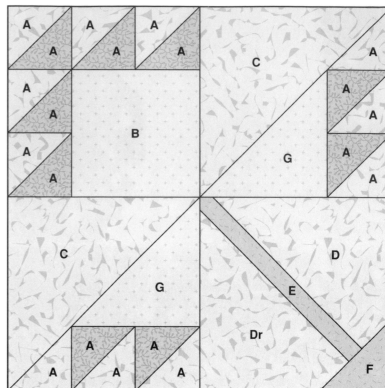

D17 Make BC, ED, and GF units; then make the 3 reverse units. Join the units to make 2 sections. Join the 2 sections with A piece (see page 309 for mitering directions). Make JIJr unit; add H to each side. Make KL and KrLr unit and add to HIJ unit, mitering the LLr seam. Join the 2 sections.

NOSEGAY

D18 Make AA unit (9 times). Join 2 AA units and add to B; join 3 AA units and add to AB section. Join 2 AA sections with A piece; add G, then C to make a square (1 time and 1 time reversed). Sew D and Dr to E; add F. Sew the 4 sections together to complete the block.

CLOVER BLOSSOM

TRADITIONAL Pieced Flowers

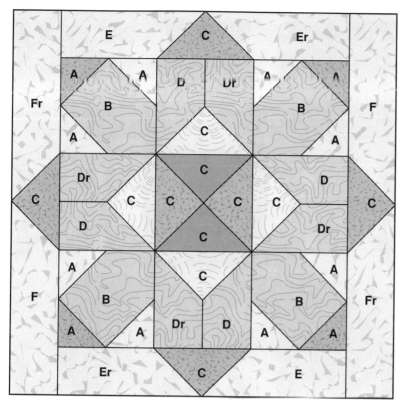

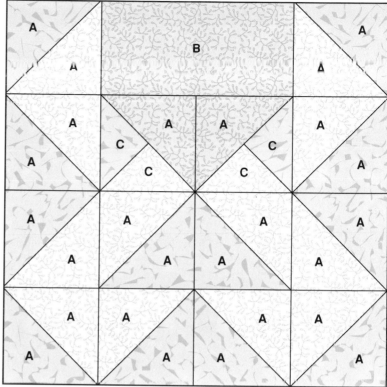

FIREWHEEL

D19 Sew D and Dr to C, mitering the DD seam (4 times). (See page 309 for mitering directions.) Sew A pieces to 3 sides of B (4 times). Join 4 C pieces to make the center section. Join the AB, CD, and center C sections as a nine-patch. (See page 309 for help in making nine-patches.) Add E and Er to C (2 times); join to opposite sides of center section. Add F and Fr to C (2 times) and join to main section to complete the block.

DAFFODIL

D20 Make AA unit (12 times). Join 2 C pieces and add to A (2 times). Add AA unit to each end of B to make top row. Join other units in rows as shown. Join rows to complete the block.

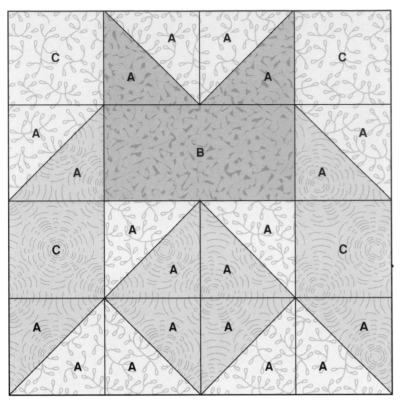

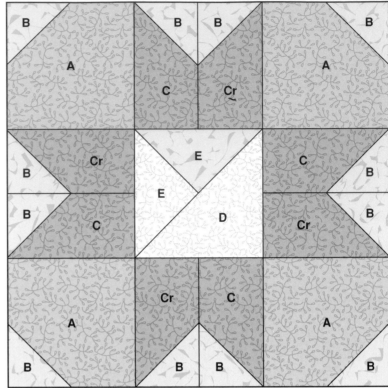

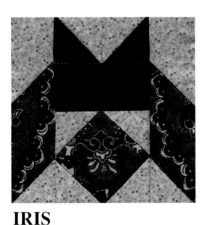

D21 Make AA unit (10 times). Join units with B and C pieces to form rows: C/AA/AA/C, AA/B/AA, C/AA/AA/C, and AA/AA/AA/AA. Join rows to complete block.

IRIS

D22 Make center EED unit. Sew B to C (4 times) and B to Cr (4 times); join BC and BCr (4 times). Add B to A (4 times). Join the units as a nine-patch. (See page 309 for help in making nine-patches.)

PRIMROSE

TRADITIONAL Pieced Flowers

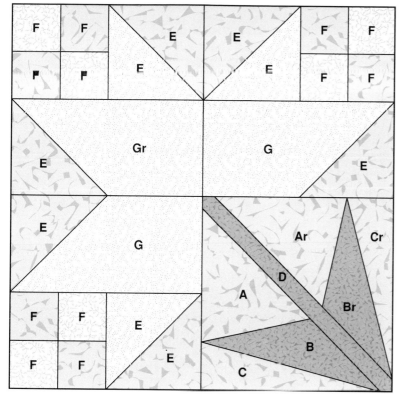

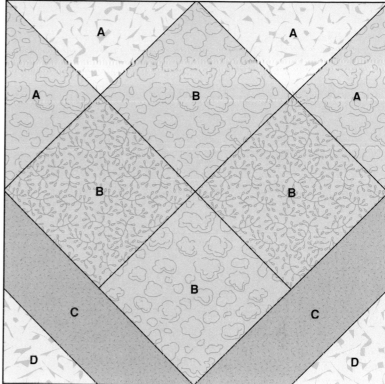

D23 Join A to B to C, and Ar to Br to Cr; add each unit to D. Make EE units (3 times). Make F four-patches (3 times). Add E to G (2 times) and E to Gr (1 time). Referring to the diagram, combine the units to make the 4 sections of the block, then join the sections.

TULIP

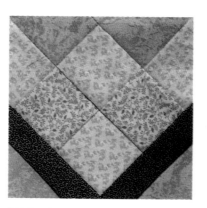

D24 Combine B pieces to make center four-patch. Make AA unit (2 times). Make CD unit (2 times). Add AA unit to 2 adjoining sides of B unit. Add CD units to 2 remaining sides to complete the block.

BEAUTIFUL TULIP

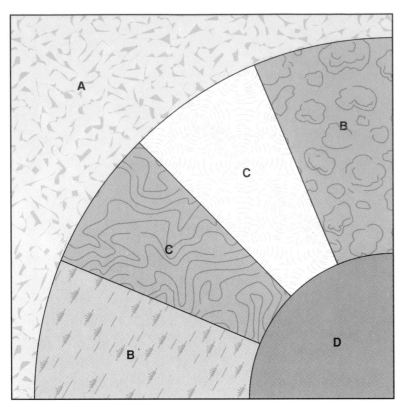

GRANDMOTHER'S FAN

D25 Cut a 4-inch square (plus seam allowances) of background fabric (A). Join B to C (2 times), then join the C edges to make the fan unit. Appliqué unit to background square. Finally, appliqué D in place.

SUNBONNET SUE

D26 Cut a 4-inch square (plus seam allowances) of background fabric. This block is appliquéd. (See page 308 for appliqué information.) Embroider the line on the hat.

TRADITIONAL The 1930s

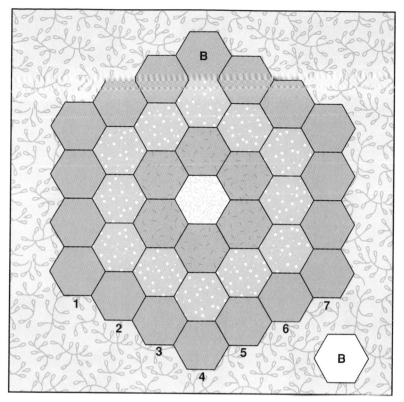

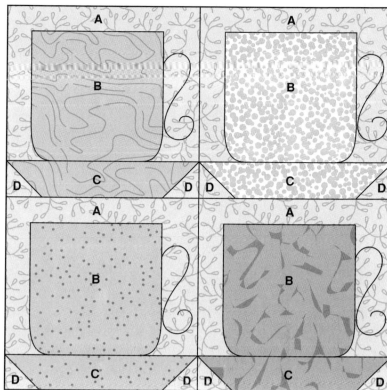

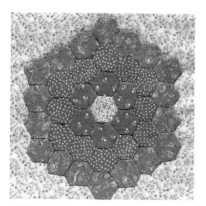

GRANDMOTHER'S FLOWER GARDEN

D27 Cut a 4-inch square (plus seam allowances) of background fabric. This block is pieced by hand, then appliquéd to the background. We pieced vertical rows (as numbered), then sewed the rows together, pivoting where the point of one piece fits in the notch of the next row. The template (B) is given in the lower right corner.

TEACUPS

D28 For each saucer, join D onto each end of C (4 times). The cups are appliquéd to A (4 times). Embroider the handles with stem stitch. Join AB with CD units (4 times), then join the 4 sections to complete the block.

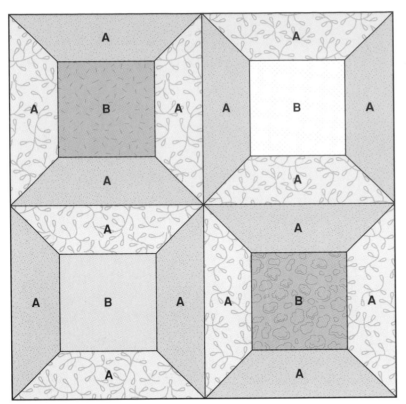

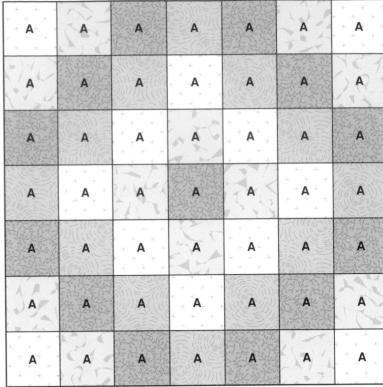

D29 Sew A pieces to opposite sides of B, being careful not to sew in the end seam allowances. Add A pieces to the remaining sides of B, then miter the AA seams. (See page 309 for mitering directions.) Make this unit 4 times, then join the 4 units to complete the block.

SPOOLS

D30 This block has just one template. The 49 pieces are stitched together in rows of 7, then the rows are joined to complete the block.

TRIP AROUND THE WORLD

TRADITIONAL The 1930s

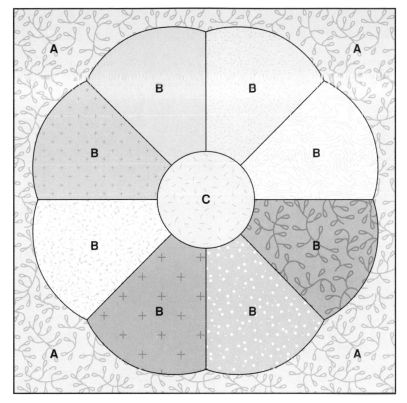

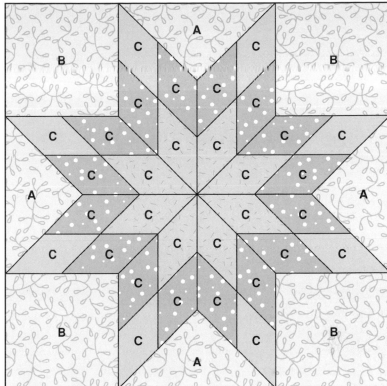

DRESDEN PLATE

D31 Cut a 4-inch square (plus seam allowances) of background fabric. Sew B pieces together in pairs, then sew 2 pairs together, then join the 2 units. (Do not sew in the seams of the outer edges.) Appliqué outer edges to the background square. Finally, appliqué C piece to center.

LONE STAR

D32 Make CCCC unit as you would a four-patch (see page 309 for help in making four-patches), to make each star point section (8 times). Sew the sections together in pairs, being careful not to sew in the seam allowances that will be mitered. Sew the pairs together to make two halves, then join the halves. Set in the A pieces (see page 309 for mitering directions), then set in the B pieces.

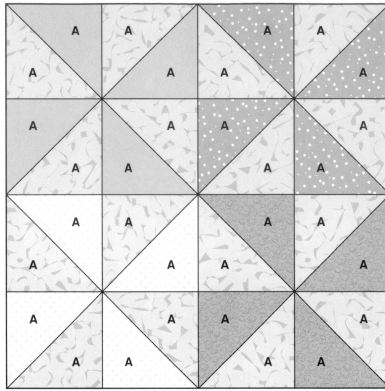

D33 Cut a 4-inch square (plus seam allowances) of background fabric. Appliqué the figure. (For more information on appliqué see page 308.) Try using the wrong side of pants' fabric for the pants' cuffs. Embroider the line on the hat.

OVERALL ANDY

D34 Make AA unit (16 times). Sew the units together in rows, then sew the rows together to make the block.

PINWHEEL

TRADITIONAL The 1930s

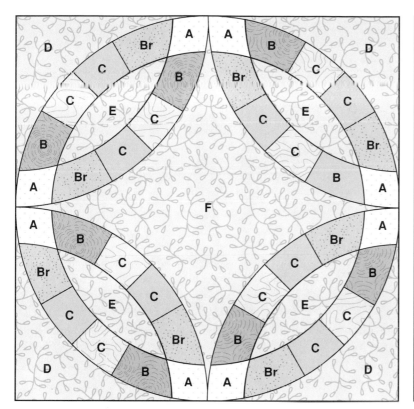

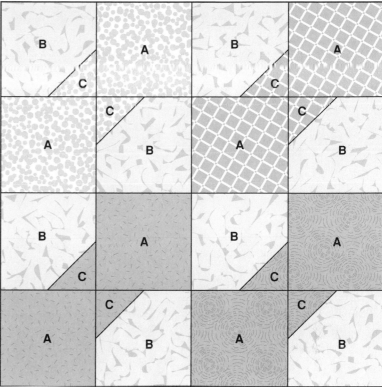

DOUBLE WEDDING RING

D35 Yes! This was pieced on the sewing machine! (See page 309 for help with sewing curved seams.) Piece arc BCCBr (4 times). Add one unit to each E piece, being careful to avoid stitching in the end seam allowances. Then piece arc unit ABCCBrA and add to the other side of E (4 times). Sew each arc unit to F, then add D corner pieces.

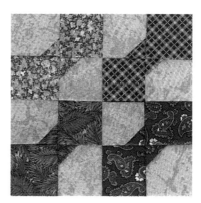

BOW TIE

D36 Make BC unit (8 times). Join the BC units with the A pieces to make rows, then sew rows together to complete the block.

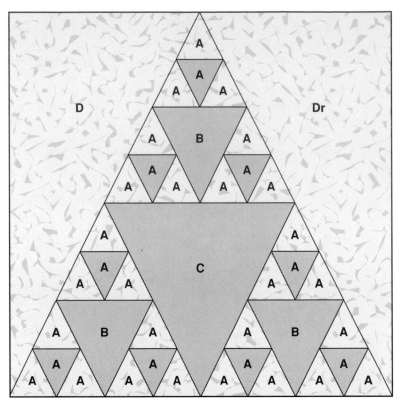

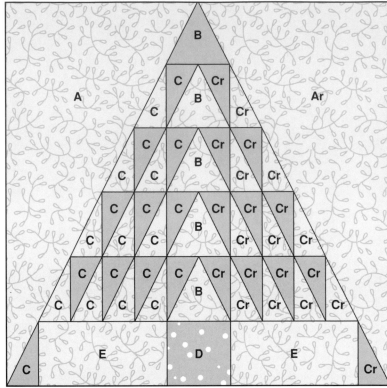

DIAMOND SPRUCE

D37 Make AAAA triangle unit (9 times). Add 3 A units to each side of B (3 times). Attach the AB units to all sides of C; add D and Dr to complete the block.

PINE TREE

D38 Make CC unit (10 times) and make CrCr unit (10 times). Join into rows with B pieces. Make CEDECr row and add to top section. Add A and Ar pieces to each side of tree.

TRADITIONAL Trees and Leaves

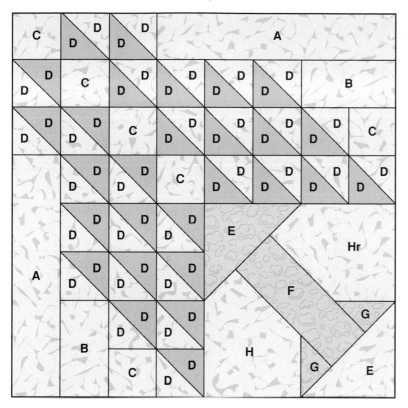

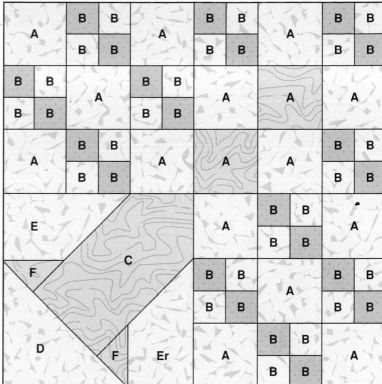

TREE OF LIFE

D39 Make DD unit (28 times). Sew G to H, and G to Hr; add each unit to F. Join FGH with E pieces to complete trunk section. Assemble DD units with C, A, and B pieces to make the 3 top rows and join the rows into top section. Make left section in 4 vertical rows and join the rows. For right section, add a row of DD units to trunk section. Join the left and right sections, then add to top section to complete the block.

TREE OF TEMPTATION

D40 Make a four-patch of B pieces (11 times). Join F and E, then join F and Er; add to C, then add D to make the trunk section. Join B units with A pieces to make nine-patches. Combine the 4 sections to complete the block.

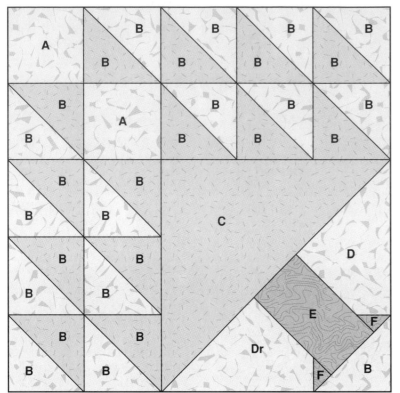

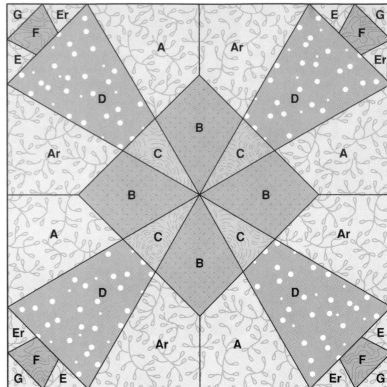

D41 Make BB unit (14 times). Join F to D and F to Dr; add to E. Add C and B to DEF to make trunk section. Assemble BB units and A pieces to make and join 2 top rows. Make left section of BB units; join with CDEFB section, then join to top section.

TEMPERANCE TREE

D42 Join and miter B with A and Ar (4 times). Add E and Er to F, then add G; add D, then C (4 times). Join AB unit with CDEFG unit (4 times). Join 2 sections (2 times); then join the 2 parts to complete the block.

LANCASTER TREE

TRADITIONAL Trees and Leaves

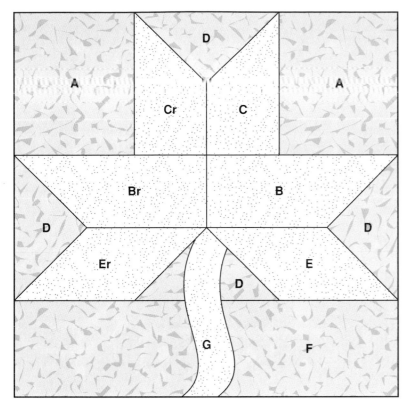

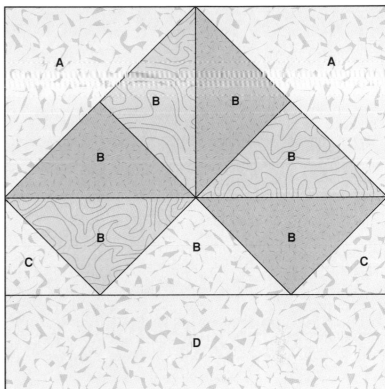

SWEET GUM LEAF

D43 Join and miter C and Cr with D. (See page 309 for mitering directions.) Add A to each side. Join and miter B and E with D; join and miter Br and Er with D. Join and miter these 2 units with D. Add to top unit, then add F piece. Appliqué G to complete the block.

IVY LEAF

D44 Make BB unit and add A (2 times). Join these 2 units to make top of block. Make second row by joining CBBBC. Add to top unit; add D to complete the block.

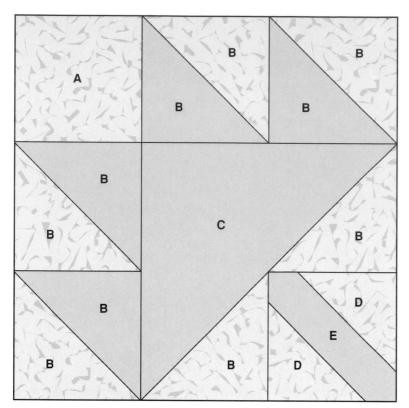

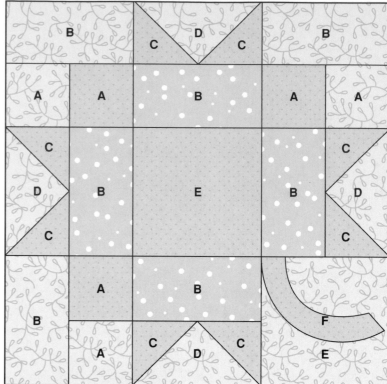

D45 Make BB unit (4 times). Add D to 2 sides of E, then add B pieces to unit; add C to make a square. Make top row A/BB/BB. Join 2 BB units and add to trunk unit. Join with top row to complete the block.

APPLE LEAF

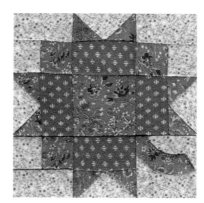

D46 Appliqué F piece to E. Make CDC unit; add B (4 times). Make AA unit; add B (3 times). Join units into 3 rows, referring to the block pattern above; join rows to complete.

MAPLE LEAF

TRADITIONAL Trees and Leaves

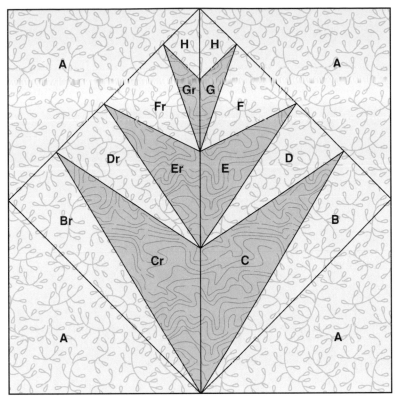

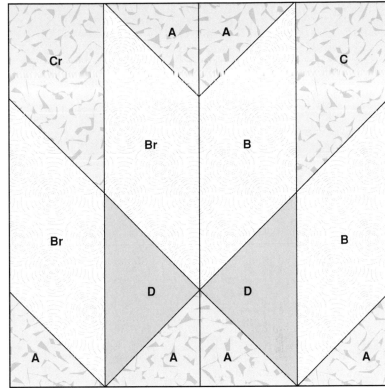

PALM LEAF

D47 Make BCDEFGH unit; then make the reverse unit. Join the 2 units; add A to all 4 sides.

TEA LEAF

D48 This block is pieced in vertical rows. Make CBA unit and the reverse unit. Make ABDA unit and the reverse unit. Join the 4 rows to complete the block.

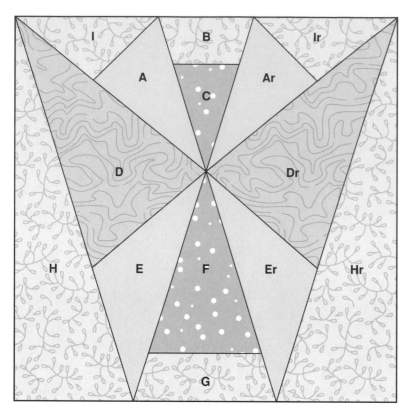

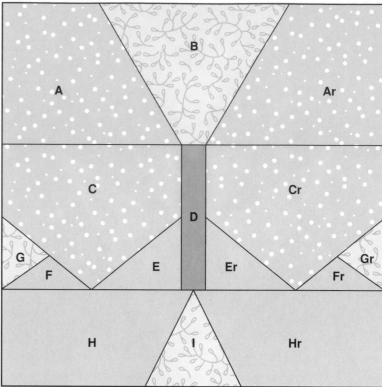

**OLD-FASHIONED
BUTTERFLY**

D49 This block is made in 2 asymmetrical sections. Left section: Sew B to C; I to A; D to E. Join these units and add H. Right section: Sew Ar to Ir; Dr to Er; F to G. Join these units and add Hr. Sew the 2 sections together to complete the block.

BUTTERFLY I

D50 Construct the block in horizontal rows. Row 1: Sew A and Ar to B. Row 2: Sew G to F, add GF to C, and add E. Repeat in reverse for other side. Join the 2 units with D. Row 3: Sew H and Hr to I. Join the 3 rows to complete the block.

TRADITIONAL Birds and Butterflies

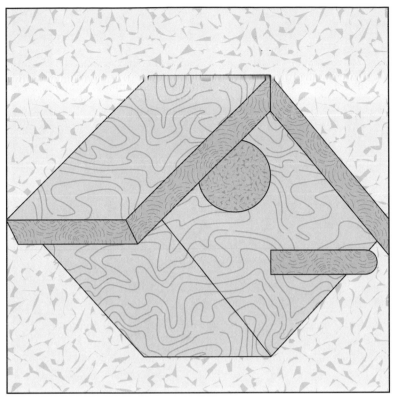

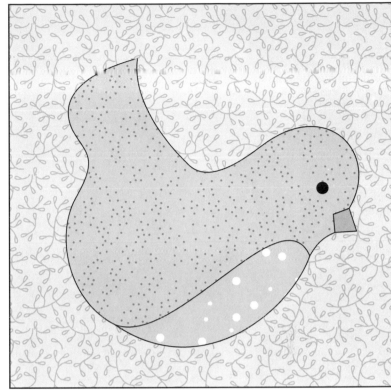

D51 Cut a 4-inch square (plus seam allowances) of background fabric. Piece the house section and the roof section, mitering the roof as needed. (See page 309 for mitering direction.) Appliqué roof and house to the background square. Appliqué the perch and doorway last.

WREN HOUSE

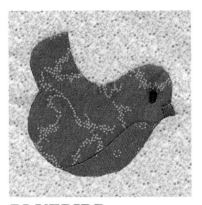

D52 Cut a 4-inch square (plus seam allowances) of background fabric. Appliqué bird in place. (See page 308 for appliqué information.) Use a little black bead or French knot for eye. Embroider line on beak.

BLUEBIRD

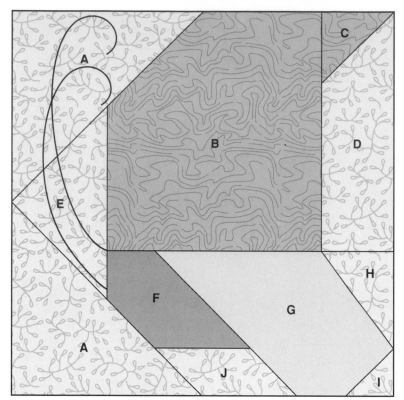

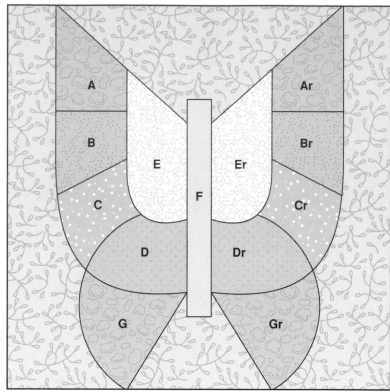

D53 Sew C to D; add to B. Join F and J, then add FJ unit, I and H to G. Join BCD unit with FGHIJ; add E. Add A pieces to complete the block. Embroider antennae with stem stitch.

BUTTERFLY II

D54 Cut a 4-inch square (plus seam allowances) of background fabric. Piece ABCD wing section and then the reverse section. Appliqué E and G to left section, Er and Gr to right section. Appliqué both sections to background square, then appliqué F.

BUTTERFLY III

TRADITIONAL Birds and Butterflies

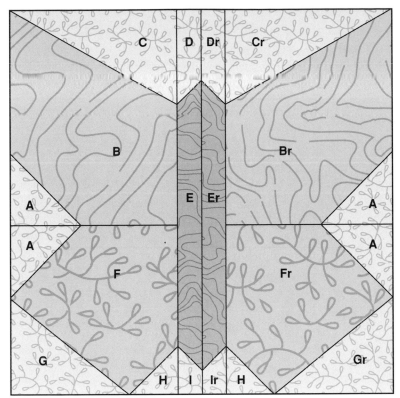

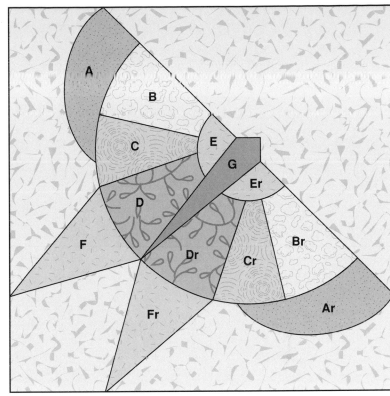

BUTTERFLY IV

D55 Piece ABC and ABrCr sections. Piece FGHA and FrGrHA sections. Join the 2 left sections and the 2 right sections. Piece DEI and DrErIr sections; join them, then add left and right sections to complete the block.

BUTTERFLY V

D56 Cut a 4-inch square (plus seam allowances) of background fabric. Piece BCD and BrCrDr units. Appliqué A and Ar, F and Fr, E and Er, and G to BCD units. Appliqué the entire unit to the background square.

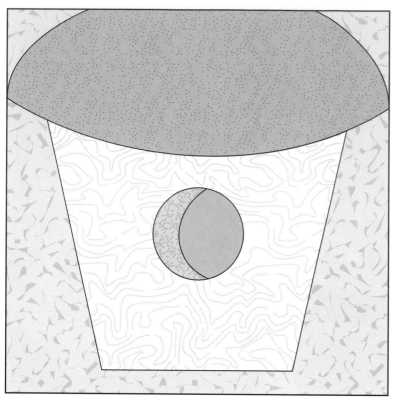

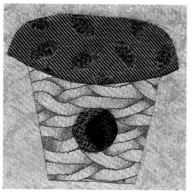

D57 Cut a 4-inch square (plus seam allowances) of background fabric. Appliqué pieces in place.

CLAY BIRDHOUSE

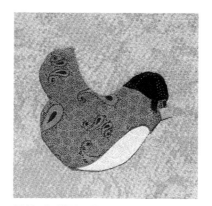

D58 Cut a 4-inch square (plus seam allowances) of background fabric. Appliqué bird to background. Use black bead or a French knot for eye.

BLACK-CAPPED CHICKADEE

TRADITIONAL Birds and Butterflies

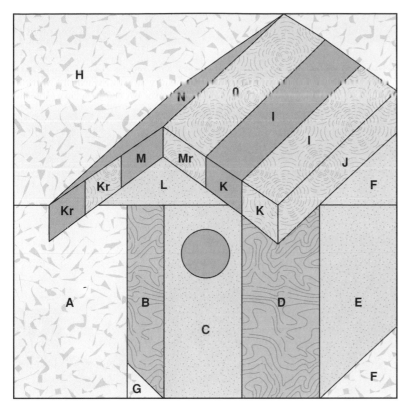

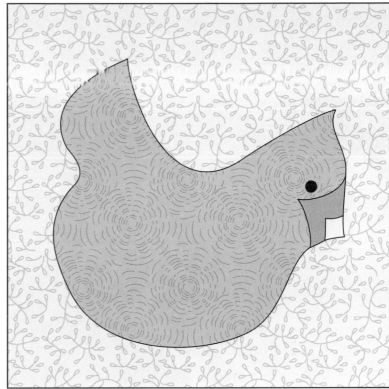

BLUEBIRD HOUSE

D59 Sew G to B and E to F. Join this section: A/BG/C/D/EF. For top section, note that H piece is 2" x 4" (plus seam allowances). Join H to bottom section, then piece the roof top. Sew OIIJF unit and MrKK unit. Sew MKrKr unit; add N. Join and miter the roof sections, then miter with L piece. (See page 309 for mitering directions.) Appliqué the roof section in place. Appliqué circle to C piece, so the birdies can get into their house.

CARDINAL

D60 Cut a 4-inch square (plus seam allowances) of background fabric. Appliqué bird to background square; use a black bead or French knot for eye.

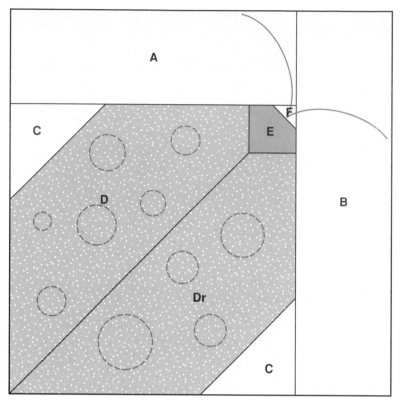

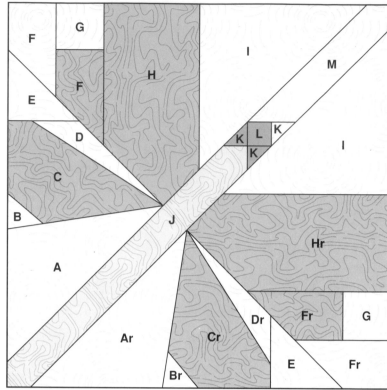

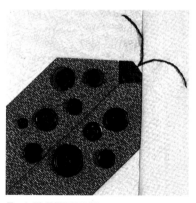

LADYBUG

DRAGONFLY

D61 Make CD unit and CDr unit. Make EF unit and miter into CDCDr. (See page 309 for mitering directions.) Add A to top of main section, then add B to adjoining side. Appliqué dots to ladybug and stem-stitch antennae. You can use varied sizes of black buttons instead of appliqué for the black spots.

D62 Make BCD unit; add A and E. Make FG unit; add F to one side and H and I to other side. Join the 2 sections. Repeat the process with the reverse pieces to make the other wing section. For the center body section, make KLK unit; add to M. Add K to J; join with KLM unit. Join the center body section with the 2 wing sections.

TRADITIONAL Birds and Butterflies

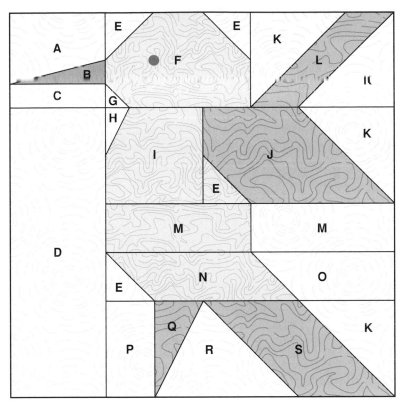

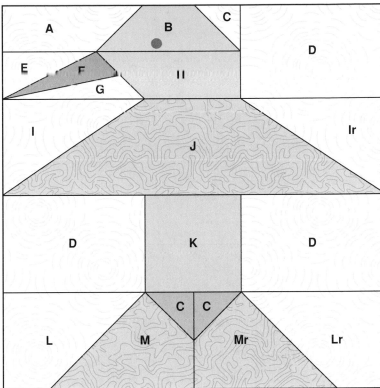

HUMMINGBIRD I

D63 Make ABC unit, EEFG unit, and KLK unit; join the 3 units for the top row. Make HI unit and EJK; join them. Make MM and join to the last section. Make ENO and add to MM edge. Join PQRSK and add to ENO edge. Add D to left side of this bottom section, then join to the top row. Use a French knot or bead for the eye.

HUMMINGBIRD II

D64 Make ABC unit. Make EFG and add H; join this unit with ABC and add D. Make IJIr unit and add to first section. Make DKD unit and add to previous section. Make LMC unit and LrMrC unit and join them; add to main section to complete the block. Use a French knot or tiny bead for the eye.

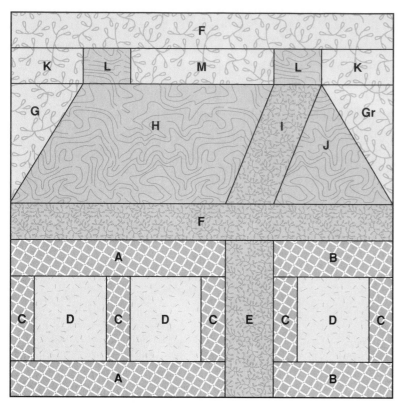

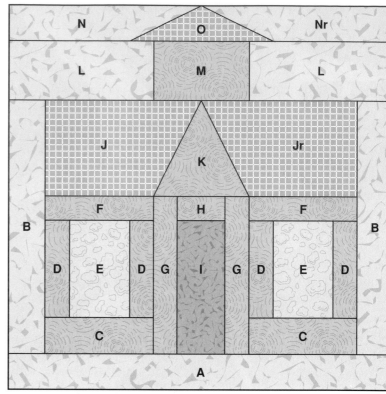

D65 Make KLMLK unit; add F. Make GHIJGr; join to first section, and add F. Make CDCDC unit, add A pieces; join with E. Make CDC unit, add B pieces; join to other side of E. Join this section with the top section to complete the block.

HOUSE I

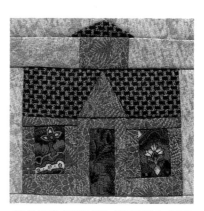

D66 Make NONr unit, and LML unit; join the 2 units. Add J and Jr to K. Make DED unit; add F and C (2 times). Add H to I, add G to each CDEF unit, and join both with HI. Add this section to roof section, then add B pieces; join to top section. Add A to bottom to complete the block.

COUNTRY CHURCH

TRADITIONAL Building Blocks

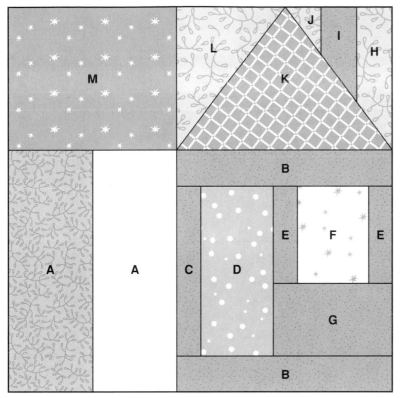

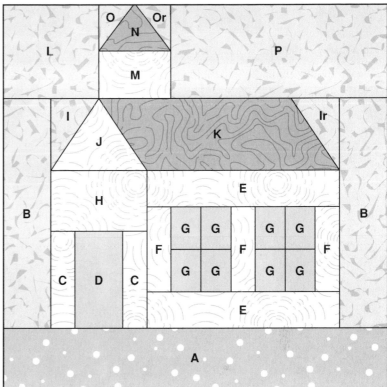

D67 Join A pieces, add to M. (This unit is a flag. If you're from Texas—or wish you were—add a star to the M piece.) Make EFE unit, add G, then add D and C. Join B pieces to CDEFG unit. Sew J and H to I; add unit to K. Join L to other side of K. Join HIJKL section with BCDEFG section; add to MAA section.

COURTHOUSE SQUARE

D68 Join O and Or to N, add M, then add L and P. Join J to K; add I and Ir pieces. Make G sections (or cut 1 piece the size of 4 G pieces, and embroider the lines), join with F pieces, then E pieces. Join C pieces to each side of D; add H. Join CDH to FGE and add the JKI section. Add B pieces to each side, then add A. Join to top section.

OLD COUNTRY CHURCH

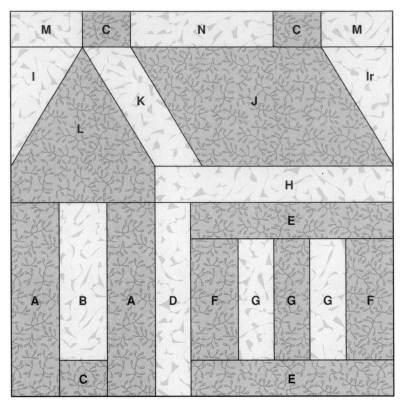

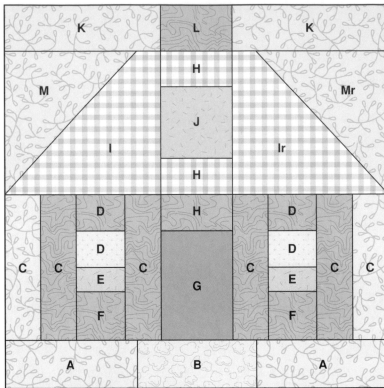

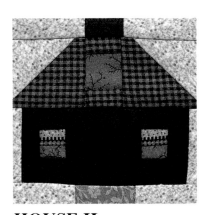

D69 Join K and Ir to J and add to H. Join I to L; miter with HIrJK unit. (See page 309 for mitering directions.) Make FGGGF unit. Add E pieces to top and bottom. Join B and C, add A pieces to each side, then add D; join to FGE unit. Add to roof section. Make MCNCM unit and add to top.

SCHOOLHOUSE

D70 Join K pieces to L. Join M to I and Mr to Ir. Join H pieces to J, add MI and MrIr units, then add to KLK. Make DDEF unit and add 3 C pieces as shown (2 times). Join G and H, and add to CDEF units. Add this section to the roof. Make ABA and add to the bottom of the block.

HOUSE II

TRADITIONAL Building Blocks

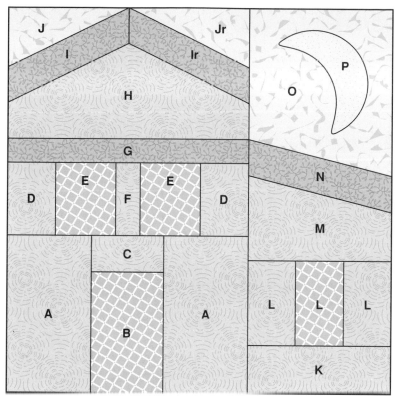

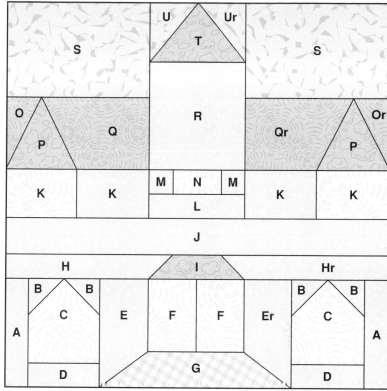

D71 Sew I and Ir to H, then miter the II seam (See page 309 for mitering directions.) Add J pieces, then add G. Make DEFED unit. Join to roof section. Join B and C; add A pieces. Join to top section. Make LLL unit. Add K, M, N, and O. Join to left section. Appliqué P to O.

BARN

COURTHOUSE

D72 Join U and Ur to T; add R. Make MNM unit, add to UTR, then add L. Make OPQ unit and QrPOr unit. Make 2 KK units, add to OPQ units; add S pieces. Join KQPOS sections to LMNR-TU and add J. Join H and Hr to I; add to roof section. Make BBCD unit; add A (2 times). Join F pieces, add E and Er pieces to 2 sides, then add G and miter EG seams. (See page 309 for mitering directions.) Add ABCD sections to each side of GEF unit. Join the top and bottom sections.

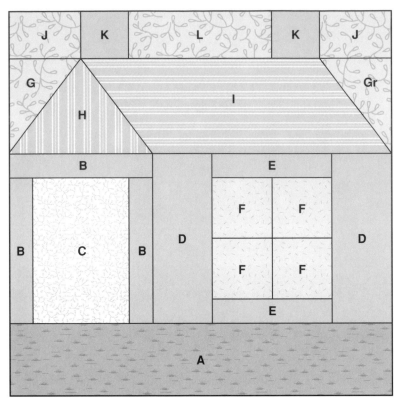

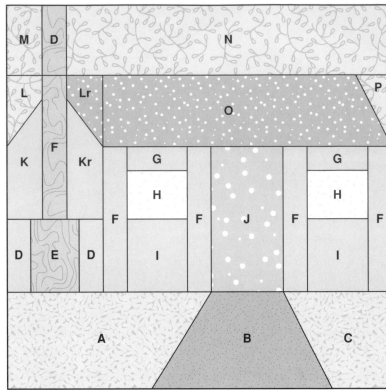

D73 Make JKLKJ unit. Join H to I, add G and Gr and join unit to top row. Make F unit; add E pieces, then D pieces. Add 2 B pieces to C, then add the top B piece. Join BC unit to DEF unit; add A. Join the 2 sections to complete the block.

HOUSE ON THE HILL

D74 Make MDN unit. Join L to K, Lr to Kr; add LK units to F. Make DED and add to LKF. Join O to P. Make GHI unit (2 times), join with F pieces, then J piece; add to OP. Join left and right sections and add to top section. Join A, B, and C; add to bottom of block.

HONEYMOON COTTAGE

TRADITIONAL Building Blocks

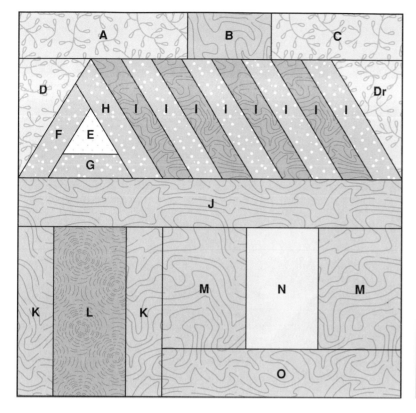

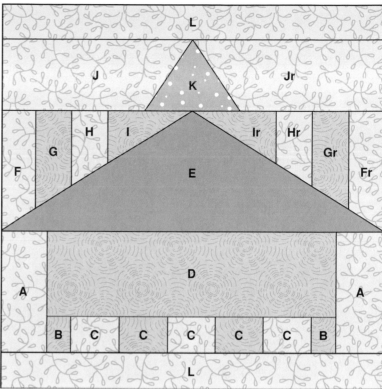

D75 Join A, B, and C. To E add G, then F, and then H. Join the I pieces. Join EFGH to I unit; add D and Dr. Join ABC unit to roof unit, and add J. Join M pieces to N, and add O. Join K pieces to L; add to MNO unit. Join to roof unit.

LOG CABIN

D76 Join J and Jr to K. Join L to top. Join FGHI and FrGrHrIr. Join units to E. Add to JKL section. Join B pieces and C pieces; add D, then add A pieces. Join to first section. Add L to bottom.

VILLAGE CHURCH

215

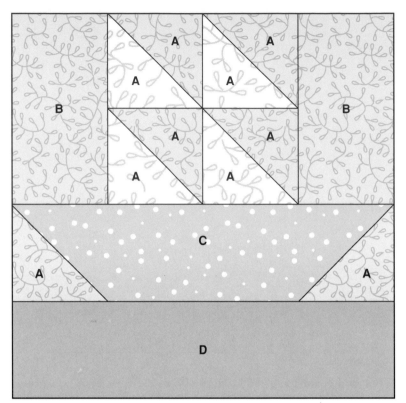

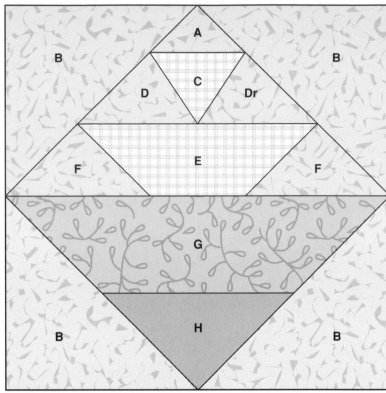

D77 Make AA unit (4 times); join into a four-patch.(See page 309 for help in making four-patches.) Add B pieces to 2 sides. Add A pieces to C. Add AC unit to top section. Add D piece to bottom.

MAYFLOWER

D78 Attach F pieces to E, and D and Dr to C. Add A to DCDr, then attach FEF, G, and H. Finally, add B pieces to all 4 sides.

SAILBOATS

TRADITIONAL Ships and Planes

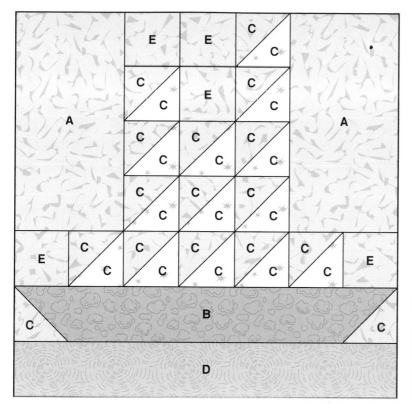

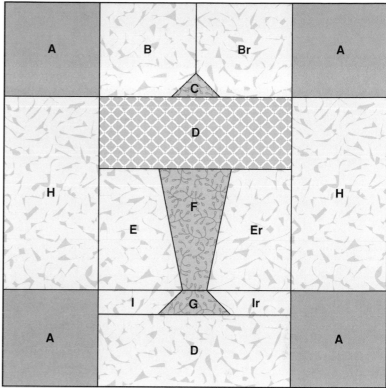

D79 Make CC unit (14 times), and combine with E pieces to make horizontal rows. Join the top 4 rows; add A pieces to each side. Add the next row of E and CC units. Sew C pieces to B; add unit to main section. Add D to the bottom to complete the block.

TALL SHIPS OF '76

D80 Join B and Br to C, mitering the BBr seam. (See page 309 for mitering directions.) Add A pieces to each end. Add E and Er pieces to F, then add D; add H pieces to each side. Join I and Ir pieces to G; add D, then add A pieces. Join the 3 sections to complete the block.

AIRPLANE II

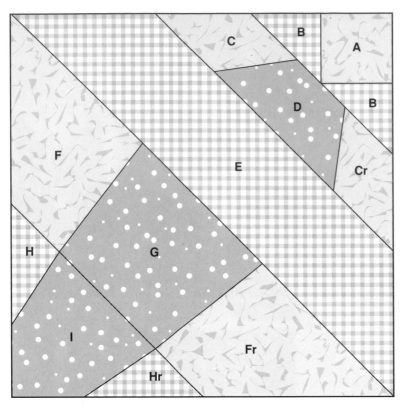

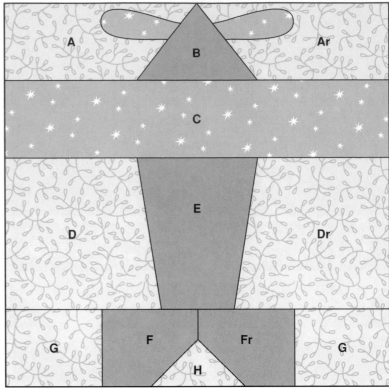

D81 Make FH and FrHr units. Make GI unit. Join FH, GI, and FrHr units. Make ABA and CDCr units. Join FGHI section with E, then CDCr, then BAB to complete the block.

AIRPLANE III

D82 Appliqué propellers to A and Ar. Add A pieces to B, then add C. Make DEDr unit; add to first section. Add F and Fr pieces to H, mitering the FFr seam (see page 309 for mitering directions.) Add G pieces, then add this final unit to the block.

AIRPLANE IV

TRADITIONAL Ships and Planes

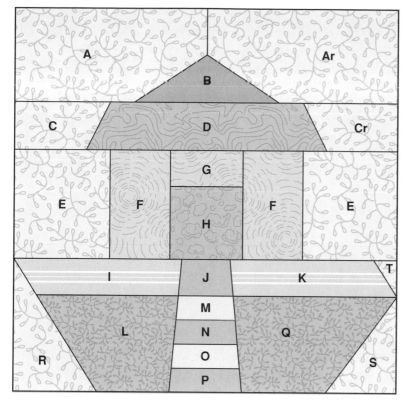

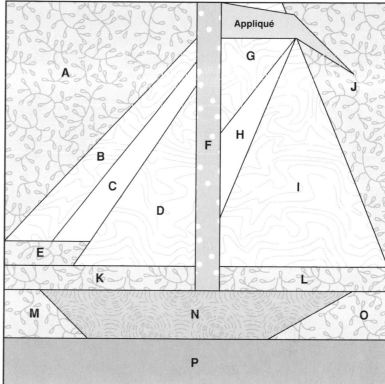

NOAH'S ARK

D83 Add A and Ar to B, mitering the AAr seam. (See page 309 for mitering directions.) Attach C and Cr pieces to D; add to ABAr unit. Join G and H; add F pieces, then add E pieces. Join to top section. Join JMNOP (or use a striped fabric for the entire unit). Add T to K, Q to S; join and add to JMNOP. Join I and L, add R; join to JMNOPQKST. Join this section to the top section.

SAILING SHIP I

D84 Join A, B, and C; add E, then D and K. Join G, H, and I; add J, add L, then appliqué flag. Join the 2 sail units with F. Add M and O to N; add P. Join the 2 sections to complete the block.

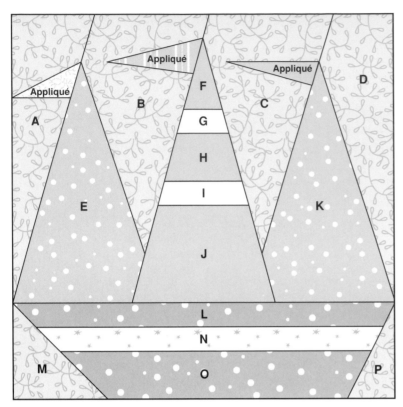

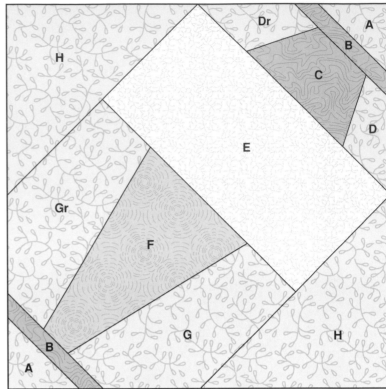

D85 Appliqué flags to A, B, and C. Join FGHIJ to make center sail (or use striped fabric with the entire unit as a template). Sew D to K; add C; join to center sail. Sew B to E, add A; join to center sail. Make LNO unit; add M and P. Join to sail section to complete the block.

SAILING SHIP II

D86 Make AB unit (2 times). Make GrFG unit; add E; join with AB unit. Make DrCD unit, add AB; join to E. Add H pieces to complete the block.

AIRPLANE I

TRADITIONAL Ships and Planes

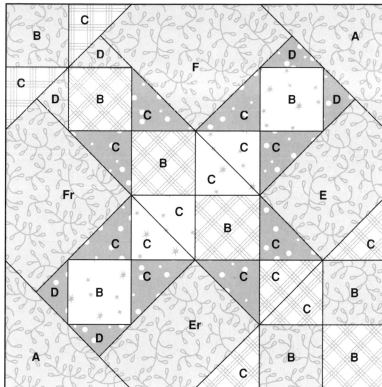

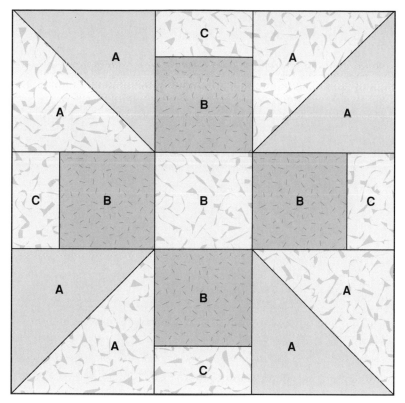

D87 Make AA unit (4 times) and BC unit (4 times). Make 2 rows of AA/BC/AA units and 1 row of CB/B/BC. Join the rows to complete the block.

PROPELLER AIRPLANE

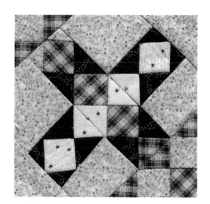

D88 Make DDBCCC unit (2 times). Add E and F to one unit; add Er and Fr to other DBC unit. Piece center section with D, B, and C pieces; join to wing sections. Join C pieces to B and add to upper left corner. Piece tail section of B and C pieces; join to main section. Add A pieces to complete the block.

ALTA-PLANE

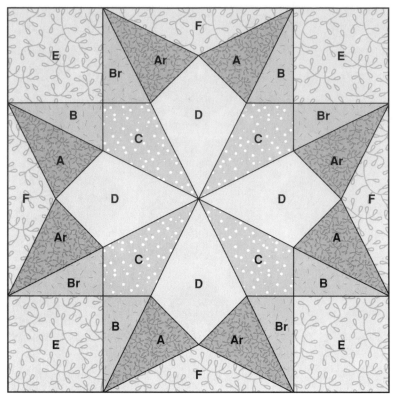

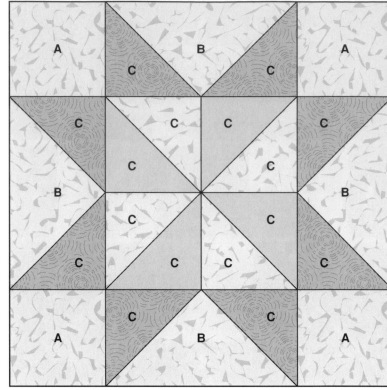

D89 Sew A and Ar to D; miter F at A/Ar edge(4 times). (See page 309 for mitering directions.) Sew B and Br to C; miter E with B pieces (4 times). Join the ADF unit with the BCE unit. Repeat 3 times to make 4 sections. Join the sections in pairs, then join the 2 sections to complete the block.

BROKEN CRYSTALS

D90 Make CBC unit (4 times). Make CC unit (4 times); join to form center square. Add CBC units on 2 opposite sides to make center row. Sew A pieces to each end of CBC unit (2 times) to make top and bottom rows. Join rows to complete the block.

STAR OF THE WEST

TRADITIONAL Stars

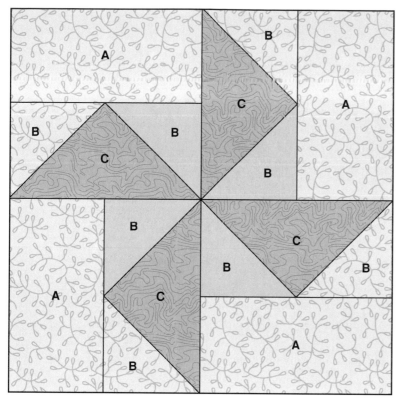

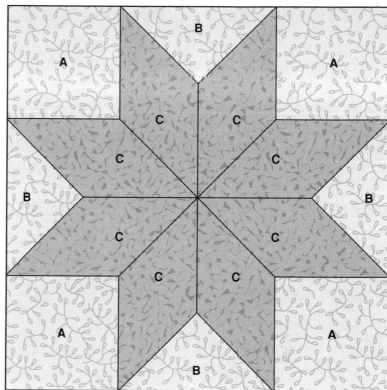

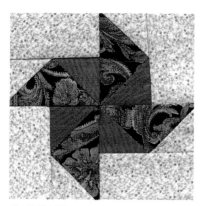

D91 Make BCB unit and join with A (4 times). Join the ABCB units as you would a four-patch. (See page 309 for help in making four-patches.)

LOUISIANA

D92 Sew C pieces together in pairs, then sew pairs together to form 2 units, then join the 2 units. (Be careful to avoid sewing into the seams where the A and B pieces will be set in.) Miter B into place (4 times), then miter the A piece (4 times). (See page 309 for mitering directions.)

EIGHT-POINTED STAR

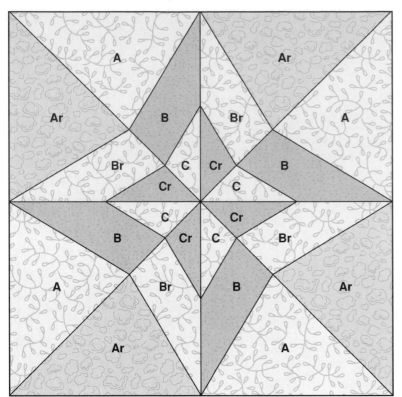

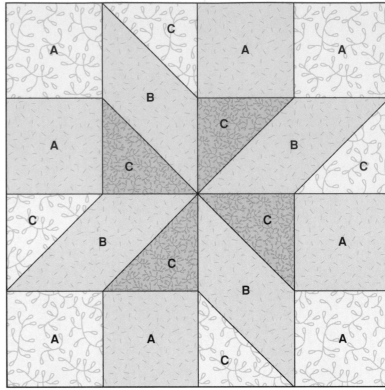

D93 Make ABC unit (4 times) and ArBrCr unit (4 times). Join ABC with ArBrCr to make a square (4 times). Join the 4 squares to make the block.

NORTH STAR

D94 Make AA unit (4 times), and CBC unit (4 times). Join AA with CBC to make a square (4 times). Join the 4 sections to complete the block.

CLAY'S CHOICE

TRADITIONAL Stars

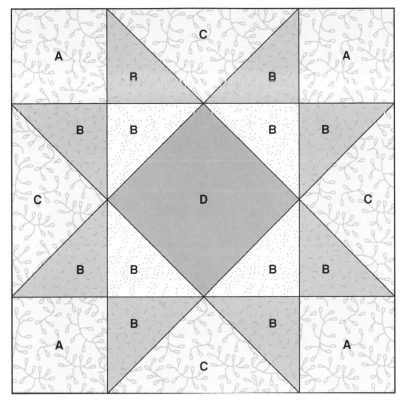

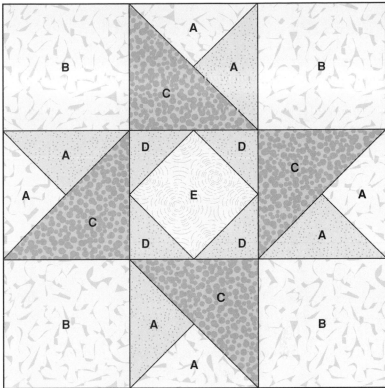

VARIABLE STAR

D95 Make BCB unit (4 times). Sew B pieces to 2 opposite sides of D, then to 2 remaining sides. Sew BCB units to 2 opposite sides of BD unit to make center row. Sew A pieces to each end of BCB unit (2 times) to make top and bottom rows. Join the rows to complete the block.

TWISTED STAR

D96 Make AA unit and join with C (4 times). Sew D to 2 opposite sides of E, then to 2 remaining sides. Join AAC units to 2 opposite sides of DDEDD unit to make center row. Sew B pieces to each end of AAC unit (2 times) to make top and bottom rows; join rows to complete the block.

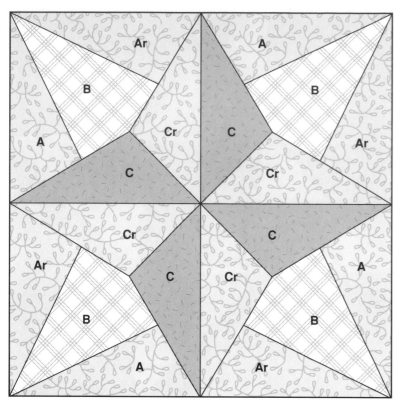

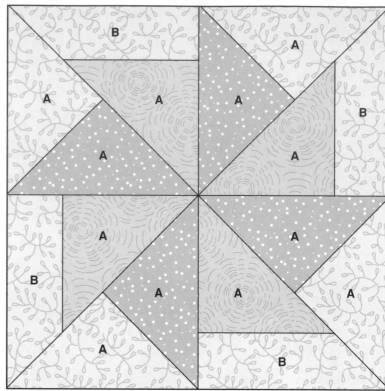

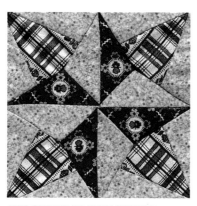

D97 Make ABAr unit (4 times) and CCr unit (4 times). Miter ABAr with CCr to form a square (4 times). Join the squares as a four-patch. (See page 309 for help in making four-patches and mitering directions.)

EIGHT-POINTED STAR VARIATION

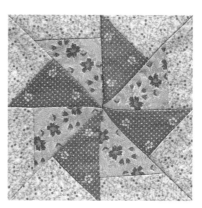

D98 Make AA unit (4 times), and AB unit (4 times). Join AA and AB to make a square (4 times). Join squares as a four-patch. (See page 309 for help in making four-patches.)

WINDMILL

TRADITIONAL Stars

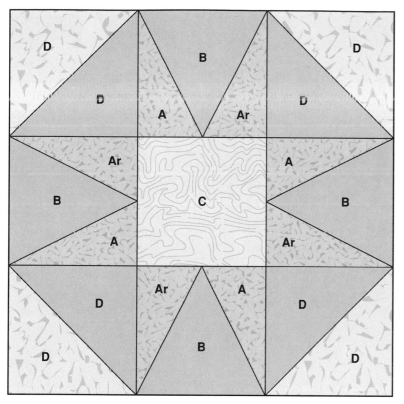

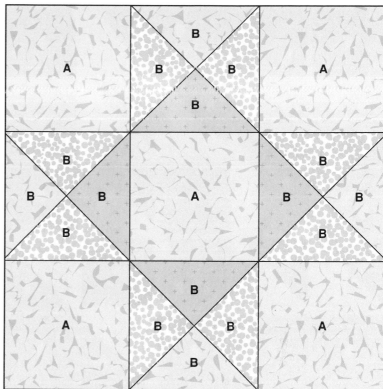

JUDY IN ARABIA

D99 Make DD unit (4 times) and ABAr unit (4 times). Sew DD to 2 sides of ABAr (2 times) to make top and bottom rows. Sew ABAr to 2 opposite sides of C to make center row. Join the rows to complete the block.

OHIO STAR

D100 Make BBBB unit (4 times); join with A pieces in a nine-patch. (See page 309 for help in making nine-patches.)

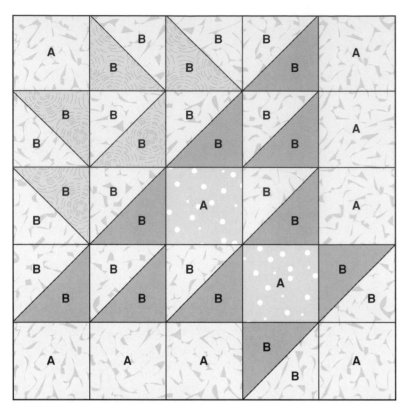

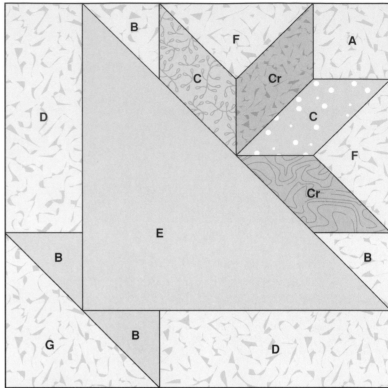

D101 Make BB unit (15 times). Join BB units with A pieces into 5 rows. Join the rows to complete the block.

FRUIT BASKET

D102 Join all the C and Cr pieces, avoiding stitching into seam allowances where F and A pieces will be set in. Set in F pieces, then A pieces (see page 309 for mitering directions). Add B pieces. Join section to E. Make DB units; add to sides of basket. Add G to complete the block.

FLOWER POT

TRADITIONAL Baskets

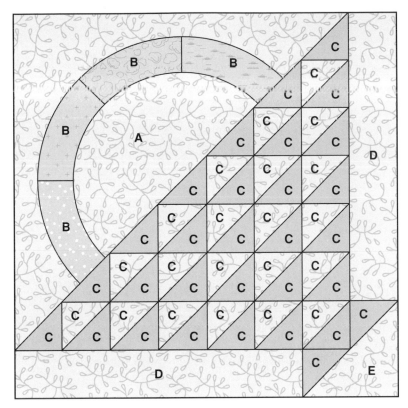

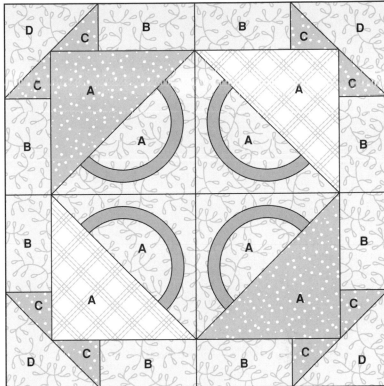

FLOWER BASKET I

D103 Make CC unit (21 times). Assemble in vertical rows with single C pieces at top of each row. Join the rows to make the basket. Join B pieces and then appliqué the handle to the A piece; join the AB unit with the basket section. Make CD unit (2 times) and add to sides; add E to complete the block.

STAMP BASKET

D104 The handles may be embroidered with a chain stitch (as shown in block photo). Or, the handles can be made from bias tubes (see page 309 for directions), cutting a ⅞ x 3-inch piece for each handle. Appliqué the tubing handle in place, then trim the excess tubing so it is even with the edge of A. Join the A handle and A basket piece (4 times). Make BC unit (8 times); add BC to 2 adjoining sides of AA (4 times). Add D (4 times). Assemble the 4 sections as a four-patch (see page 309 for help in making four-patches.).

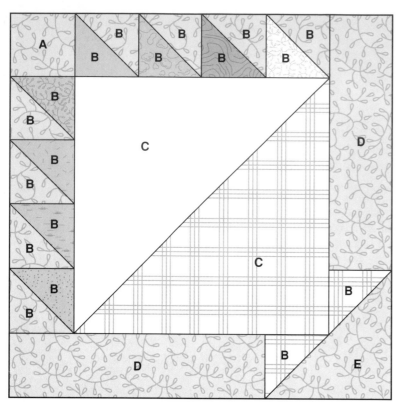

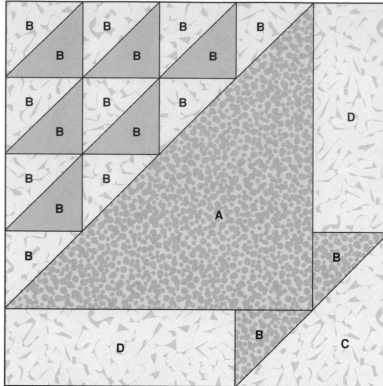

D105 Make CC unit. Make BB unit (8 times); join 4 BB units and attach to CC. Join 4 BB units and add A piece to end; attach to CC. Make DB unit (2 times), and add to each side of basket. Attach E.

CAKE PLATE

D106 Make BB unit (6 times); join in vertical rows, adding single B piece to the bottom of each row. Join rows, adding a B piece to complete the section; add to A. Make DB unit (2 times), add to basket sides. Add C.

BASKET

TRADITIONAL Baskets

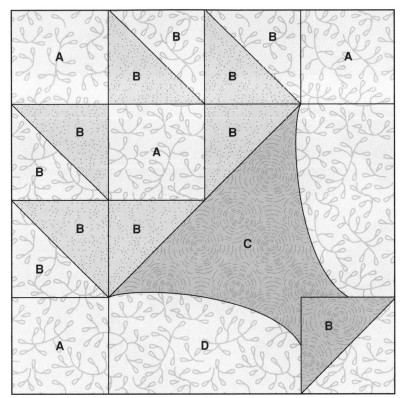

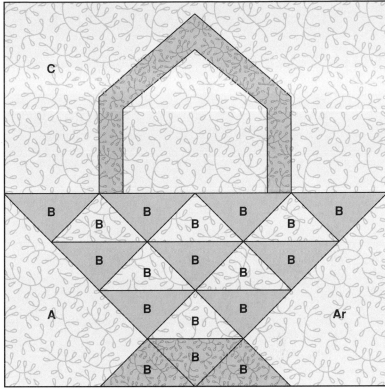

TEA BASKET

D107 Appliqué B and C pieces to D. Make BAB unit and attach to BCD unit. Make BB unit (4 times). Join 2 BB units with A and attach to ABCD section. Make row of 2 A pieces and 2 BB units and attach to main section to complete the block.

COLONIAL BASKET

D108 The handle can be appliquéd using a template or made from tubing from a 6 x 1-inch piece of fabric. (See directions for making a bias tube on page 309, although this piece does not need to be cut on the bias.) Appliqué handle to C. Make BB units (6 times); join in diagonal rows with a single B piece at the end of each row. Join the rows, adding B to complete basket. Make AB and ArB units and add to basket section. Join the handle and basket sections to complete the block.

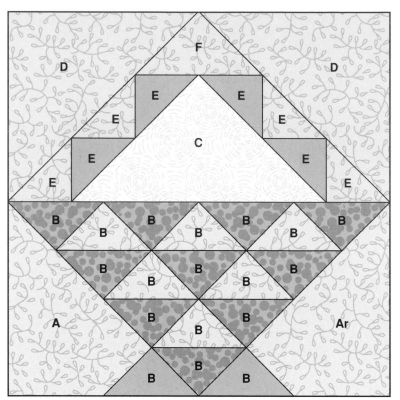

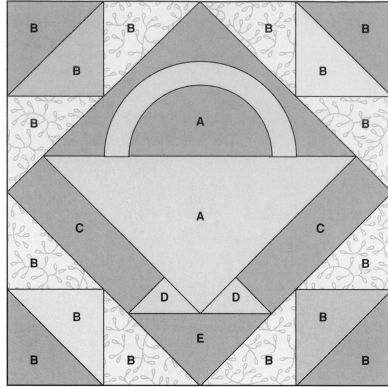

D109 Make BB unit (6 times); join in diagonal rows, adding single B pieces. Join the rows; add B to complete the basket section. Make AB and ArB units and add to sides of basket. Join 4 E pieces for handle (2 times) and attach to sides of C. Add F, then add D pieces. Join top and bottom sections to complete the block.

FLOWER BASKET II

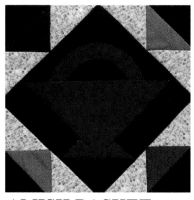

D110 Appliqué handle made from 1 x 4¼-inch bias strip (see page 309 for information on bias tubing) to A piece. Join basket piece A to handle piece A. Make CD unit (2 times) and add to sides of basket, then add E. Make BBBB unit (4 times) and add to all 4 sides of center basket section.

AMISH BASKET

TRADITIONAL Baskets

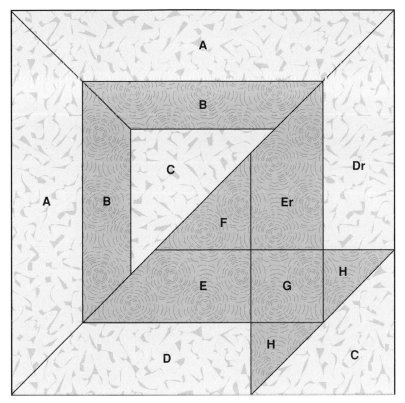

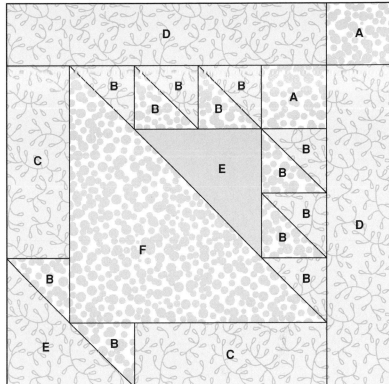

**GEOMETRIC
BASKET**

D111 Make AB unit (2 times); join units with C and miter the AB seam. (See page 309 for mitering directions.) Make DE and DrEr units. Make GHH unit and join to DrEr; add C. Add F to DE; join the DEF unit with the DrErGHHC unit. Join the 2 sections to complete the block.

HANGING BASKET

D112 Make BB unit (4 times). Join 2 BB units with a single B piece and join to E. Combine 2 BB units with a single B and A and add to first section; join to F. Make BC unit (2 times), attach to F, then add E. Join D to one side. Join A and D and attach to second handle edge to complete the block.

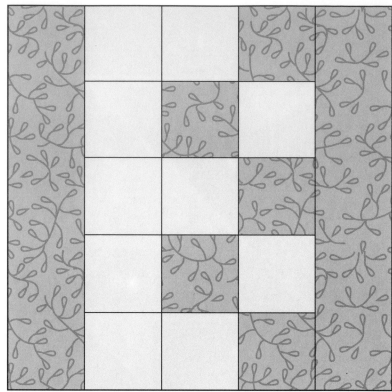

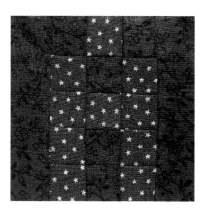

E1 Only 2 templates are used. Piece the letter in horizontal rows; join the rows to make center section; add strips of background fabric to each side.

LETTER A

E2 Piece B in horizontal rows; join rows to form center section; add strip to each side.

LETTER B

ALPHABET

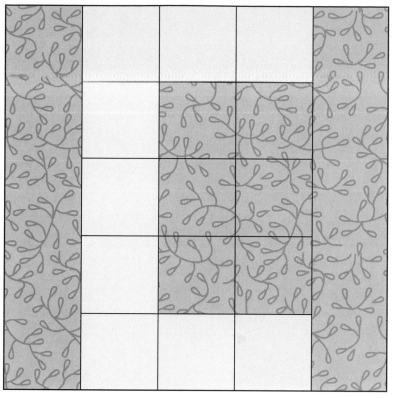

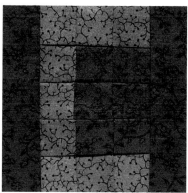

E3 Piece C in 5 horizontal rows with 3 squares in each row. Join the rows; add strips to each side.

LETTER C

E4 Make center section by piecing horizontal rows, then joining the rows. Add background fabric strips to each side.

LETTER D

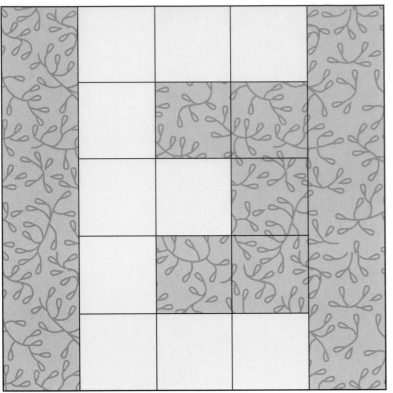

E5 Only 2 templates are used. Piece the letter in horizontal rows; join the rows to make center section; add strips of background fabric to each side.

LETTER E

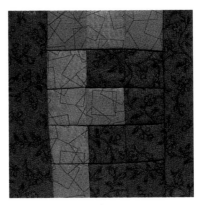

E6 Join 5 rows of 3 squares each to make center section; add a strip to each side to complete the block.

LETTER F

ALPHABET

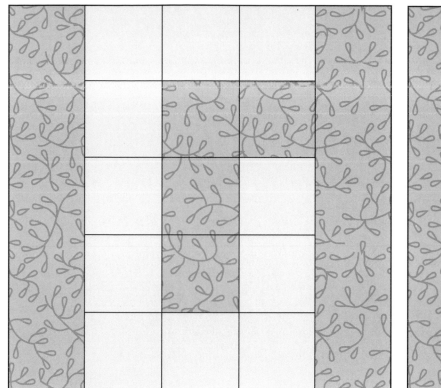

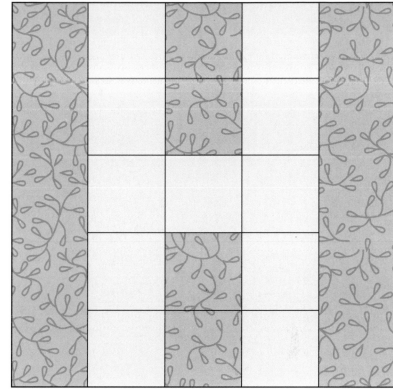

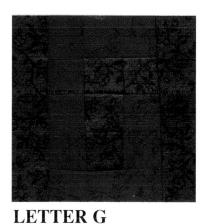

E7 Only 2 templates are used. Piece the letter in horizontal rows; join the rows to make center section; add strips of background fabric to each side.

LETTER G

E8 Piece the H using square template, joining 3 squares in horizontal rows. Join rows and add strip to each side.

LETTER H

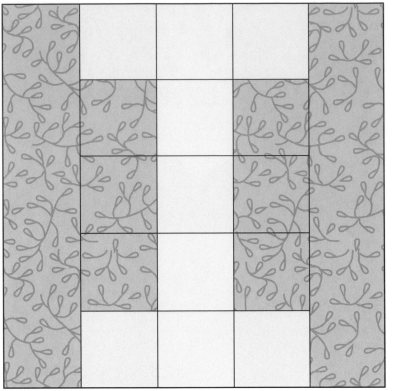

E9 Make center section by piecing horizontal rows, then joining the rows. Add background fabric strips to each side.

LETTER I

E10 Piece J in horizontal rows; join rows to form center section; add strip to each side.

LETTER J

ALPHABET

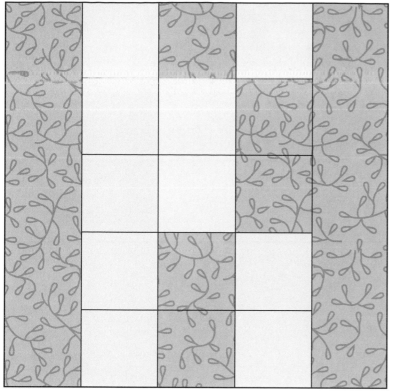

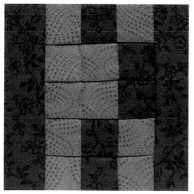

E11 Only 2 templates are used. Piece the letter in horizontal rows; join the rows to make center section; add strips of background fabric to each side.

LETTER K

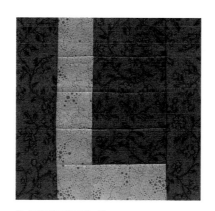

E12 Piece L in 5 horizontal rows with 3 squares in each row. Join the rows; add strips to each side.

LETTER L

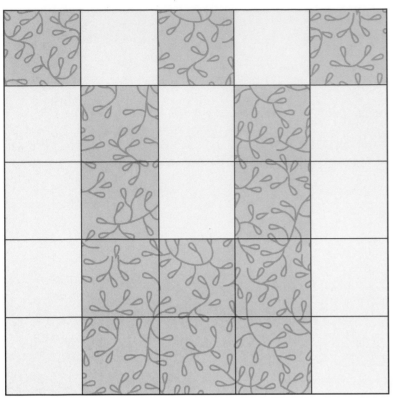

E13 This letter is pieced using only 1 template. Join the squares in horizontal rows; join the rows to complete the block.

LETTER M

E14 Join 5 rows of 3 squares each to make center section; add a strip to each side to complete the block.

LETTER N

ALPHABET

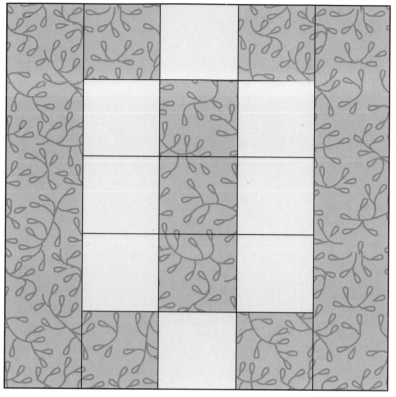

LETTER O

E15 Only 2 templates are used. Piece the letter in horizontal rows; join the rows to make center section; add strips of background fabric to each side.

LETTER P

E16 Make P in 5 horizontal rows with 3 squares in each row. Join the rows; add strips to each side.

E17 This letter is pieced in 5 rows of 4 squares each. Join the rows and then add a strip to the left side.

LETTER Q

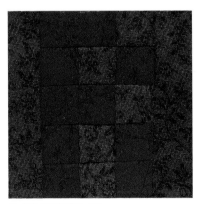

E18 Make center section by piecing horizontal rows, then joining the rows. Add background fabric strips to each side.

LETTER R

ALPHABET

E19 Only 2 templates are used. Piece the letter in horizontal rows; join the rows to make center section; add strips of background fabric to each side.

LETTER S

E20 Piece T in 5 horizontal rows with 3 squares in each row. Join the rows; add strips to each side.

LETTER T

E21 Piece in horizontal rows; join rows to form center section; add strip to each side.

LETTER U

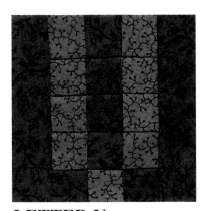

E22 Make center section by piecing horizontal rows, then joining the rows. Add background fabric strips to each side.

LETTER V

ALPHABET

E23 This letter is pieced using only 1 template. Join the squares in horizontal rows; join the rows to complete the block.

LETTER W

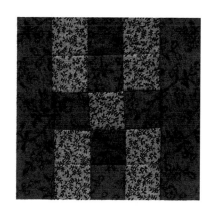

E24 Only 2 templates are used. Piece the letter in horizontal rows; join the rows to make center section; add strips of background fabric to each side.

LETTER X

LETTER Y

E25 Piece Y in 5 horizontal rows with 3 squares in each row. Join the rows; add strips of background fabric to each side.

LETTER Z

E26 Piece in horizontal rows; join rows to form center section; add strip to each side.

ALPHABET

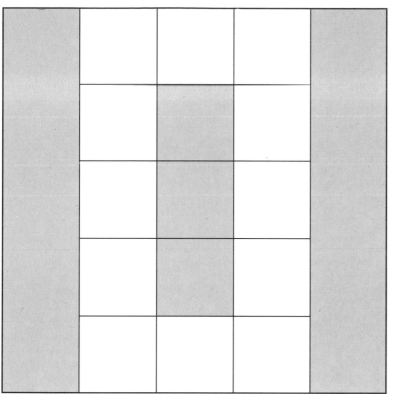

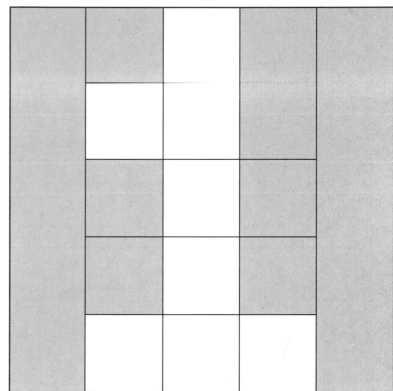

E27 Only 2 templates are used. Piece the zero in horizontal rows; join the rows to make center section; add strips of background fabric to each side.

NUMBER 0

E28 Piece the 1 in horizontal rows; join rows to form center section; add strip to each side.

NUMBER 1

NUMERALS

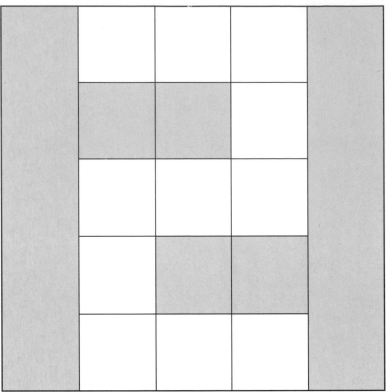

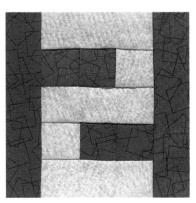

NUMBER 2

E29 Piece the number 2 in 5 horizontal rows with 3 squares in each row. Join the rows; add strips to each side.

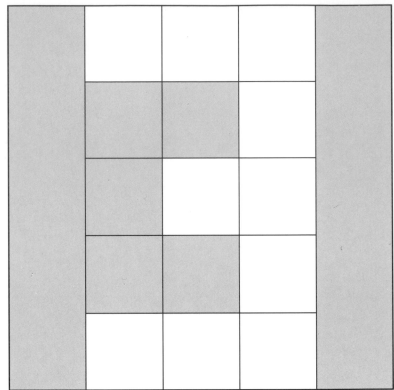

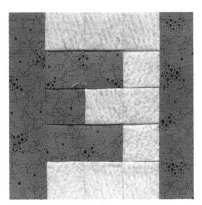

NUMBER 3

E30 Make center section by piecing horizontal rows, then joining the rows. Add background fabric strips to each side.

NUMERALS

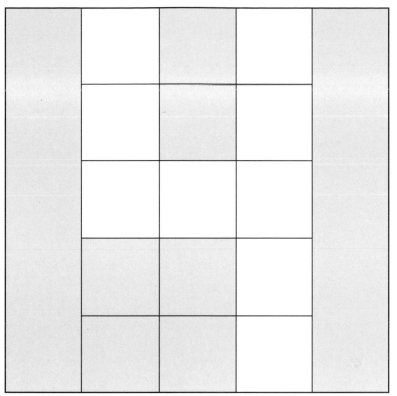

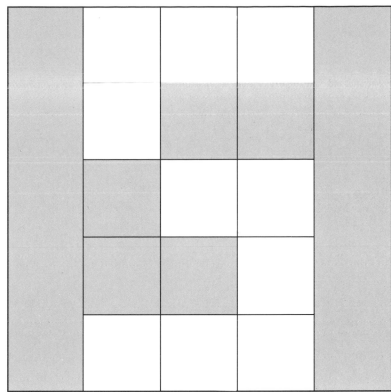

NUMBER 4

E31 Join the squares in rows to make the number 4; join the rows; add side pieces to complete the block.

NUMBER 5

E32 Only 2 templates are used. Piece the letter in horizontal rows; join the rows to make center section; add strips of background fabric to each side.

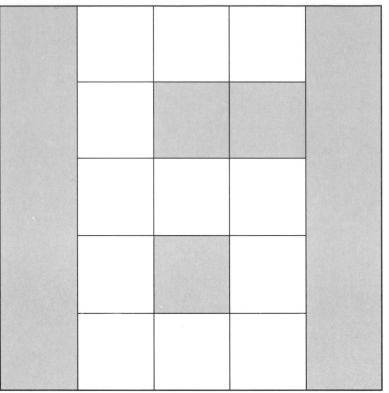

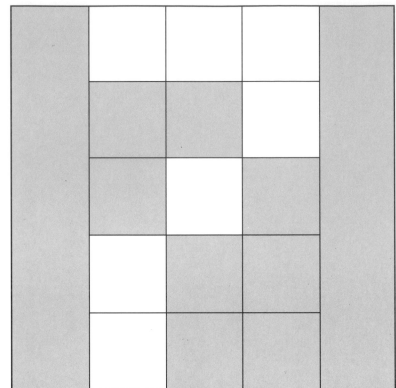

NUMBER 6

E33 Piece the 6 in horizontal rows; join rows to form center section; add strip to each side.

NUMBER 7

E34 Piece the 7 in 5 horizontal rows with 3 squares in each row. Join the rows; add strips to each side.

NUMERALS

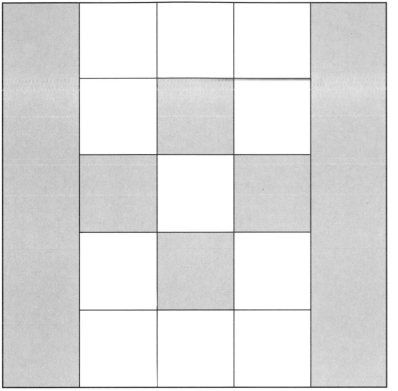

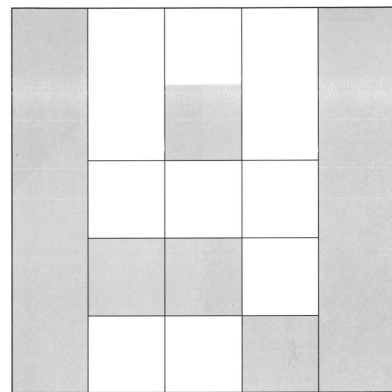

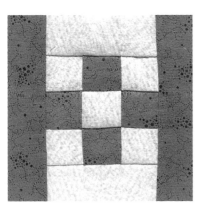

E35 Make center section by piecing horizontal rows, then joining the rows. Add background fabric strips to each side.

E36 Join the squares in rows to make the number 9; join the rows; add side pieces to complete the block.

NUMBER 8

NUMBER 9

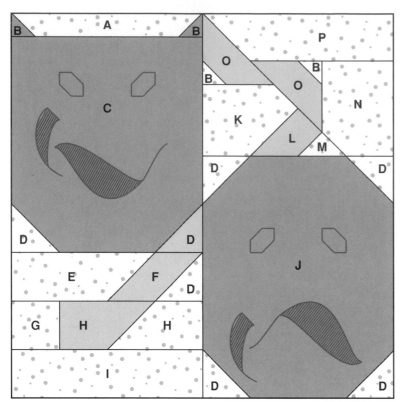

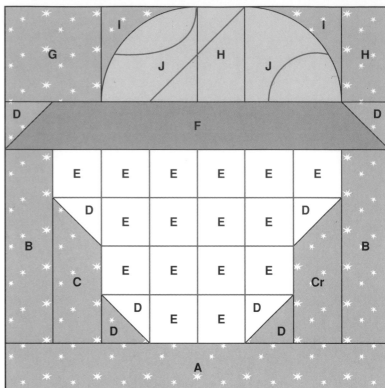

DRAMA

F1 Make left side of block: Make BAB and DCD units and join. Make EFD unit and add to first section. Make GHH unit and add to first section, then add I piece to bottom of section. Make right side of block: Sew D pieces to all corners of J. Make BO unit (2 times). Sew N to BO unit, then add P. Make KLM unit and add to second BO unit; join with POBN, then attach to bottom section. Join the left and right sections. Embroider the faces.

BASKETBALL

F2 Make IJ unit (2 times). (See page 309 for help with sewing curved seams.) Join IJ units with G and H pieces to make the top row. Make DFD unit and add to top row. Make DD unit (2 times); join with E pieces to make 4 rows of 4 squares each, then join the rows to make a square. Make EDC and EDCr units and add to sides of the square, then add B pieces to each side. Join with top section and then add A to bottom. Embroider detail on basketball net using chain stitch. Embroider basketball with stem stitch.

YOUNG AT HEART School Spirit

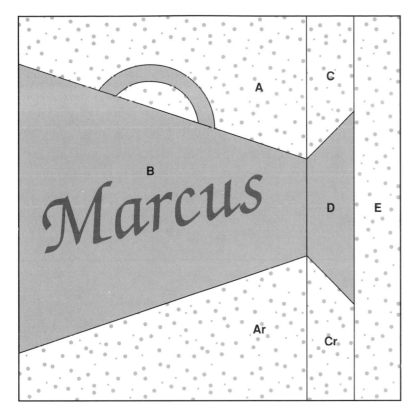

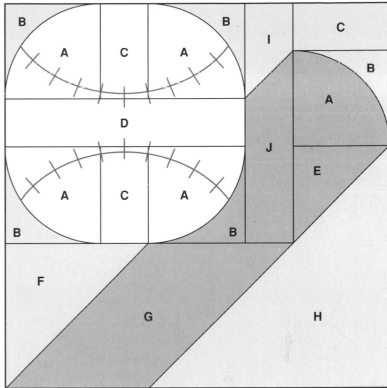

CHEERLEADING

F3 Appliqué handle to A. Make ABAr and CDCr units. Join units and add E. Embroider name on the megaphone.

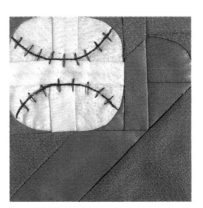

BASEBALL

F4 Make AB unit (5 times). (See page 309 for help with sewing curved seams.) Join AB to C to AB (2 times), then join the 2 units with D. Make IJ unit and add to right side of section. Make FG unit and add to bottom of section. Make CABE unit and add to right side of section; then sew H in place. Embroider detail on the baseball using stem stitch and straight stitch.

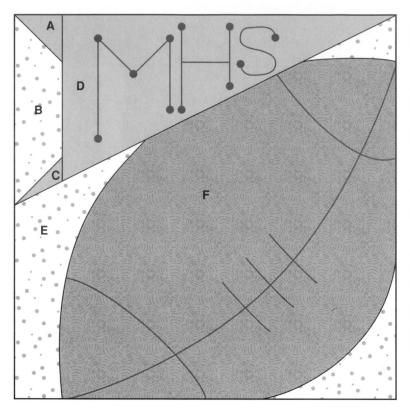

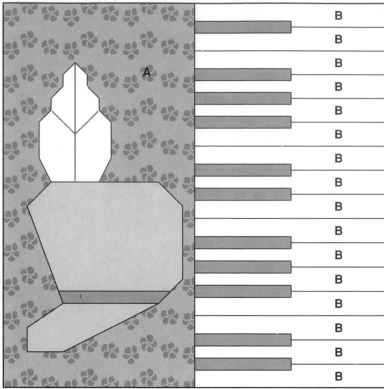

FOOTBALL

F5 Make ABC unit and add D. Appliqué F (football) onto E; join the 2 sections. Embroider detail on the football and on the pennant using stem stitch and French knots.

BAND

F6 Join 16 B pieces. Satin stitch black keys or appliqué ⅛" black satin ribbon for the keys. Join A piece to this section. Appliqué band hat to A.

YOUNG AT HEART School Spirit

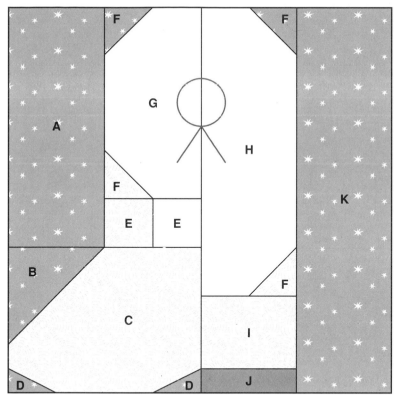

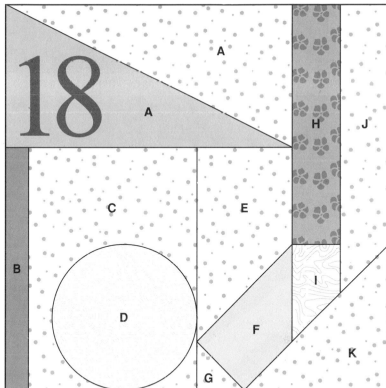

DRILL TEAM

F7 Make FGF and EE units; join the units, then add A. Make BCDD unit and add to first section. Make FHF unit, then add I and J to bottom of unit, then add K to right side. Join the 2 sections to complete the block. Embroider details or use a small silver button to embellish the boot.

GOLF

F8 Make EFG unit, then add C and B pieces to left side. Make AA unit and add to top of first section. Make HIJ unit; add to right side of first section, then add K. Appliqué D in place. Embroider the details, using stem stitch for the numeral, and embellish the golf ball with French knots.

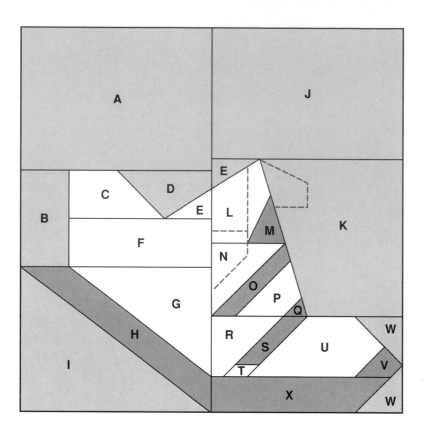

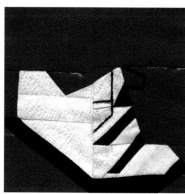

TRACK

F9 Make GHI unit. Make CDE unit; add F piece to bottom of unit and B piece on the side, then attach GHI unit and A. Make ELM and NOPQ units; join units and add K, then J. Make ST unit; add R and U, then add V. Attach X, then the 2 W pieces, and sew unit to top section. Join the left and right sides of the block. Embroider the shoelaces shown with a dashed line.

YOUNG AT HEART School Spirit

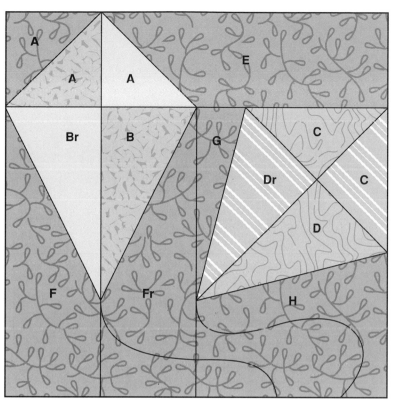

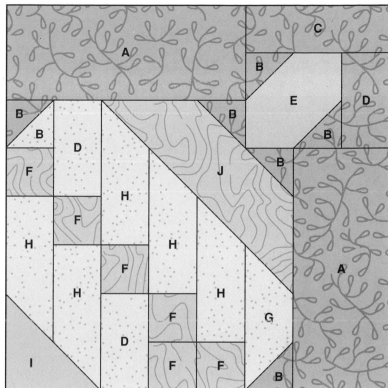

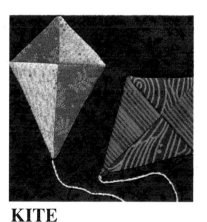

KITE

F10 Make AA unit and AE unit; join to make the top section. Make FBr unit and FrB unit; join. Make GDr and DH units and join. Make CC unit and add to GDH. Add this section to FBrBFr section; sew to top section. Embroider kite tails with stem stitch.

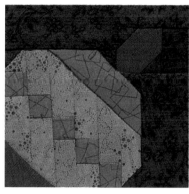

TOP

F11 Add B pieces to E; add D, then C. The top is made in vertical rows (BBFH is the first row). Make and join the 6 rows, then add I to HH edge; make BBJ unit and add to HHHG edge. Add A pieces to sides. Miter BCDE unit into place. (See page 309 for help with mitering.)

YOUNG AT HEART Juvenile

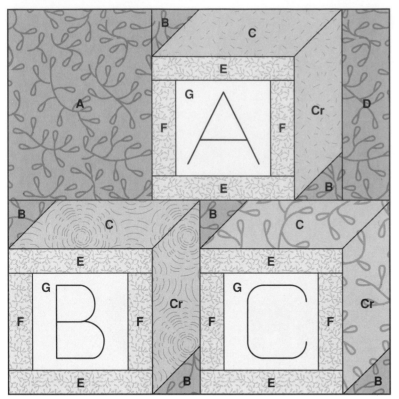

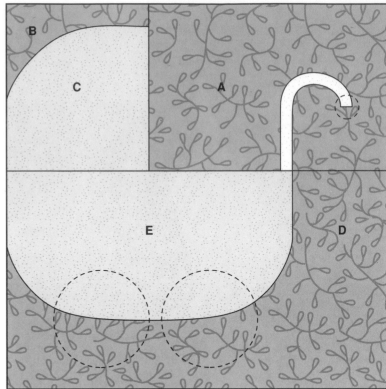

**STACKED BABY
BLOCKS**

F12 Sew F pieces to 2 opposite sides of G (3 times): then add E pieces to remaining sides (3 times). Make BC unit (3 times), and BCr unit (3 times); miter with EFG units (3 times). Join 2 block units for the bottom section. Add A and D to the remaining block; join top and bottom sections to complete.

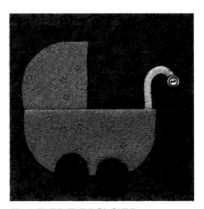

BABY BUGGY

F13 Cut background piece (D) 2¼" x 4" (plus seam allowances). Appliqué E onto D. Appliqué C piece to B (which is 1¾" x 1½", plus seam allowances). Join A to BC; join bottom section. Appliqué the handle of the baby buggy using bias tubing. (See page 309 for help in making bias tubing.) Sew a tiny button to the end of the handle. Make 2 yo-yos for the wheels (see page 308 for yo-yo directions). Appliqué yo-yos in place.

YOUNG AT HEART Juvenile

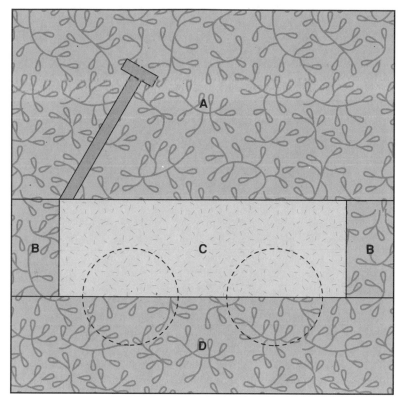

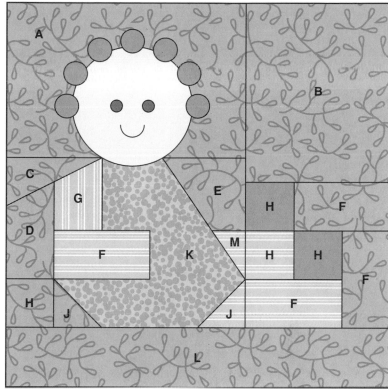

WAGON

F14 Sew B pieces to each end of C. Add A to top and D to bottom. Appliqué handle, using bias tubing (see page 309 for help in making bias tubing). Make 2 yoyos for wheels (see page 308 for yo-yo directions), and appliqué in place.

DOLL

F15 Make GF unit and appliqué to K. Make EM unit and join to GFK. Add J pieces; then make DH unit and join it to this section. Join C and then A to main section. Make HF unit; make HHFF unit and join with HF. Add B to top. Join left and right sections and add L to bottom. Appliqué the head in place. Embroider the face using French knots or beads for the eyes. Make "curls" with snaps or buttons.

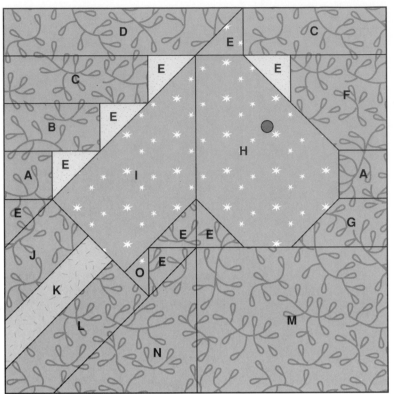

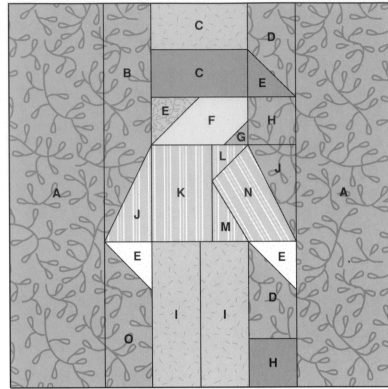

STICK HORSE

F16 Make AE, BE, and CE units; join the units and add E to bottom. Join JKL. Join OEE, add to I; join with JLKL, add N. Join with top section to make left section. Make right side by joining E to F and attaching H. Join A to G and miter with H, then miter with F. (See page 309 for help with mitering.) Add E; then add M. Join right and left sections. Join DEC and add to the top of the block. Use button, bead, or embroidery to make eye.

TOY SOLDIER

F17 Beginning at the top, join C to C. Make DE unit and add to CC. Make EFG unit, add H; join to first section. Make NJLM unit, add K; join to first section. Make EDH unit, add 2 I pieces; join to first section. Make BJ unit, make EO unit; join units and add to side of first section. Add A to each side of this center section to complete the block.

YOUNG AT HEART Juvenile

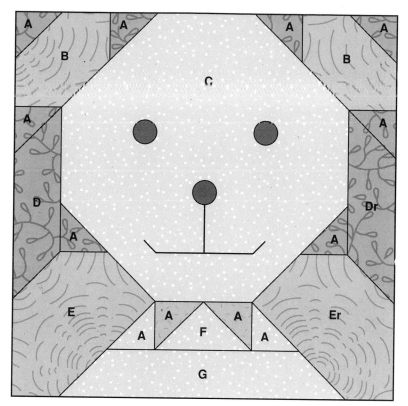

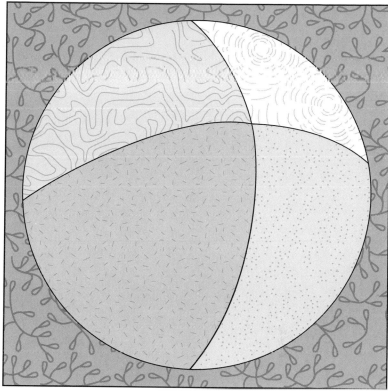

F18 Piece AAFAA unit, add G; attach C. Join A to E and A to Er; miter with CAFG unit. (See page 309 for help with mitering.) Add and miter D and Dr pieces. Make AAAB (2 times); add to CD edges to complete the block. Embroider mouth using stem stitch; use satin stitch or buttons for eyes and nose.

TEDDY BEAR

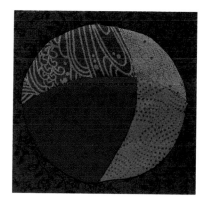

F19 Cut a 4-inch square (plus seam allowances) of background fabric. Appliqué ball in place. (See page 308 for appliqué information.)

BALL

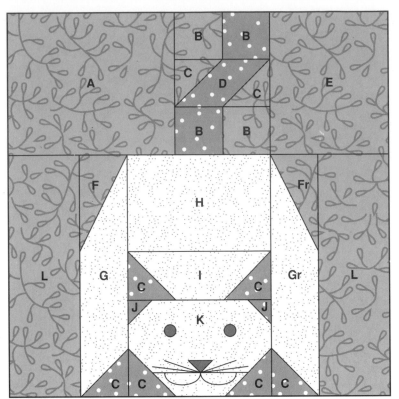

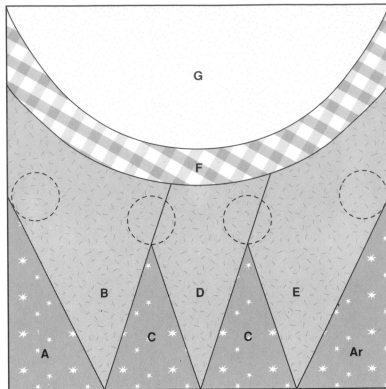

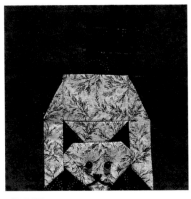

CAT

F20 Add J and C pieces to K. Make CIC unit and add to JK edge, then add H. Make FGC and FrGrC units and add to sides of first unit; then add L pieces to the sides. Make BB unit (2 times), make CDC unit, join a BB unit to top and bottom. Add A and E to the sides of this unit; join top and bottom sections. Embroider face detail; beads can be used for eyes.

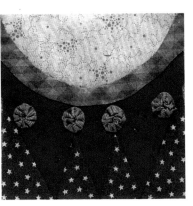

DRUM

F21 Appliqué G to F. Make AB, CD, and CEAr units; join to form lower section of drum. Appliqué F to bottom section. Make 4 yo-yos (see page 308 for yo-yo directions), and appliqué in place.

YOUNG AT HEART Juvenile

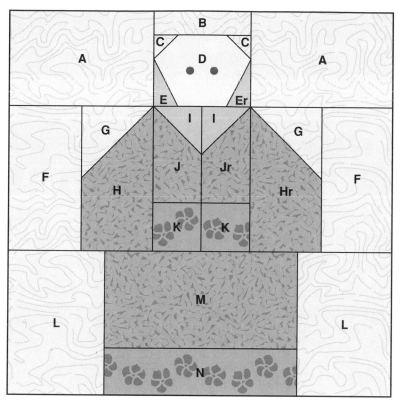

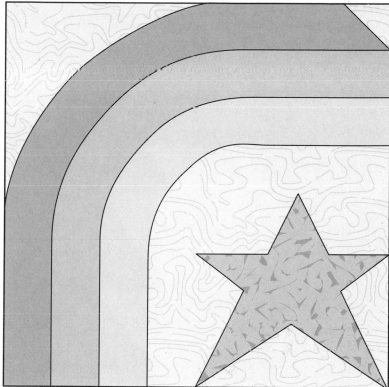

NOAH

F22 Make CCDEEr unit; add B to top, then add A pieces to each end to make top row. Make GH, IJK, IJrK, and GHr units; join the 4 units and add F pieces to each end to make center row. Join M and N; add L to each end. Join the 3 rows to complete the block. Use French knots or beads for eyes.

RAINBOW

F23 Cut a 4-inch square (plus seam allowances) of background fabric. Appliqué the rainbow and star onto the background. (See page 308 for appliqué information.)

YOUNG AT HEART Noah's Ark

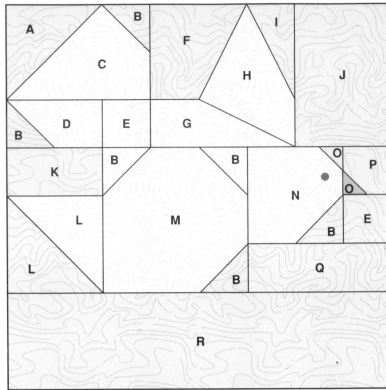

CLOUD AND LIGHTNING

F24 Cut a 4-inch square (plus seam allowances) of background fabric. Appliqué the 2 cloud pieces and lightning bolt onto the background.

DOVE

F25 Make ABC unit. Make BD unit; add E, then add unit to ABC unit. Miter F and G pieces with H (see page 309 for help with mitering); add I to H, add J, then add this section to the first section. Make LL unit and add to K. Make BBBM unit and add to KLL unit. Make NOB unit. Join O to P; add E, then attach to NOB; add Q. Add this unit to BMB edge, then attach this section to the top section. Add R to bottom of the block. Make eye with a French knot or bead. Embroider olive branch with stem stitch.

YOUNG AT HEART Noah's Ark

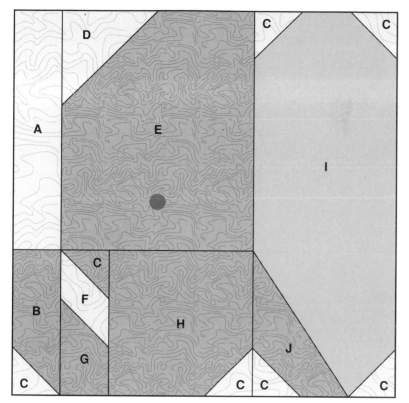

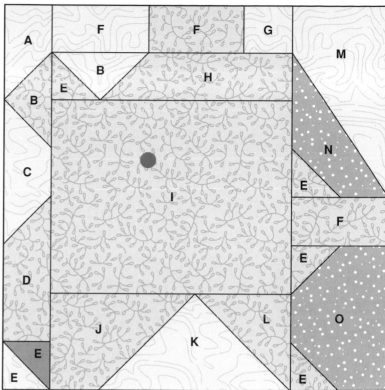

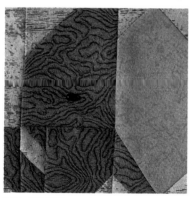

F26 Sew J to I, then add C pieces to all 4 corners. Make DE unit. Make CFG and HC units and join; combine with DE unit and add to first section. Make ABC unit and add to left side of block. Use a button for elephant's eye.

ELEPHANT

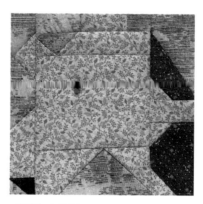

F27 Make FFG and EBH units and join; attach I. Make JKL unit and sew to I. Make MNF and EOE units; join with F and add to right side of first section. Make ABCDEE unit and add to left side to complete the block. Use a button or bead for eye.

GIRAFFE

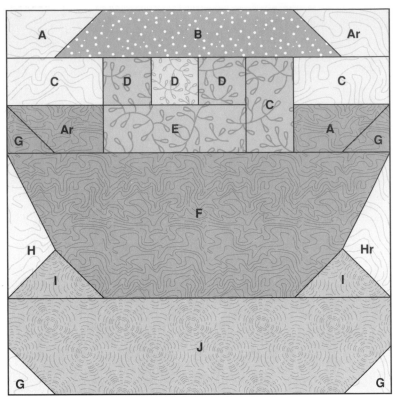

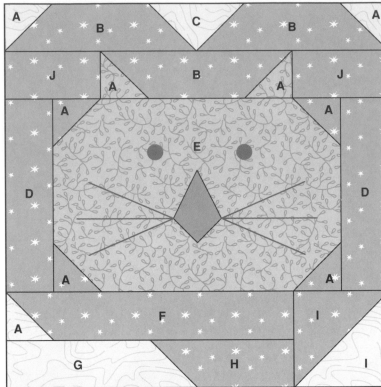

ARK

F28 Make ABAr unit. Make ArG and AG units; add a C piece to each unit. Make DDD unit and add E, then C; join with CAG and CArG units and add to top section. Miter H and I pieces with F, then miter Hr and I pieces with F. (See page 309 for help with mitering.) Add this unit to the top section. Make GJG unit and join it to the top section.

LION

F29 Make ABCBA and JABAJ units and join. Sew A pieces to 4 corners of E; join D pieces to each side of AAEAA; add to top section. Make AF and GH units and join; make II unit, join to FH edge and add to top section. Appliqué nose, embroider whiskers, and use beads or buttons for eyes.

YOUNG AT HEART Noah's Ark

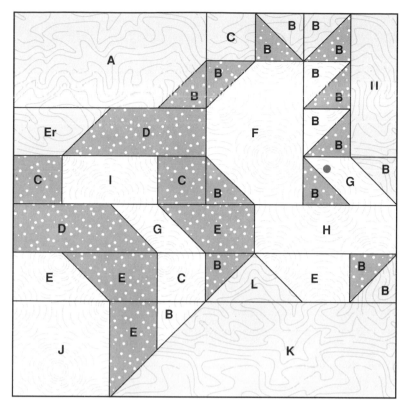

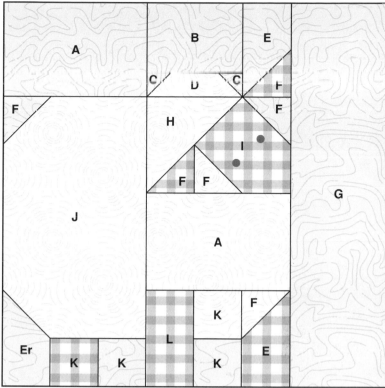

ZEBRA

F30 Make JEB unit; add K. Make EECBLEBB unit and add to bottom section. Make DGEH unit and join with bottom section. Make CIC, ErD and AB units and join together. Make BB unit (4 times). Make BFB unit, join BB unit with C, then join with BFB; add to right side of previous section. Make BGB unit; join 3 BB units and attach to H, then join with BGB unit and add to previous section. Join the top and bottom sections to complete the block. Use a button or bead for the eye.

SHEEP

F31 Make KK unit and sew to J; add F to J. Miter Er piece at JK edge (see page 309 for help with mitering). Add A to JF edge to complete left section. Make FE and KK units; combine with L and add to A. Make FFIF unit, add H, and join to A edge of section. Make CDC unit, add B; make EF unit and add to BC edge, then add this unit to previous section. Join the 2 sections and add G to right side to complete the block. Use beads for eyes.

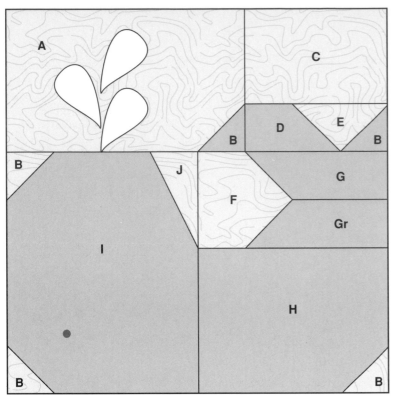

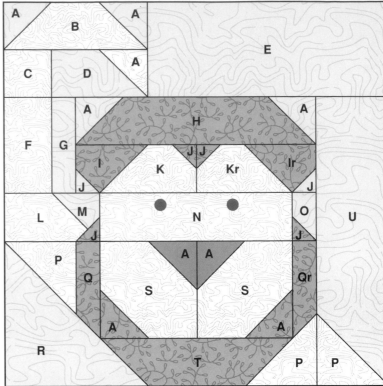

WHALE

F32 Make DEB unit and add C; make AB unit and add to CD edge. Miter F pieces with G and Gr pieces (see page 309 for help with mitering); make HB and add to FGGr unit. Make BBIJ unit and attach to FH edge, then add this section to the top section. Appliqué bubbles and add a bead or button eye.

MONKEY

F33 Make ABA and CDA units; join and add E. Make AHA unit; make and join JIKJ and JKrIrJ units and then join to AHA unit. Add F and G pieces to AIJ edge. Make LM unit and add J; make OJ unit and join with LMJ and N. Attach this unit to the top section. Make ASA unit (2 times); join units and add T. Sew Q and Qr pieces to sides of ASA units; add P to Q, then add R. Sew P to TQr edge; attach this section to previous section. Make PU unit and join. Finally, join top and bottom sections. Use beads or buttons for eyes.

YOUNG AT HEART Noah's Ark

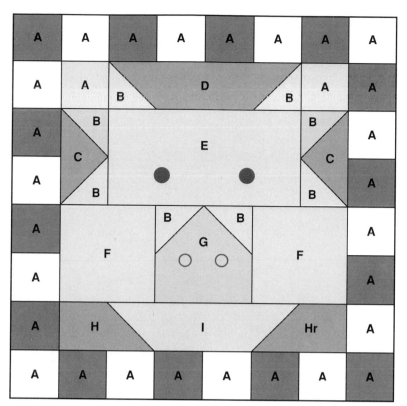

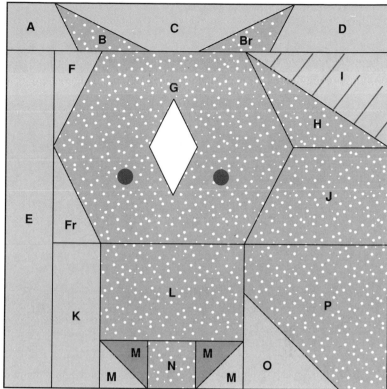

PIG

F34 Make BDB unit; add A to each end. Make BCB unit (2 times) and add to each side of E; join this unit to top section. Make BGB unit and sew F to each side; attach to top section. Make HIHr unit and join to top section. Make borders by joining 6 A pieces (2 times) and 8 A pieces (2 times). Join units of 6 A pieces to opposite sides of center section; join 8-piece units to top and bottom. Use buttons, beads, or embroidery to make eyes and nose.

HORSE

F35 Make HI unit and attach to G. Miter J piece with HI unit and G. (See page 309 for help with mitering.) Sew F and Fr to G. Make MM unit (2 times); join units with N and add to L. Make OP unit and add to side of LMN section, then add K to other side. Join this section with the first section; add E piece to left side. Make ABCBrD unit and add to top of block. Embroider mane detail with straight stitches. Appliqué diamond to face. Use buttons or embroider eyes.

YOUNG AT HEART Barnyard

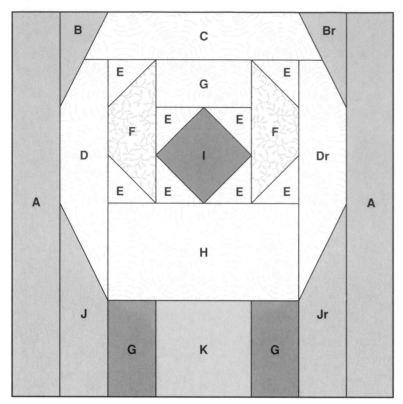

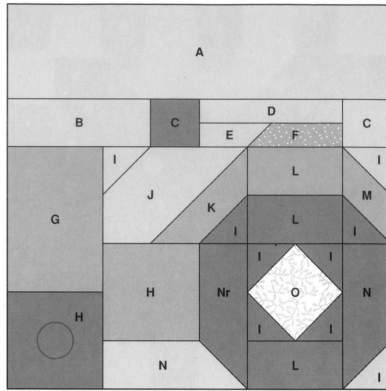

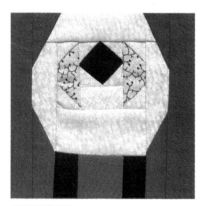

SHEEP

F36 Beginning in center of block, sew 4 E pieces to each side of I; add G. Make EFE unit (2 times); add to sides of IEG unit; sew H to bottom of the unit. Make GKG unit and add to bottom of first section. Make DJ and DrJr units and add to sides of center section. Add C piece to top of section; attach B and Br. Sew A pieces to each side to complete the block.

TRACTOR

F37 Sew I pieces to all sides of O; add 2 L pieces to top of unit and L to bottom. Make and join IMI and NI units; add to first section. Make IJKI unit. Sew N and Nr to H and miter (see page 309 for help with mitering); join with IJKI unit and attach to left side of first section. Make GH unit and sew to side of first section. Join E and F; add D, then sew C to right side and C and B pieces to left side. Add unit to bottom section; add A piece to top to complete the block. Add buttons to the wheels.

YOUNG AT HEART Barnyard

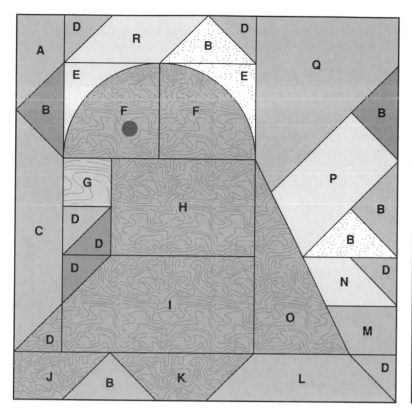

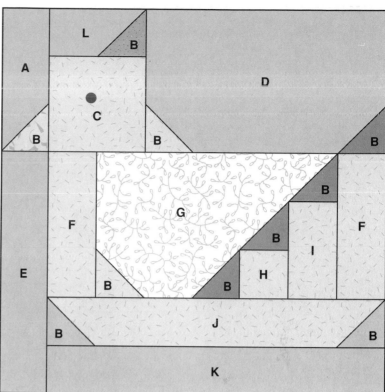

ROOSTER

F38 Make PB, BB, and ND units; join units, add Q, add M, then add O. Make DRBD unit. Make EF unit (2 times) (see page 309 for help with sewing curved seams); join units and add to DRBD unit. Make DD unit, add G, then add H; join to top unit. Sew D to I and add to bottom of section. Join the 2 completed sections. Make ABCD unit and attach to left side of main section. Make JBKLD unit and add to bottom of block. Use a button or bead for eye.

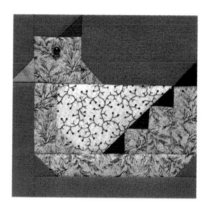

CHICKEN

F39 Make LB unit and add to C. Make BDB unit and join with LBC unit. Make BH and BI units; combine with F and B and sew to G. Add B to G, then add F. Make and attach BJB unit; add K. Join the 2 sections. Make ABE unit and sew to left side of block. Add a button or bead eye.

271

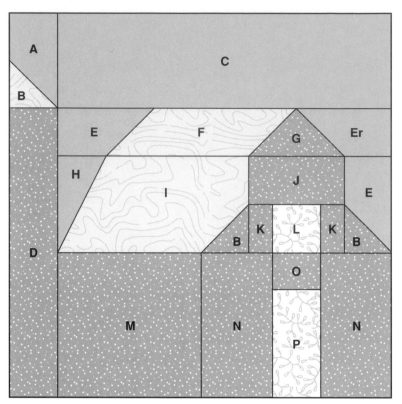

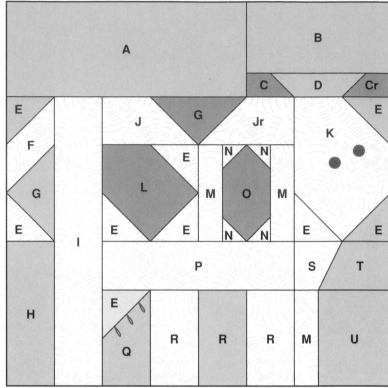

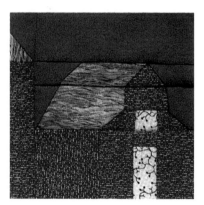

F40 Join O and P; sew N to right side, and N and M pieces to left side. Make KLK unit, add J. Make EB and HIB units; join to JKL, add to bottom section. Make EFGEr unit and attach to bottom section; add C to top. Make ABD unit and add to left side of the block.

BARN

F41 Make EQ unit; join with R, R, R, M, and U to make bottom row. Make ST unit, join with P; add to bottom row. Make LEEE unit and NNNNO unit and join with 2 M pieces. Make JGJr unit and add to LEMNO unit. Make KEEE unit and attach to right side of previous section; join this section with bottom section. Make EFGEH unit; add I, sew to left side of section. Make CDCr unit and attach B; add A; join this section to the bottom section. Embroider udder detail with straight stitches; use beads for eyes.

COW

YOUNG AT HEART Barnyard

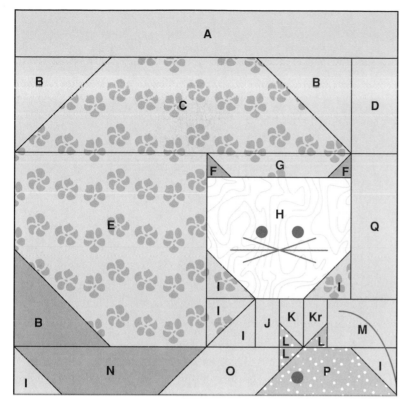

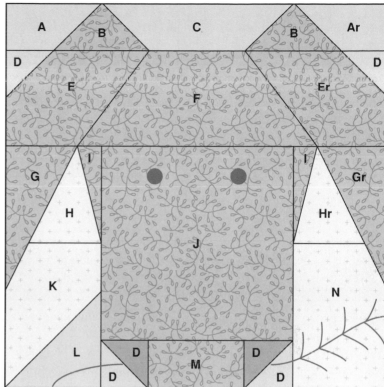

BARN CAT AND MOUSE

F42 Make INOL unit and PI unit; join. Make and join II, J, KL, KrL, and M. Make IHI and FGF units and join; add Q; join this section with IJKLM. Join B to E and add to previous section; join this section to bottom row. Make BCBD unit; join to bottom section; add A to top. Embroider mouse tail and cat face, using stem stitch; use French knots or small beads for eyes.

DONKEY

F43 Make DD unit (2 times); join with M; add J. Make IHrN unit; add Gr piece and attach to right side of center section. Make IHKL unit; add G; sew to left side of center section. Make DEFErD unit and join with first section. Make ABCBAr unit and add to top of the block. Embroider hay using stem stitch. Use buttons or beads for eyes.

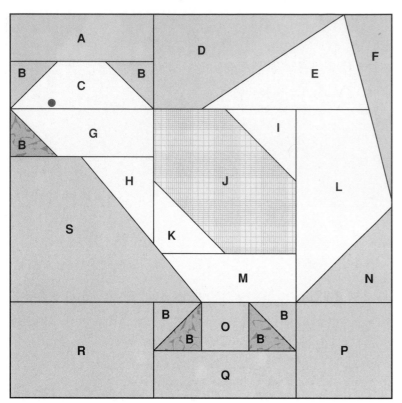

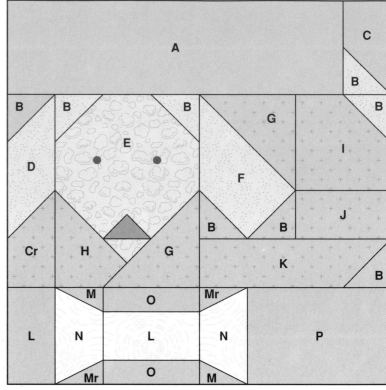

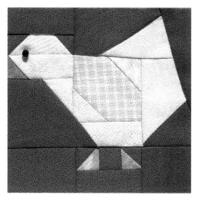

DUCK

F44 Make BCB and BG units; join together and add A to top and H to bottom. Make IJK unit, add M; make LN unit and join to IJKM. Make ED unit and add to previous section, then add F. Join this unit with the first section, then miter S in place. (See page 309 for help with mitering.) Make BB unit (2 times); join together with O, then add Q. Sew R to left side of BOQ unit and P to the the right side; add this unit to main section. Use a French knot or bead for the eye.

DOG AND BONE

F45 Make MNMr unit (2 times) and OLO unit; join the units and add L to left side and P to right side. Make GFBB unit. Join B and I pieces, add J; add this unit to GFBB, then make and attach KB unit. Make HEBB unit and add G; add this unit to left side of previous section. Make BDCr and join to previous section; add this section to bottom section. Make CB unit and attach to A; add this unit to the bottom section. Appliqué nose; use beads for eyes.

YOUNG AT HEART Barnyard

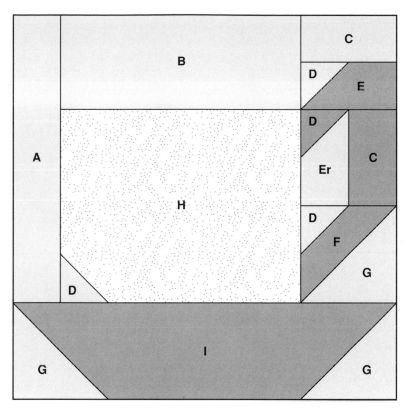

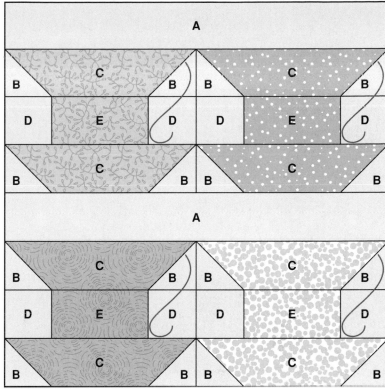

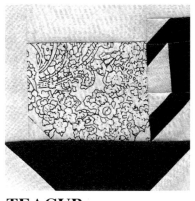

G1 Make DE unit, add C; join with B. Make DErC and DFG units, join, and add H. Sew D to H; add this section to top section, then add A to left side. Make GIG unit and add to bottom to complete block.

TEACUP

G2 Make BCB unit (8 times) and DED unit (4 times). Join BCB, DED, and BCB to make teacup section (4 times). Join 2 sections (2 times). Join bottom section with A, add second section, and add A at top to complete the block. Embroider the cup handles, using stem stitch.

SERVICE FOR FOUR

COLLECTIONS Teatime

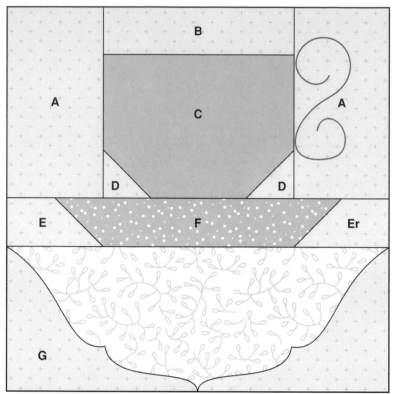

**GRANDMA'S
PRIZED
POSSESSION**

G3 Make DCD unit; add B to top, then add A pieces to sides. Make EFEr unit and join to top section. Appliqué the napkin unit to G. Join G unit to top section. Embroider the cup handle with stem stitch.

TEAPOT

G4 Cut a 4-inch square (plus seam allowances) of background fabric. Appliqué teapot. (See page 308 for appliqué information.)

COLLECTIONS Teatime

G5 Cut a 4-inch square (plus seam allowances) of background fabric. Appliqué teapot.

CONTEMPORARY TEAPOT

G6 Cut a 4-inch square (plus seam allowances) of background fabric. Appliqué teapot.

ORIENTAL TEAPOT

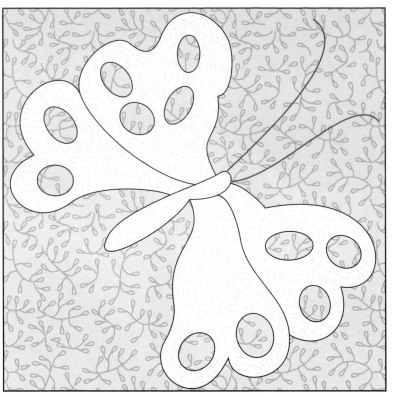

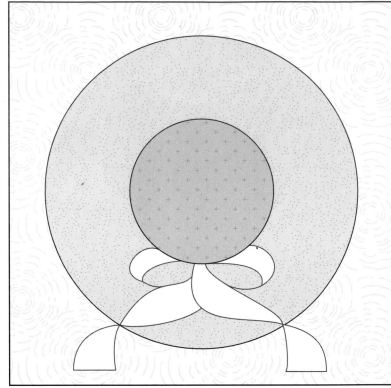

G7 Cut a 4-inch square (plus seam allowances) of background fabric. The butterfly is appliquéd and embroidered. Make the antennae with stem stitch. (See page 308 for appliqué information.)

CUTWORK
BUTTERFLY

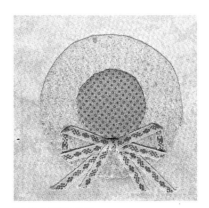

G8 Cut a 4-inch square (plus seam allowances) of background fabric. Appliqué bonnet; use ribbon for bow.

BONNET

COLLECTIONS Teatime

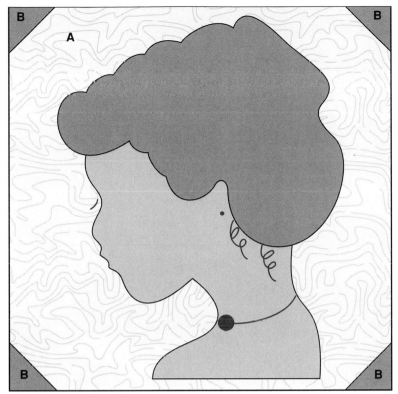

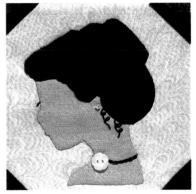

CAMEO

G9 The background block is pieced (sew B pieces to 4 corners of A). The profile is appliquéd. The details are embroidered; we used a button to highlight the necklace.

GLOVE

G10 Cut a 4-inch square (plus seam allowances) of background fabric. Appliqué glove to the background square. Embellish at the cuff, as desired.

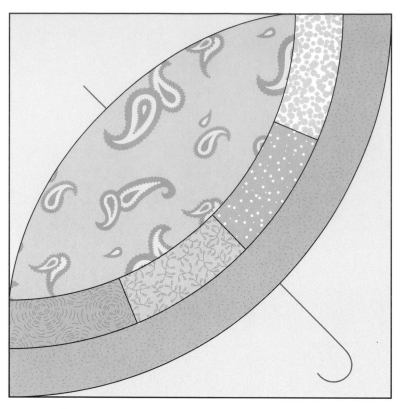

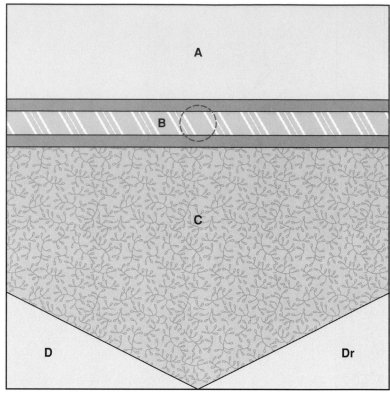

G11 Cut a 4-inch square (plus seam allowances) of background fabric. Appliqué umbrella to background square. Embroider the details.

UMBRELLA

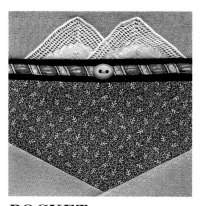

G12 Make the DCDr section, add B. Appliqué the handkerchief section to A. Join the 2 sections. Add a button to provide additional interest.

POCKET

COLLECTIONS Teatime

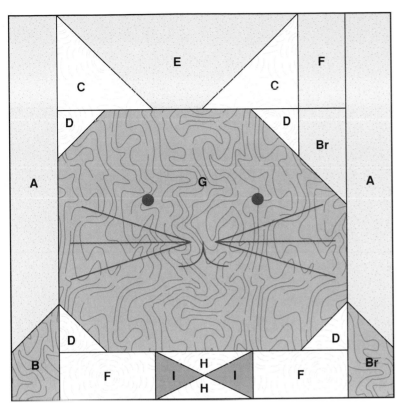

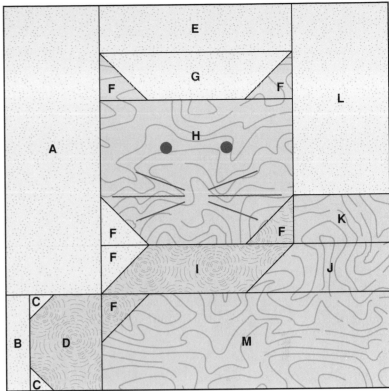

FLASH

G13 Make CEC unit; add F to right side. Make DBr unit and add to G; add 3 more D pieces to G; attach to first section. Make HI unit (2 times) and join together; add F pieces to each end; join with first section. Make AB and ABr units and sew to sides of center section to complete the block. Embroider mouth and whiskers; use beads for eyes.

SALLY

G14 Make FGF unit; sew E to top edge. Attach 2 F pieces to H; join with first section. Make LK unit and sew to right side of first section. Make FIJ unit and FM unit; join the units and attach to top section. Make CDC unit; add B to left side, then add A to top; attach to main section. Embroider whiskers; use French knots or beads for eyes.

COLLECTIONS Cats

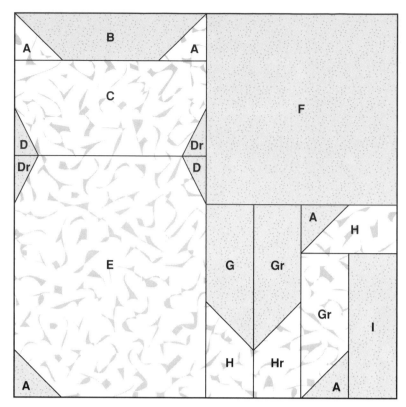

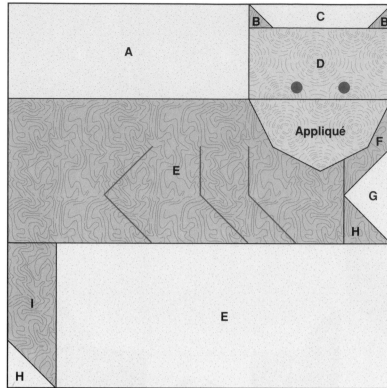

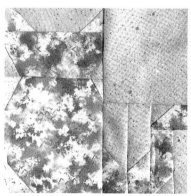

KILLER

G15 Make ABA, DCDr, and DrEDA units and join to form left side of block. Make GrA unit, add I; make AH unit and add to GrAI. Make GH and GrHr units and join together; add unit to AHGrAI unit and add F. Join left and right sides of block.

SAM

G16 Make BCB unit; add D, then attach A. Make FHG unit, add E. Appliqué the bottom half of cat's face in place. (See page 308 for appliqué information.) Join the 2 sections. Make HI unit, then attach E; join this unit to top section. Embroider the lines for legs with stem stitch. Use French knots or beads for eyes.

COLLECTIONS Cats

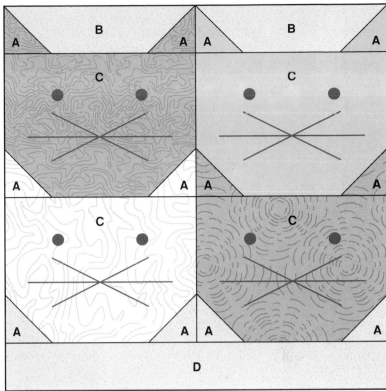

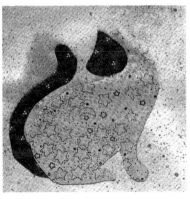

MARVIN

G17 Cut a 4-inch square (plus seam allowances) of background fabric. Appliqué cat in place. (See page 308 for appliqué information.)

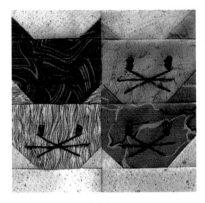

FOUR CATS

G18 Make ABA unit (2 times); make ACA unit (4 times). Join the units into rows; join rows, then add D piece to bottom of the block. Embroider whiskers; use French knots or beads for eyes.

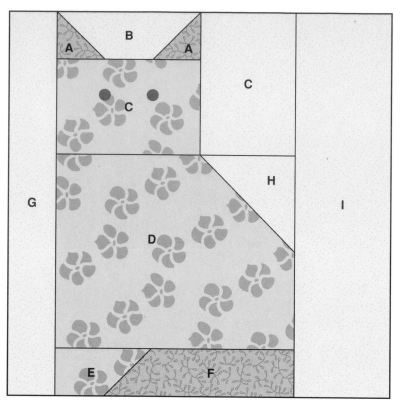

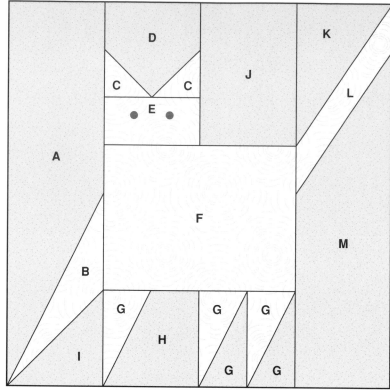

G19 Make ABA unit; add C to bottom, then to right side of section. Make DH unit and add to top section; make EF unit and add to main section. Add G and I pieces to sides to complete the block. Use tiny buttons, beads, or French knots for eyes.

AGATHA

G20 Make CDC unit and add E, then add J; add F to the first section. Make GH unit and GG unit (2 times); join units to form a row and add to top section. Make KLM unit, add to right side of block. Make ABI unit and add to left side of block. Use French knots or beads for eyes.

SAMANTHA

COLLECTIONS Cats

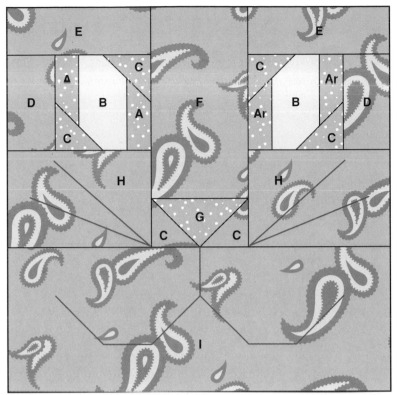

BASTET

G21 Make ABA unit and ArBrAr unit; add 2 C pieces to each unit, then add D to each. Sew H pieces to bottoms of ABCD sections and E pieces to tops of ABCD sections. Make CGC and attach to F; join the 3 top sections. Sew I to bottom of the block. Embroider whiskers and mouth.

LOUIE

G22 Cut a 4-inch square (plus seam allowances) of background fabric. Appliqué cat to block. (See page 308 for appliqué information.)

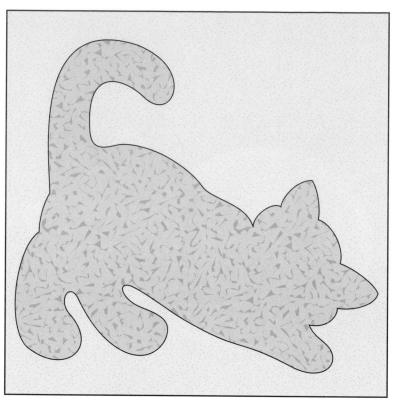

SOCKS

G23 Cut a 4-inch square (plus seam allowances) of background fabric. Appliqué cat to the block.

MOLLY

G24 Cut a 4-inch square (plus seam allowances) of background fabric. Appliqué cat to block. Embroider face with straight stitches and stem stitch; use French knots or beads for the eyes.

COLLECTIONS Cats

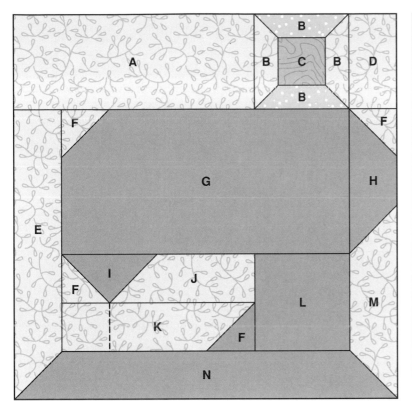

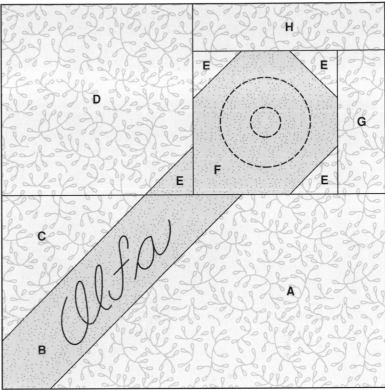

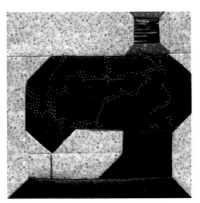

SEWING MACHINE

G25 Sew B pieces to 2 opposite sides of C, then add B pieces to remaining 2 sides and miter BB seams. (See page 309 for help with mitering.) Add A to one side of BC unit and D to the opposite side. Make FIJ unit and KF unit; join and add L. Sew F to G and add to FIJKFL unit. Make FHM unit and add to right side of this section; add E to opposite side. Then join N to bottom, mitering the EN and MN seams. Add the first section to second section to complete the block. Embroider the machine needle.

OLFA CUTTER

G26 Make the EEEF unit, add G, then add H. Add E to D and join to first unit. Join A to B to C and join with top section. Embroider "Olfa" on handle. Appliqué one round piece onto F; add a clear button on top.

COLLECTIONS Sewing

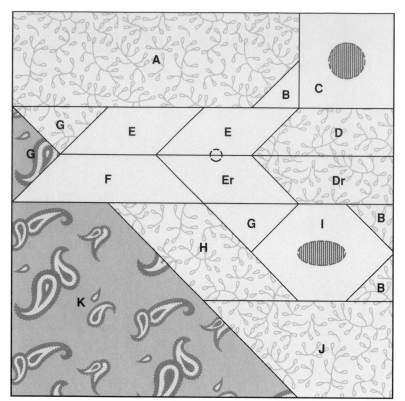

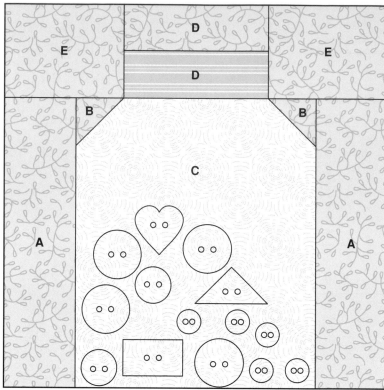

G27 Add B to A; join C to make top row. Make EED unit and FErDr unit and join the 2 units. Make GG unit and add to EF edge; join to top section. Make GIBB unit; add H, then add J; join with K and add to top section. Satin-stitch finger openings and add a tiny button where the screw would be.

SCISSORS I

G28 Make DD unit (use a striped fabric or embroider lines on the lid piece later). Add E to each side of DD unit. Add B pieces to C, then add A pieces to opposite sides. Join the 2 sections. Sew buttons on C.

BUTTON JAR

COLLECTIONS Sewing

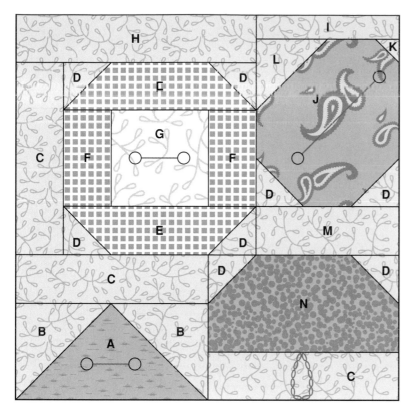

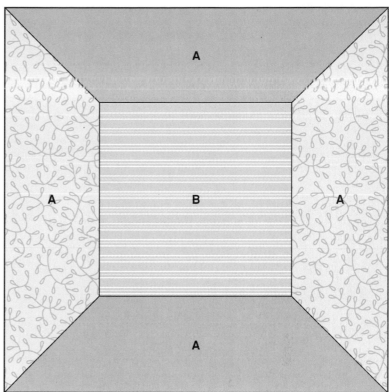

BUTTONS

G29 Make FGF unit; make DED unit (2 times) and add to top and bottom of FGF unit; add C, then add H. Make JKLDD unit; add I to top and M to bottom; join with first unit to make top section. Make ABA; add C to the top. Make DND unit, add C; join to ABBC unit. Join bottom section to top section. Embellish with embroidery and tiny buttons.

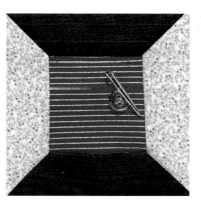

SPOOL

G30 Sew A to 2 opposite sides of B, then to 2 remaining sides, mitering the AA seams. (See page 309 for help with mitering.) A pinstripe fabric for B puts thread on your spool. Accent your block with a button and real needle or embroider a needle.

289

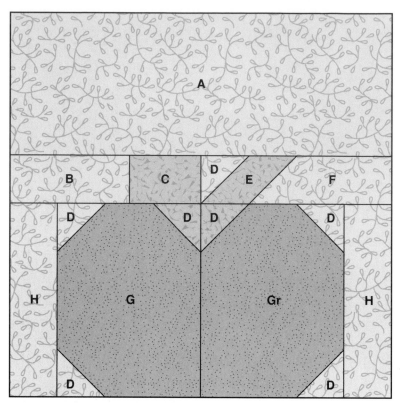

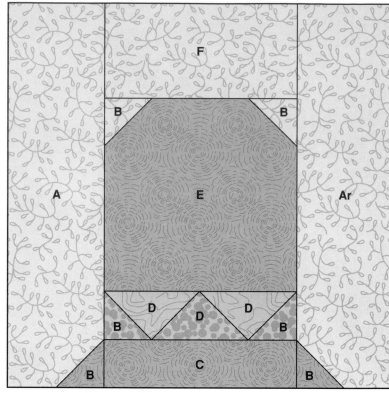

PINCUSHION

G31 Make DDDG and DDDGr units; add H to each unit. Make BC unit and add to DDGH; make DEF unit and add to DDDGrH. Join these 2 sections, then add A to complete the block. Embroider pins and needles.

THIMBLE

G32 Make BBE unit and BDDDB unit; join and add C and F. Make AB and ArB units; join to center section to complete the block.

COLLECTIONS Sewing

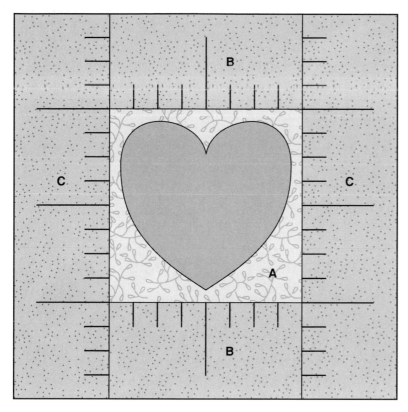

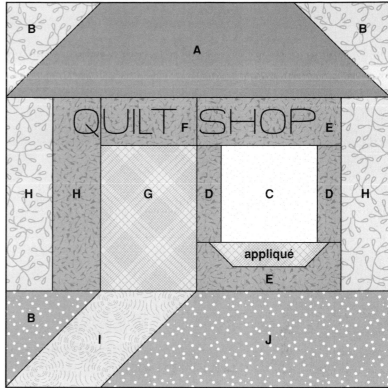

RULER

G33 Sew B pieces to opposite sides of A; add C pieces to 2 remaining sides. Appliqué the heart onto A. Embroider black lines on B and C at 1-inch and ¼-inch intervals.

QUILT SHOP

G34 Make BAB unit. Make DCD unit; appliqué window sill to E, then add E pieces to top and bottom of DCD; add H to right side. Make FG unit; add 2 H pieces to left side and join with CDEH; add to top section. Make BIJ unit and add to main section to complete the block. Embroider the name of your favorite shop.

291

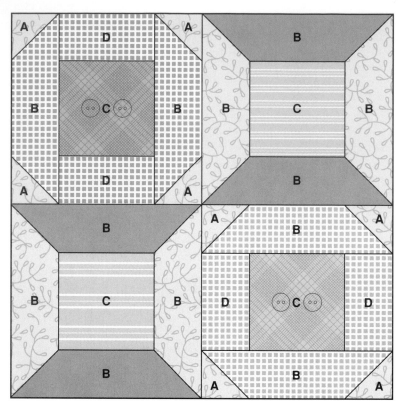

G35 Make ABA unit (4 times); make DCD unit (2 times). Sew ABA units to 2 sides of DCD (2 times). Sew B pieces to 2 opposite sides of C, then to 2 remaining sides, and miter BB seams (2 times). (See page 309 for mitering directions.) Join 2 sections in a row (2 times); join the 2 rows. Add tiny buttons as shown.

BUTTONS AND SPOOLS

G36 Cut a 4-inch square (plus seam allowances) of background fabric. Appliqué the scissors. Embroider the lines on the wing section. Embroider the eye or use a tiny black button or bead.

SCISSORS II

COLLECTIONS Sewing

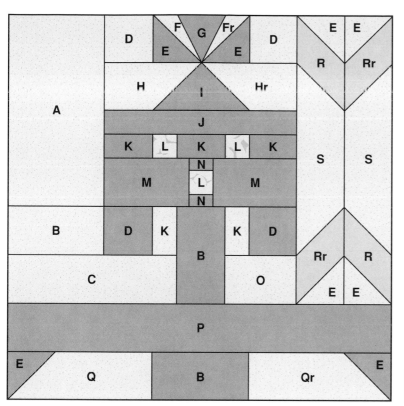

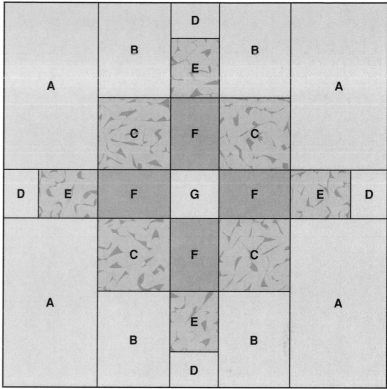

KACHINA DOLL

G37 Make FE and FrE units; join the 2 units with G, add D to each end. Make HIHr unit and add to first section, then add J. Make KLKLK unit and add to J edge of section. Make NLN unit, add M to each side, and add to main section. Sew A to left side of this section. Make DK unit (2 times). Sew B to one DK unit, then add C. Sew O to second DK unit, add B, then join with BCDK section and add to previous section. Following pattern, make ERSRrE (2 times); join the 2 units and add to right side of main section. Add P to bottom. Make EQ and QrE units; join the 2 units with B; add to main section to complete the block.

GEOMETRIC I

G38 Following pattern, make ABC unit (4 times). Make DEF unit (4 times). Combine units to make 2 rows of ABC/DEF/ABC. Sew DEF unit to each side of G; join this row with the top and bottom rows to complete the block.

COLLECTIONS Southwest

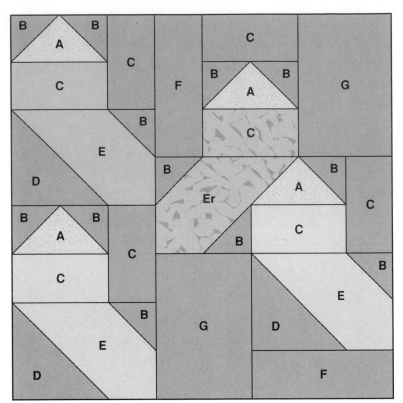

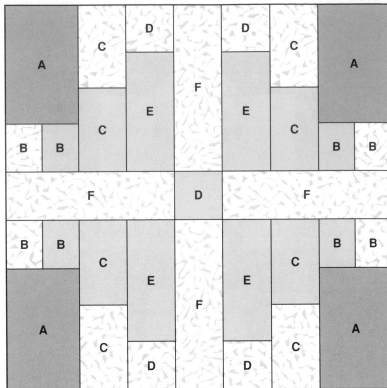

CHILI PEPPERS

G39 Construct the left section by making 2 blocks. Make BAB unit, add C to the bottom edge, then to right side. Make DEB unit and add to top section. Repeat to make a second block; join the blocks to complete the left side. Make BAB unit, add C to top and bottom of unit; add F and G pieces to sides. Sew B to A, sew B to C; join the 2 units and and add C to right side. Make BEr unit and add to ABBCC unit; add this section to the ABCFG section. Make DEB unit, add F to bottom, add G to left side. Attach this unit to the top section. Join the left and right sections to complete the block.

GEOMETRIC II

G40 Referring to pattern for placement, make ABB (4 times), CC (4 times), and DE (4 times). Combine the units to make 4 square sections. (Note, 2 sections are reversed.) Join one section and its reverse with F to make a row (2 times). Make FDF unit and join with the 2 completed sections.

COLLECTIONS Southwest

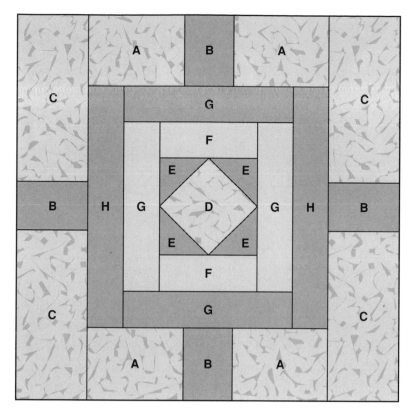

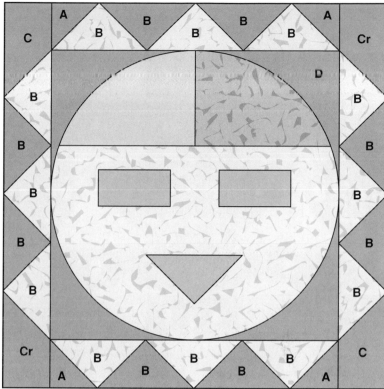

GEOMETRIC III

G41 Begin in the center by making EEEED unit; add F to 2 opposite sides, then add G to 2 remaining sides. Add G to top and bottom of section, then attach H pieces to sides. Make ABA unit (2 times) and sew to top and bottom of center section. Make CBC unit (2 times) and attach to sides of center section to complete the block.

SUN

G42 Cut D for center section and appliqué the sun face onto D. (See page 308 for appliqué information.) Make ABBBBBA unit (2 times); attach to top and bottom of center block. Make CBBBBBCr unit (2 times); attach to 2 sides of center section to complete the block.

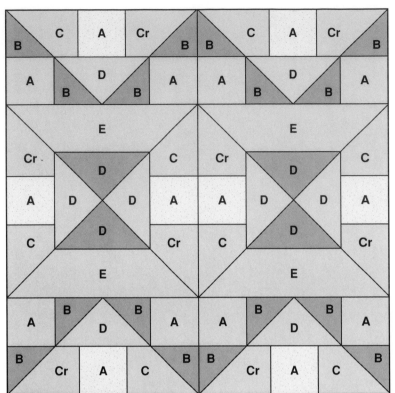

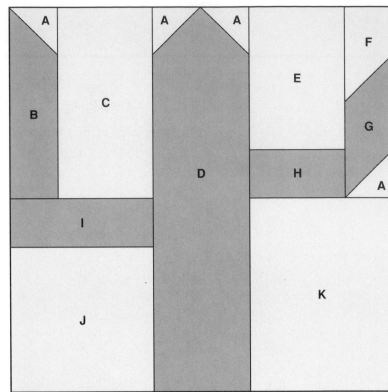

NAVAJO RUG

G43 Make BAB (8 times) and CACr (8 times). Add D to CACr (8 times). Sew 2 BAB units to CD edges (4 times). Make ED unit (4 times); combine 2 ED units with 2 ACCrD units to make a square (2 times). Attach ABCD units to 2 sides of square (2 times) to form left and right sides of the block; join the 2 sections to complete the block.

CACTUS I

G44 Make AB unit; attach C to right side, add I and then J. Make ADA unit and join with first section. Make FGA unit and EH unit; join the 2 units and add K. Join the 2 sections to complete the block.

COLLECTIONS Southwest

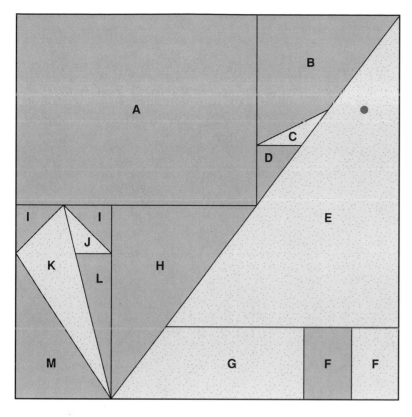

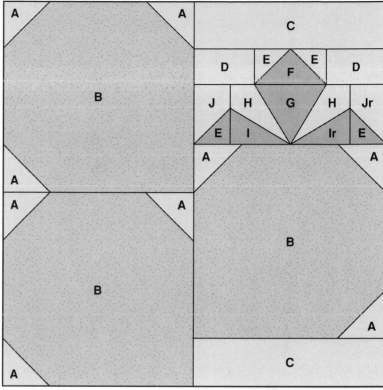

COYOTE

G45 Make BCD unit and sew to A. Make IJL unit and MKI unit; join the 2 units, add H; then add this section to the bottom edge of A. Make GFF unit; add to E. Join the 2 sections diagonally to complete the block. Embroider or use a button or bead for eye.

CACTUS II

G46 Make AAAB unit (3 times); join 2 of the units to make the left section. Make EFE unit; attach D pieces to each side, add C to top. Make HI and HIr units and join with G. Make JE and JrE units and sew to sides of GHI unit; join this unit to top section. Add AAAB unit to the top section, then add C. Join left and right sections to complete the block.

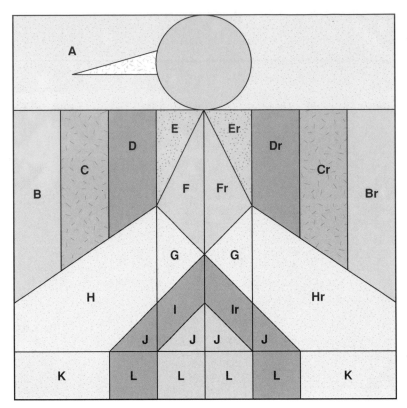

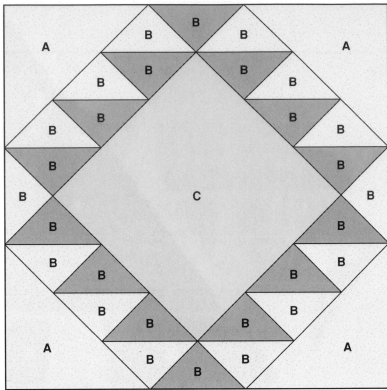

G47 Appliqué 2 pieces to A. Make BCD unit and add H, then add J. Make DrCrBr and add Hr, then add J. Make EFGIJ unit and ErFrGIrJ units and join them; add left and right sections; join to A. Make KLLLLK unit and sew to bottom of block.

THUNDERBIRD

G48 Make square BB unit (12 times). Join BB units into 4 rows of 3 units each; attach 2 rows to opposite sides of C. Sew B pieces to each end of 2 remaining B rows and sew to remaining sides of C. Sew A pieces to all 4 corners.

GEOMETRIC IV

COLLECTIONS Southwest

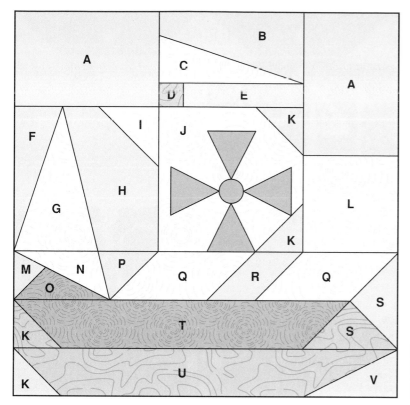

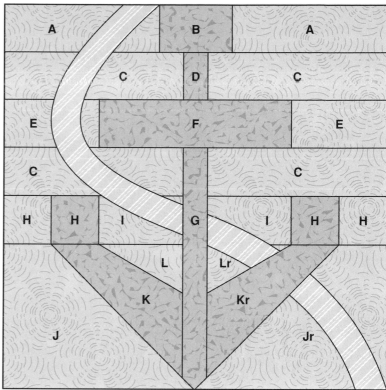

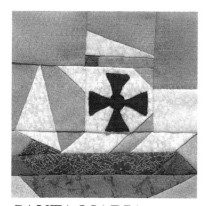

SANTA MARIA

G49 Make FGHI unit, add A. Make DE and CB units; join. Sew 2 K pieces to J; join this unit with BCDE; attach to AFGHI section. Join A and L; add to first section. Join M and O, add N; make PQRQ unit and add to MNO. Sew K to T; add to MNOPQRQ unit. Join 2 S pieces and add to TQ edge. Attach K and V to U; sew to to KTS edge. Join top and bottom sections. Appliqué cross to center sail.

ANCHOR

G50 Beginning at top, make and join 3 horizontal rows: ABA, CDC, and EFE. Make HHI unit (2 times); join C to top of each unit. Make JKL unit and attach to left section; make LrKrJr unit and attach to right section. Join the left and right sections with G. Join the top and bottom sections. For the rope, use bias tubing made from striped fabric. (See page 309 for help with bias tubing.)

COLLECTIONS Columbus

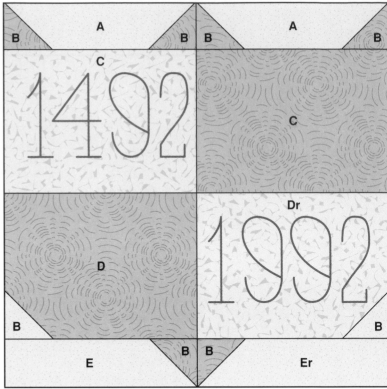

G51 Make EDDDD unit for center. Make BCCCBr unit (4 times). Add BCCCBr unit to 2 opposite sides of center section. Join A to each end of remaining BCCCBr units and add to remaining sides of center section. Embroider face using satin stitch and stem stitch.

SUN

G52 Make BAB unit (2 times), add each unit to a C piece. Make BD unit and DrB unit and add each to C edge of first units. Make EB and BEr units; attach to BD and DrB. Sew the left and right sides together. Embroider the dates, using stem stitch.

SHIELD—COAT OF ARMS

COLLECTIONS Columbus

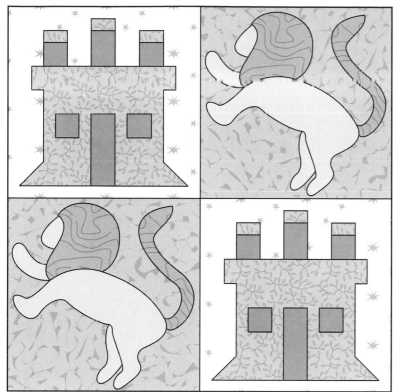

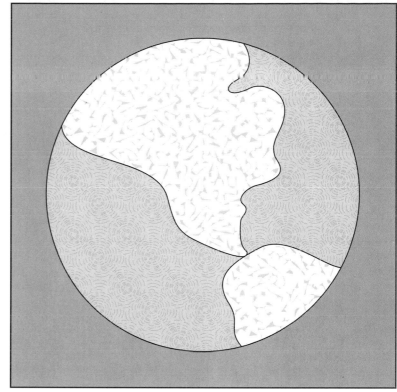

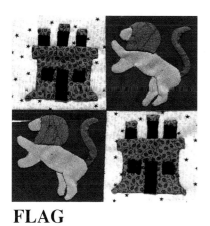

G53 Cut four 2-inch squares (plus seam allowances). Appliqué designs to the individual blocks. Join as a four-patch. (See page 308 for appliqué information and page 309 for help in making four-patches.)

FLAG

G54 Cut a 4-inch square (plus seam allowances) of background fabric. Appliqué Earth.

WORLD

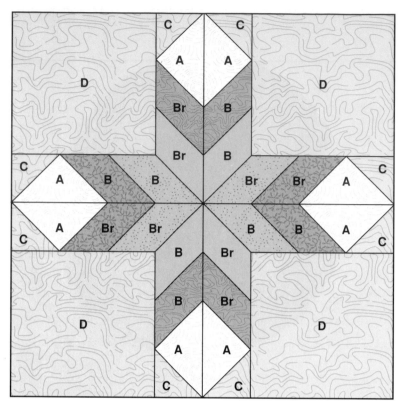

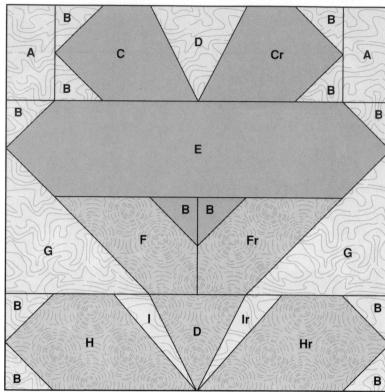

G55 Make CABB unit (4 times) and CABrBr (4 times). Join CABB and CABrBr with D, mitering the BBr seam (4 times). Join the 4 units as a four-patch to complete the block. (See page 309 for mitering information and for help in making four-patches.)

FEATHERS

G56 Sew B pieces to C and Cr; join the 2 units with D and add A pieces to each end. Make and join FB and FrB units; sew to E; add B pieces and then add G pieces to this section. Join to top section. Make BBHlI and BBHrIr units; join the 2 units with D and attach to top section to complete the block.

STYLIZED ROSE

COLLECTIONS Columbus

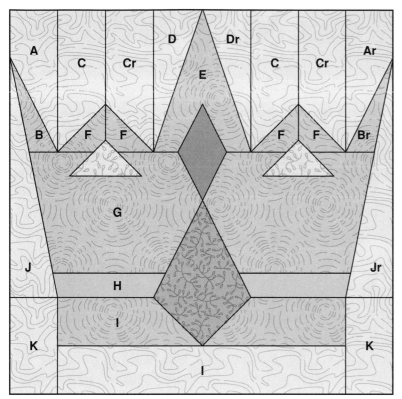

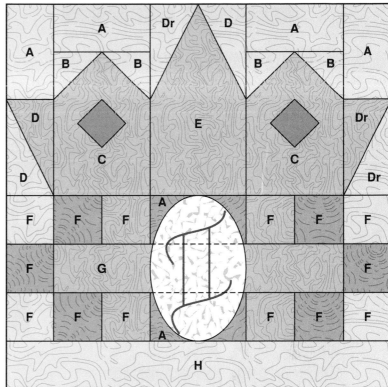

CROWN—
FERDINAND

G57 Make AB, CF (2 times), CrF (2 times), DEDr, and ArBr units; join the units in sequence to make the top row. Join G and H; add to top row, then add J and Jr pieces to each side. Make II unit, add K pieces to each side, then join to top section. Appliqué the "jewels" onto the crown. (See page 308 for appliqué information.)

CROWN—
ISABELLA

G58 Make ADD, ABBC (2 times), DrED, and ADrDr units; join in sequence to make the top row. Make FFFAFFF unit (2 times) and FGF unit; join the units and add H, then join this section to top section. Appliqué the oval section of the crown and the "jewels." Embroider the initial.

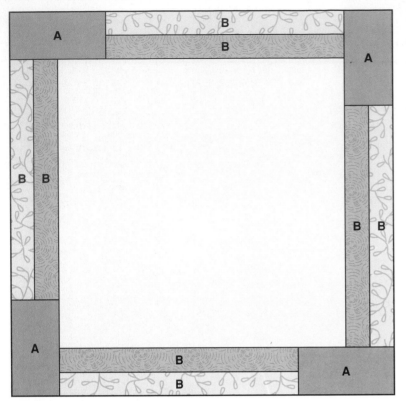

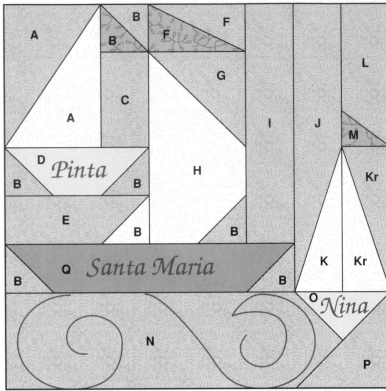

FLAG BORDER

G59 This block is designed to hold a commemorative patch. Make BB unit (4 times); add A to each unit. Sew one ABB unit to side of block, then add the remaining 3 units using the stop-and-start method. (See page 309 for stop-and-start directions.)

PINTA, NINA, AND SANTA MARIA

G60 Make BB unit; add C. Make AA unit; join with BBC. Make BDB unit; add to first section. Make EB unit and add to BDB edge. Sew G and B to H; make FF unit and add to BHG. Sew BHGFF to first section; add I to right side. Sew B pieces to Q; join to bottom of first section. Make KrKr unit and LM unit; join the units. Make JK unit and add to LMKrKr; add this unit to right side of first section. Sew O to N; add P; then join to top section to complete the block. Embroider names on ships and waves on the sea.

COLLECTIONS Columbus

TIPS AND TECHNIQUES

Everything you need to know to make the quilt blocks and projects in this book.

TIPS AND TECHNIQUES

Methods used in making the quilt blocks and projects, from laying in supplies to making yo-yos.

All of the blocks in this book were made using templates. Strip-piecing methods could be used if you were making multiples of one block. (But you already know how we feel about making the same block over and over again!) In the interest of accuracy and ease, we recommend that you use templates.

Most of the blocks can be pieced on the sewing machine, but some require hand-appliqué and embroidery. Instructions for appliqué are on page 308; the embroidery stitches you'll need are given on pages 311–2.

SUPPLIES

Beyond your sewing machine, straight pins, and thread, you'll find the following items either necessary or very useful.

Template Plastic

Use the kind that is slightly frosted. You can still see through it, but can find it more easily than the clear, shiny kind, and you can mark on it easily. Do not use the template plastic with a grid printed on it for these blocks. Don't use cardboard for templates; it doesn't hold its shape well with continuous use.

Clear Ruler

Use the clear ruler to add seam allowances after you have traced

around the template onto the fabric. You need a clear ruler printed with a fine-line ⅛-inch grid. Many of these are not accurate— the ¼-inch mark may be different on opposite sides of the ruler. If

you own one of these, choose one edge and use *only* that edge.

Red Rule

A useful alternative to the clear ruler, the red rule is exactly ¼ inch thick, and you use it to add

seam allowances around the seam lines on the fabric. It is about 1 inch high, so it lifts your fingers up, keeping them out of the way as you trace. Its bright red color makes it easy to spot on your sewing table.

Floss-Away Bags

Small plastic zipper-lock bags available at cross-stitch or craft stores are perfect to hold the templates for one block, and they are easily labeled.

Permanent Markers

Label your templates with fine-line permanent markers. We use the Staedtler Lumocolor 313, but there are others you might like just as well.

Masking Tape

To maintain the correct seam allowance when machine stitching, use two or three layers of ¼-inch masking tape, placed ¼ inch from the sewing machine needle, as an edge along which to guide the cut edge of the fabric

Little Foot by Lynn Graves

Little Foot is a sewing machine attachment. One side has a perfect ⅛-inch seam allowance guide, and the other has a perfect ¼-inch seam allowance guide. It is sold according to the type of shank on your sewing machine.

Number 2 Pencil

Mark around the template onto

the fabric, and add the seam allowances with a pencil. Mechanical pencils are excellent, because they stay sharp. Don't choose one with lead that is too thick—the 0.7mm size is large enough. You can buy a package of leads inexpensively.

Colored Pencils

You cannot see a black pencil line on dark fabric. Colored pencils, such as Eagle Verithin, are handy markers. They come in several colors that work well: silver, white, and yellow, for example. Colored leads are also available for mechanical pencils.

Scissors

You will need one pair of scissors for cutting fabric and another for cutting template plastic. Don't cut anything but fabric with your fabric scissors (and don't let anyone else, either!).

Fabric

The easiest fabric to work with is 100-percent cotton, muslin weight. It presses well without melting, as some man-made fibers will do. If you really want to use a particular fabric that doesn't fit this description, try it; it may work with careful handling. Heavy fabric, such as velvets and corduroys, are probably too cumbersome to manage for small blocks. In choosing patterns, don't limit yourself to tiny prints or solids. Some medium- and large-scale prints are very interesting cut into little pieces.

Sandpaper Board

A masonite board with sandpaper glued to one side keeps fabric from shifting as you trace around the template.

Appliqué Needles

We use Number 12 sharps. If you like needles that are even longer and skinnier, you might try milliner's needles

Appliqué Thread

Fine thread works best for appliqué. One brand is J P Coats Dual Duty Plus for machine embroidery. You can also use one strand of embroidery floss.

MAKING TEMPLATES

Lay the template plastic over the block pattern drawing in this book and trace, using a permanent marker and a ruler.

Label each piece with the appropriate letter. (See Appliqué, page 308, for marking appliqué pieces.) Remember, the letters in each block are for that block only; piece B in one block isn't the same as B in another block.

It is not necessary to move the template plastic when tracing each template; if several pieces are grouped together, draw them that way, then cut them apart later.

As you draw the templates, note any edge that will be on the outside of the block. Mark the template with an arrow along this edge to remind you to cut the fabric with the arrow on the straight

of the grain. This will help keep your block from stretching.

After drawing the templates for a block, cut them apart carefully and put them aside until you are ready to use them. (Store them in those little plastic bags mentioned in our supply list.)

MARKING FABRIC

Before you do any tracing and cutting of the fabric, you must decide if your quilt will ever need to be washed. If so, you must pre-wash the fabric. If the fabric is going to shrink, or the dyes are going to run, you want it to happen before you make the quilt.

Lay your fabric out smoothly, wrong side up. Try using elements of the fabric print to enhance the design of the block, centering a flower or a stripe.

Position the template, wrong side up, on the fabric. It is a good practice to always place the template wrong side up on the fabric, even when it doesn't seem to matter. There are times when it is *very* important, and this habit will help you avoid redrawing.

Trace around the template. This is the line on which you will sew.

Once the template is traced, add ¼-inch seam allowances to all sides, using a clear ruler or a red rule.

Mark the templates to show which edges are to be sewn together. Then make these marks in the seam allowances of the

fabric. This helps you line up the correct edges. It is especially helpful when, for instance, a triangle has two sides of similar length.

Marking fabric for appliqué is done differently. It is marked on the right side of the fabric. The seam allowance (between ¼ and ⅛ inch) is added as you cut out each piece.

Cut out the pieces you have drawn, remembering to cut along the seam allowance lines. If your scissors are sharp, you will be able to cut more easily and more accurately.

SEWING BY MACHINE

Little blocks and little pieces require little stitches. Adjust the stitch length to 12 to 14 stitches-per-inch.

Although you will have sewing lines to follow, other guides are also helpful. We have noticed that different machine models have different interpretations of a quarter-inch.

To make a seam guide with masking tape, draw two lines on paper, ¼ inch apart. Cut along one line. Put the paper in your unthreaded sewing machine, positioning the needle on the remaining drawn line.

Take a few stitches on the line to make sure the paper is in the machine straight. Then, lay a strip of masking tape along the edge of the paper. Make the tape extend an inch or two behind and in front of the presser foot. When you have the tape in place, remove the paper. Place another strip of tape over the first piece. You can even add a third strip. This builds a ridge against which the fabric can ride as you move it through the machine.

PIECING

For each of the blocks in this book we've provided a piecing diagram and instructions for putting the block together. The instructions tell you the sequence in which the pieces are assembled.

As you begin to feed the pieces into your sewing machine, it is not necessary to backstitch; you will be sewing over the ends of the seams, so they aren't in danger of coming unsewn. Also (we hate to bring this up), it is easier to rip out a seam that is not back-stitched.

As each seam is pieced, you may want to trim away some of the points that protrude beyond the end of the seam allowance. Some of the seams may also need to be trimmed if they will be caught in the next seam you sew.

Just to keep us amused while we made these blocks, we saved the snipped "points" in a jar as we trimmed them. (You can see them in the photo on page 305.)

APPLIQUÉ

There are several ways to do

appliqué. We turn the edges of our blocks under with the needle as we sew. Basting beforehand is another option. (Never use a colored thread for basting. A contrasting thread can leave little, unsightly dots of color on the piece.)

Trace the entire design onto template plastic, as described in the section, Marking Fabric. Number the pieces in the design, and also number the corresponding pieces on the template plastic. Then, cut out the individual template pieces.

Trace around the template pieces on the right side of the fabric with the template right-side up. Make a dotted line on the template to indicate areas that will be lying under another shape. As shown in illustration A1 below, piece number 2 would fit under piece number 3 along their common seam line, so a dotted line on template number 2 is a reminder not to baste here.

Concave (inward) curves should be clipped before basting. Clip around the curve only up to

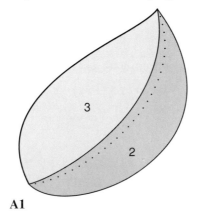

A1

1/16 inch from the seam line. (If you clip right up to the line, you will get points along the curve.)

To baste each piece, roll the seam edge under along the marked line. Do not turn under seams that will lie under another shape, as this produces bulky ridges on the finished surface.

Our method of appliqué is to layer and build the smaller pieces of the design onto each other as much as possible before applying them to the background. This reduces the awkwardness of handling a large background piece, and allows you to clip away fabric from the back of the piece if it shows through.

The actual application of one fabric piece to another is done with blind stitching. Using thread to match the piece being applied, bring your needle from the back to the front, catching a few threads of the rolled edge. Pull thread through. Re-enter the base fabric at the exact spot and slightly under the rolled edge. Make a

YY-1

linear stitch on the back, following the outline of the shape, coming up again through all layers. The linear stitches should be no more than 1/8 inch in length, less for very small or intricately-shaped pieces.

When all application is finished, remove all basting threads. Any embroidery should be done now.

YO-YOS

Making yo-yos is hardly an exact science. Historically, they were a first sewing project for children: "And you have to finish 12 yo-yos before you can go play."

To determine the cutting size of the yo-yo piece, decide how large you want the finished product and double the diameter. Thus, for a 1-inch finished yo-yo, draw a 2-inch circle and add 1/8 - to 1/4-inch seam allowance.

If you are going to make several yo-yos of the same size, make a plastic template. You can trace onto fabric once, make three or four layers of fabric, and cut several at one time. (The sharper your scissors, the more layers you can cut.)

To sew the yo-yos, use quilting thread, and knot the end. Turn a scant ¼-inch as you stitch (see IllustrationYY-1, opposite).

End where you began, on the opposite side of the fabric from the knot. Pull thread firmly to draw the yo-yo closed. Tack with a few stitches to secure it.

Yo-yos are not the place for tiny, dainty stitches. Little stitches will put too many gathers in the circle and make the hole too big.

The other tip for yo-yo success is to stitch very close to the edge of the fold. This avoids a belly-button effect in the center of the completed yo-yo.

GLOSSARY OF TERMS AND TECHNIQUES

Some terms and techniques are used many times throughout this book. In the following review, we explain the terms we use and share our methods for the basic procedures you'll employ.

Reverse

In the block patterns you will see pieces marked with a letter followed by a lower-case r (as in B and Br). This means that you must reverse (flip over) the B template to trace and cut this piece. You don't need two templates to cut B and Br: you simply use the other side of your B template.

Repeat

Instructions for making the blocks will often include a direction such as (4 times). This means that you create the unit described a total of 4 times.

Four-Patch

A four-patch is a square made of four smaller squares. To assemble, sew two together two times (making two pairs of squares); then join the two pairs into a square.

Nine-Patch

A nine-patch (also known as a three-patch) is a square made up of nine smaller squares—three rows of three squares each. To make a nine-patch, sew three squares together in a row three times, making three rows; then sew the rows together to make the larger square.

Mitering

This technique is also referred to as "setting in." Some blocks, such as the Eight-Pointed Star, must have pieces mitered or set in. The most important thing to remember about mitering is: *Do not sew into the seam allowance for the third seam.*

Begin your mitered unit by sewing the first two pieces together. When you reach the end of the marked seam (that is, before you go into the seam allowance), stop and backstitch a few stitches to lock the stitching.

As shown in illustration M-1 below, align one edge of the third piece and sew from the outer edge to the point where you stopped stitching for the first seam; backstitch, remove from machine, and break the thread.

Then sew the third seam the same way, beginning at outer edge.

Stop-and-Start Seams

Perhaps there is another term for this procedure, but this is our method. It is used in blocks that seem to have no beginning and no end, such as Block G59 (page 304), where the flag borders go around the center section, but there really isn't a natural place to begin the addition.

The illustration below (SSS-1)

shows the attachment of the B1 piece to the A piece. Notice that B1 is even with A at the edge where the next piece will be joined, and that the stitching stops about 1½ inches from the opposite A edge.

Press the B1 piece, then add B2 in the normal way of adding one piece to another, lining up the edges. Add B3 and B4 in the same way. Then complete the first seam, including the B4 piece.

Curved Seams

Make the templates in the usual way, but note on them the center of both the concave piece (the one that makes a "cave") and the convex piece (the one with the bulge). Trace around the templates onto the wrong side of the fabric and make a mark in the seam allowance of the curved seam to note the center.

Clip into the concave seam allowance, close but not up to the seam line.

Pin the two pieces together, matching both end points and the center. Stitch the curve, easing the seam lines together as you sew.

Bias Tubing

This is a wonderful way to make curvy pieces without templates. There are many uses for this technique in appliqué; flower stems are a prime example.

To begin, decide how wide you want the finished stem to be. For our example, we'll say ¼ inch.

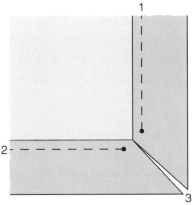

M-1

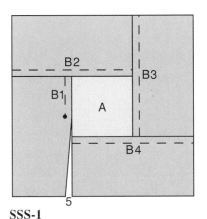

SSS-1

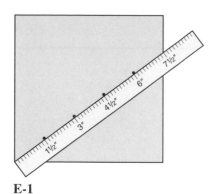

E-1

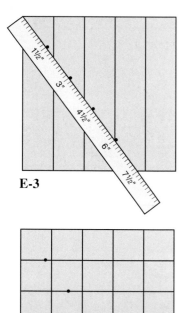

E-2

E-3

E-4

Double this measurement and add two ¼-inch seam allowances. That would make the piece you cut 1 inch wide.

Cut a piece of bias fabric (cut at a 45-degree angle from the grain), 1 inch wide and the length needed, say 3 inches.

Sew the piece into a tube, using ¼-inch seam allowance, stitching with wrong sides together. Trim the seam allowance to about ⅛ inch.

Press the tube so that the seam is in the center of one side. (There are little flat plastic tools that can be used to help you with this pressing.)

Now, simply appliqué one pressed edge in place (with the seam on the under side), and then appliqué the other edge.

Enlarging and Reducing

When you are in creative high gear, you may want to make some of our blocks in a size different than our 4-inch squares.

To enlarge (or reduce) a quilt block, you must first determine what increments it is divided into. For instance, is it a five-patch? Are there five equal divisions across the block and down the side?

Many blocks are easily redrafted by simply going to a size divisible by the increment of the block. By that we mean, if the block is a five-patch, you can most easily redraft it to a 7½-inch block (increments of 1½ inches) or a 10-inch block (increments of 2 inches). But what if you want

to make a 6-inch five patch?

Begin by drawing a 6-inch square. Lay your ruler on the square (Illustration E-1) with the zero end exactly in the lower left corner, and the 7½-inch point exactly on the right vertical line. Make a mark on the block at each 1½-inch increment, as shown.

Next, draw lines through the marks you made. The lines should be perpendicular to the bottom edge of the block (Illustration E-2).

Now, repeat this process, placing the zero end of the ruler in the upper left corner, and the 7½-inch point on the bottom edge. When you complete this set of lines, you should have a square marked off in a perfect five-patch.

This same technique applies to any block that you want to enlarge or reduce.

The photocopying machine is certainly a temptation, but we warn you that this is not accurate. There is distortion in the enlarging and reducing process that makes the copying machine an unreliable method.

Enlarging or Reducing Appliqué

Appliqué can be enlarged or reduced by two methods. The first is by superimposing a grid over the original drawing. Make a grid of the same number of squares in the block size you want, then draw what is in each square of the original drawing into the squares of the enlarged

(or reduced) drawing.

The second way is to use a copying machine. Yes, we told you not to do this in the preceding section. That was for piecing, and this is for appliqué! To reduce any distortion, make the first copy with the block in a vertical position; then make the second copy with the (enlarged) block in a horizontal position.

Drafting a Hexagon

Drafting a hexagon is one of the easiest jobs in the world of geometry. We just love how this works out–so cosmic! Geometry would have been much more interesting if it had been related to quilting when we went to school!

Begin by using a compass to draw a circle the size you want.

Now, using the same radius, put the point of the compass anywhere on the circle and draw an arc. Move the compass point to where the arc and the circle intersect, and draw another arc. Continue around the circle in this manner until you have 6 arcs.

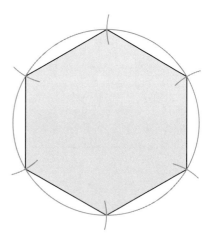

H-1

(See Illustration H-1, opposite). Now connect the arc/circle intersections to make the hexagon. Amazing!

Drafting An Eight-Pointed Star
Begin with a square the size you want, and mark diagonal lines to locate center. Adjust your compass so that its radius is the same distance as from one corner to the center point (Illustration S-1). Make an arc from each corner that goes through the sides of the block. Number the points where the arcs and block edges intersect, as shown (Illustration S-2).

Now, connect the points as shown in Illustration S-3; then draw the lines you need for the block as you see in Illustration S-4. The heavy lines are the lines you need to make the simplest eight-pointed star. The dotted lines give you some other ideas of how this block can be made even more interesting.

EMBROIDERY
Many of our blocks are embellished with embroidery. A few stitches can add just the right accent and extra texture.

The illustrations below and on the following page show how to execute stem stitch, satin stitch, lazy daisy stitch, chain stitch, French knot, herringbone stitch, and feather stitch.

We generally use two strands of six-ply embroidery floss for

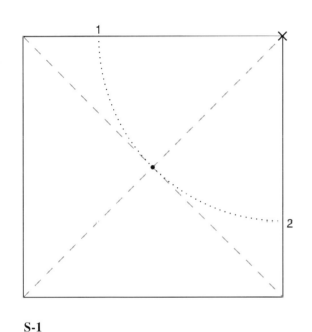

S-1

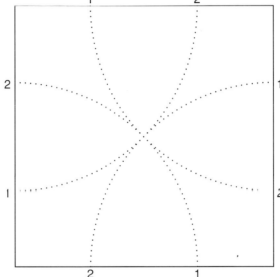

S-2

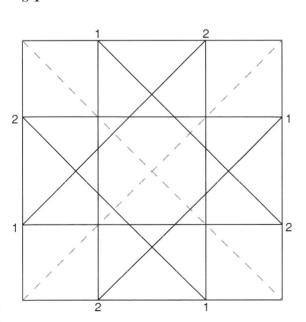

S-3

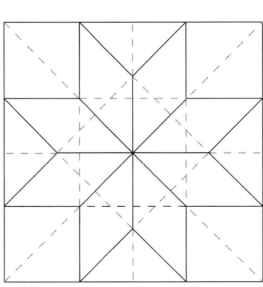

S-4

STEM STITCH

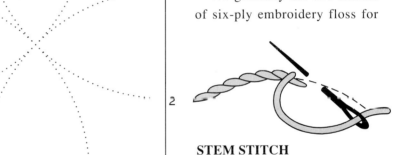

SATIN STITCH

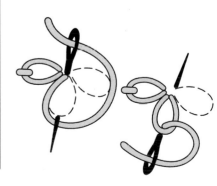

LAZY DAISY STITCH

311

CHAIN STITCH

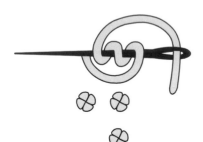

FRENCH KNOT

HERRINGBONE STITCH

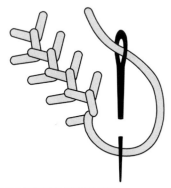

FEATHER STITCH

embroidery, though there may be occasions when you will want to use more than two strands—for example, to make larger French knots, heavier chain stitch, or for other decorative stitchery.

PRESSING

Pressing is very important to the finishing of a block. In hand piecing, press the block after all the sewing is done. But in machine piecing, press each seam after you sew it. The seams are generally pressed to one side or another (making the seam sturdier than if it were pressed open). You can often plan your pressing so that the seams of one row fall one way and the seams of the next row fall the opposite way. This makes the joining of the two rows easier, since the seams butt up against each other, forming a good, sharp intersection.

Note: Appliqué is pressed from the wrong side of the block.

Press so that the seams lie flat, but don't press so aggressively that the edges of the block are distorted.

After pressing, measure your block; it should measure 4½ inches square. If it is more than about ⅛ inch off, the block will not fit with the others. A variation of ⅛ inch can usually be eased to fit.

If your block doesn't measure 4½ inches square, check to see that you stitched on the stitching lines. If there are many pieces in the block, and the stitching is off-line, there can be a relatively large discrepancy in the size of the block.

BACKING AND BINDING

To back a quilt, you simply cut a piece of the fabric you have chosen, making it a few inches larger than the quilt top. (The larger the quilt, and the more quilting you plan to do, the more extra fabric you should allow on all sides.) If the quilt is larger than the fabric you want to use, you will have to piece the backing to make it the right size.

Layer the top, batting, and backing, with wrong sides of the top and backing toward the batting. Baste the layers together and quilt as desired.

We use two sizes of binding, depending on the size of the quilt. They are both made in the same manner; just the measurements and the seam allowances are different. This procedure makes a nice mitered corner on the front and back.

Quarter-Inch Binding

Cut binding 2 inches wide. Use ¼-inch seam allowances.

Half-Inch Binding

Cut binding 3 inches wide. Use ½-inch seam allowances.

Binding the Quilt Choose ¼- or ½-inch binding and cut as described above, and long enough to go all the way around the quilt (with a few inches to spare). Piece the binding as necessary to reach the required length, pressing seams open.

Then press the binding in half (wrong sides together) along the length.

Trim the backing and batting even with the edge of the quilt front. Lay the binding along the raw edge of the quilt, folding over edge of binding before you

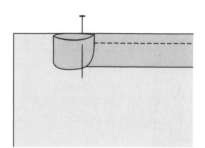

BB-1

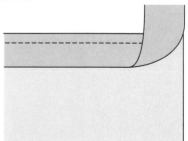

BB-2

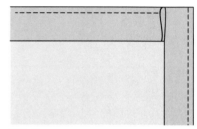

BB-3

stitch it (Illustration BB-1). Stitch, using the correct seam allowance.

Stop stitching a seam's width from the edge. Backstitch and break the thread. Fold the binding up, as shown in Illustration BB-2, then down (Illustration BB-3), and stitch from edge. Repeat the process at each corner of the quilt.

Turn binding up and over the edge of the back of the quilt. Tuck binding in at corners on back to make a miter. Hand stitch the binding to the backing, being careful not to sew through to the front.

INDEX

A Guide to the
Themes, Techniques,
and Block patterns

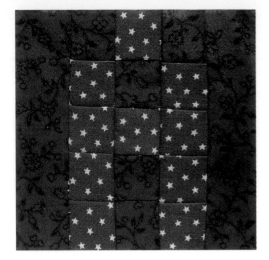

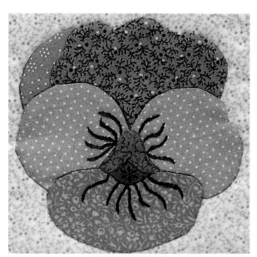

SOURCES

Red Rule For this useful tool and many other quilting supplies: Itchin' to Stitch, 311 S. Walker Way, Sun Prairie, WI 53590; 608-837-4419 (Shown in photo on page 305.)

Little Foot This quilter's presser foot is available from Little Foot, Ltd., 605 Bledsoe, NW, Albuquerque, NM 87107; 505-345-7647 (Shown in photo on page 305.)

Jack-O'-Lantern Cross Stitch Pattern used in Thanksgiving Table Runner: "Seasonings" Leaflet #100, Cross-eyed Cricket, Box 6367, Chesterfield, MO 63006 (Photo page 40.)

Buttons and Button Covers Sunbonnet and Barnyard Buttons QT Crafts, 3318 Ivanhoe, Abilene, TX 79605; 915-692-7143 (Used on shirts photographed on pages 27, 28, and 29.)

Patchwork Shirt Pattern Available from: A Quilter's Wardrobe, 612 Huntington Court, Grapevine, TX 76051; 817-488-1167 (Used to make barnyard shirt on pages 28-29 and Southwest shirt on page 27.)

Western Bib Simplicity Pattern #8326 (Used to make bibs shown on page 26.)

Patchwork Jacket Butterick Pattern #6595 (Used to make jacket shown on pages 28 and 29.)

Tea Cozy Simplicity Pattern #8106 (Project shown on page 37.)